The e-Assessment Handbook

Also available from Continuum:

Shirley Bennett, Debra Marsh and Clare Killen:
Handbook of Online Education

The e-Assessment Handbook

Geoffrey Crisp

continuum

Continuum International Publishing Group
The Tower Building
11 York Road
SE1 7NX

80 Maiden Lane, Suite 704
New York, NY 10038

www.continuumbooks.com

British Library Cataloguing-in-Publication Data

A catalogue record for this book is available from the British Library.

ISBN: 0–8264–9628–8 (paperback)
       0–8264–9627–X (hardcover)

Library of Congress Cataloging-in-Publication Data
A catalog record for this book is available from the Library of Congress.

Typeset by Fakenham Photosetting Limited, Fakenham, Norfolk

Printed and bound in Great Britain by Antony Rowe Ltd, Chippenham, Wiltshire

BRIEF CONTENTS

Detailed Contents

List of Figures and Tables

Why write another book on assessment?

There are many excellent books, monographs, guides and journal articles specifically covering assessment in tertiary education. Some of these touch briefly on e-assessment, whereas others have been written explicitly for tertiary educators and e-learning designers wishing to incorporate e-assessment into particular learning designs. It is certainly the case that much more has been written on e-learning than on e-assessment, and much of the literature on e-learning has been written from the point of view of explaining to tertiary teachers why they should invest time and effort in acquiring new skills that will enable them to participate in the digital world.

This book brings together some of the key ideas from the literature on e-learning and e-assessment and sets it in context within the traditional literature on learning and assessment. It presents a realistic view of what is possible in terms of the use of computers and the Internet in assessment today and what will be possible in the near future. It specifically discusses the dynamic interrelationship between learning, teaching and assessment, and presents to tertiary teachers and instructional designers a number of frameworks for aligning e-learning activities and e-assessment tasks.

The book presents a continuum of assessment possibilities for tertiary teachers, from the use of simple computer-marked multiple-choice questions, through to elaborate role-plays and interactive simulations and scenarios. The book is certainly not proposing that e-assessment will replace all other forms of traditional assessment, but highlights the absolute necessity for teachers and educational institutions to be aware of the significant opportunities for enhancing the student experience and the quality of tertiary education through the use of e-assessment. The book also emphasizes, as do many of those already published, that the process of engaging with, and the product resulting from, the actual learning activities that students undertake must be aligned with the most appropriate form of assessment for those activities. So if students are using the Internet or interactive digital applications as part of their learning environment, they should also use these tools to complete their assessment tasks.

The book is not trying to convince tertiary teachers that they should pursue e-assessment in order to give the appearance that they are 'up to date' with their teaching methodologies, but rather it is encouraging them to reflect on the design principles behind their choice of learning activities and associated student assessment tasks. The various chapters highlight the possibilities available for aligning authentic learning activities and assessment tasks that will engage students and provide numerous examples that illustrate how this is currently being achieved in the online environment.

Authentic learning activities, such as role-playing and scenario immersion will become more significant in tertiary education as we move towards a more genuine articulation of the generic or transferable attributes (capabilities, skills) that graduates will need in their professional lives in the workplace. Students will require transcripts that are much richer than many currently used, and the e-portfolio will become more commonly accepted as an appropriate format for reporting learning outcomes and achievement.

e-Assessment issues have been driving a renewed examination of assessment itself. This has occurred as proponents of e-assessment have had to justify the validity and reliability of the methodologies used, and this has resulted in a review of the characteristics and properties used in more traditional forms of assessment that have been accepted as the norm. e-Assessment use will continue to increase, and it will certainly become more sophisticated in terms of the range of possible tasks available and the level of feedback provided to students. The technology will move to a simpler, more transparent interface for both teachers and students.

The context for this book is not to present e-assessment as a solution seeking a problem; it is not an end in itself but rather a component of the framework for a well-designed learning, teaching and assessment model. Tertiary teachers and academic developers, who have embraced the culture of adaptation and adoption, will already be exploring new ways to improve the quality of their designs and student outcomes. The use of e-assessment will be a natural progression along this enhancement continuum. e-Learning and e-assessment should not be viewed as a disruptive technology; they are really only alternative ways to engage teachers and students in a richer, more sustaining learning environment.

What does this book cover?

This book has been divided into seven sections, each section based on the type of question that a teacher might ask about e-assessment. Readers should be able to read the chapters in any order, depending on their particular interest and current needs.

Section 1: How does assessment affect learning?

This section looks at the impact assessment has on learning, and draws mainly from the traditional learning and teaching literature. The fundamental principles of assessment are the same for e-assessment and the more traditional forms of assessment. The alignment of learning, teaching and assessment applies irrespective of the methodologies used for the construction and delivery of the activities and tasks.

Section 2: How will I make an e-assessment?

Teachers would be interested in the types of e-assessment frameworks that are available, the types of questions and tasks that could be presented to students through the Internet or a computer interface and the characteristics of the software required to construct, deliver and report e-assessments. A number of professional groups, as well as individual researchers, have provided very useful guidelines on the use of e-assessments in tertiary education. Teachers and institutions are required to make many decisions when contemplating the use of computers and the Internet for assessment. Some of these relate to technical issues, some relate to the often significant costs associated with enterprise level systems, some relate to the increasing workload of teachers and the increased demand for staff development. This section sets out some of the critical factors that teachers and institutions should consider, and the risks and major consequences that flow from making a particular decision. Guidelines are provided that relate the objectives of a learning activity with an appropriate framework for its assessment.

Section 3: What does an e-assessment look like?

This section provides discipline-based examples of e-assessments. It is often difficult for teachers to visualize what an interactive e-assessment might look like for their particular discipline. This section will enable teachers to view examples of e-assessments from a number of disciplines, so that they can reflect upon and perhaps adapt a particular approach or example. It is interesting and informative to view how divergent and convergent student responses are used by different disciplines.

Science-based disciplines have provided numerous examples of 'helper applications' that can be used within an e-assessment. These are typically Java applets, Shockwave or Flash files that allow students to interact with information, data or a concept, in order to produce a response. This section illustrates how e-assessments can provide opportunities for students to respond at the multistructural and relational levels of the SOLO taxonomy.

Section 4: What are the practical issues when doing an e-assessment?

This section covers many of the practical issues that will confront teachers and institutions as they develop and deliver e-assessments. The use, and reuse, of questions through the construction of item banks is discussed. How will teachers decide if questions are suitable for an item bank, and whether they should continue to use a particular question? Where can teachers obtain questions for their particular discipline, and how much will it cost?

An increasingly important issue for institutions is the cost associated with moving from one software system to another. Will the content and assessment questions in one learning management system be able to be used in another? Will questions need to be reformatted over time? How secure is the Internet for high stakes summative assessments? This section provides examples of how questions can be designed for multiple systems, and how metadata standards may be used to provide questions that may be repurposed.

The issues of validity and reliability apply to all assessments, but the use of computers often makes it easier to analyse students' responses and scores so that comparisons can be made between students' actual and anticipated results. This section provides a brief introduction to Classical Test Theory and Item Response Theory, without being overly technical. It is important for teachers to engage with an analysis of the assessment responses in order to enhance the quality of the questions.

Security is a major concern for teachers and institutions alike when high stakes assessments are conducted using the Internet. This section highlights some of the risks, and associated mitigations, that apply when delivering assessments on computers or though the Internet. The risks and opportunities afforded by mobile communication devices are also discussed.

Whenever technology is used to deliver an assessment, accessibility issues must be considered. It is clear that despite the ability of computers to provide exciting and engaging formats for learning and assessment, they also provide significant barriers for some students. Teachers will need to be aware of these barriers, and the assistive technologies that are available for reducing these barriers. In some cases, it may be necessary to design alternative forms of assessment for some students when the barriers are so high that students are prevented from showing the capabilities they have developed.

Section 5: How do I make e-assessments interactive?

The online environment is interactive. If students are using the Internet to respond to questions in an assessment, they will be expecting some form of interactivity that will engage their senses and allow them some control over the process. This ability to explore and create a responsive environment is fundamental to the way in which computers are used. e-Assessments should be designed so that they record the full range of capabilities developed by the student. Through the Internet, students have access to resources from across the world that can be incorporated into their responses in a synchronous or asynchronous manner. Good assessment designs harvest these possibilities and enrich the student experience.

This section provides examples of the use of computer-mediated communication, discussion boards and online group activities. The assessment of group activities and online discussions requires careful planning, and students should be given clear criteria on the assessment of both the process and product of group activities, and on the quality and quantity of entries required in discussion boards.

Role-plays and scenario-based activities are becoming increasingly popular in tertiary education as they provide authentic learning environments where students can develop capabilities for the relational and extended abstract sections of the SOLO taxonomy. Teachers need to plan carefully for the assessment of these activities and some examples are provided in this section.

Interactivity can be incorporated into assessments through the use of packaged files based on Java applets, Shockwave or Flash. They provide opportunities for authentic assessment tasks, ones that more closely resemble those that the student will encounter in their professional practice. Numerous examples of these approaches to interactivity are included in this section.

Section 6: What about the future?

This section looks at where e-assessment is heading. It discusses what is possible now, and what will be possible in the near future. Will teachers be expected to be multimedia producers as well as discipline experts? The concept of the culture of adaptation and adoption is explored, as well as the notion that individual teachers, or even institutions, might consider being specialist assessors rather than content creators and deliverers.

Section 7: Appendices, Glossary, References, Index

This section provides some examples of marking rubrics for online discussions, and more examples for discipline based Java applets. The e-assessment landscape is littered with acronyms and technical terms, so a brief glossary is provided for the perplexed teacher.

Section 1 How does assessment affect learning?

1 Overview

1.1 Why do we assess?

Why do we assess students and their learning outcomes in educational institutions? Before we can begin any discussion on e-assessment, we must first consider assessment itself, and the impact it has on learning. Setting and responding to assessment tasks, and marking or grading an assessment, all consume significant amounts of time and effort for both students and teachers. Assessment activities are expensive and produce stress for all those involved in the process. How often do we question the benefits of our assessments and whether all our assessment tasks are justified, or indeed required?

If we look at the assessment literature, discuss assessment issues with colleagues at conferences and in our own institutions, we will encounter a variety of perspectives on why we inflict this time-consuming task on our students and ourselves. Some of the reasons generally proposed for assessment activities include:

- it encourages learning
- it provides feedback on learning to both the student and the teacher
- it documents competency and skill development
- it allows students to be graded or ranked
- it validates certification and licence procedures for professional practice
- it allows benchmarks to be established for standards.

(Broadfoot *et al.*, 2004)

Teachers' epistemologies for learning and assessment are closely linked, and range from a teacher-centred focus on knowledge reproduction through to a learning-centred focus on knowledge transformation (Samuelowicz *et al.*, 2002). Teachers can justify assessment tasks as an accepted, and expected, step along the educational journey of students, and would be confident that the general community, the professional organizations associated with the discipline and their colleagues would all be expecting some form of assessment. Indeed, it is certain that if a teacher did not assess the students in their course using some form of recognizable assessment task, those responsible for the quality assurance protocols at the institution would be demanding an explanation!

If we can justify assessment activity from the teacher's perspective, can we also justify it from the perspective of the student? Are students always expecting to be assessed, and should the general community expect educational institutions to validate all learning activities? Are students and the community expecting holistic changes in behaviour, attitude, skills, knowledge and capabilities from the assessment process, or only selective changes? Assessment tasks can be designed to provide students with an understanding of their own learning behaviour, or they may be designed to provide teachers with an understanding of the impact of their teaching. Assessment tasks may be undertaken for the benefit of the student, the teacher, the community or, more often, the same assessment activity is expected to provide simultaneous benefits to each group.

1.2 Relationship between learning and assessment

1.2.1 Assessment for learning

The instructional design methodology used in the creation of a learning activity will have a significant influence on how students learn and how you will assess that learning. The design methodology that you choose allows you to highlight the learning objectives and construct appropriate learning activities, and assessment tasks that align specifically with those objectives.

Assessment methodologies in schools and tertiary education institutions have traditionally been validated through their origins in cognitive psychology, and the universal requirement for objective methods to rank students for selection processes and to differentiate various student performances for reporting purposes (Dunn *et al.*, 2004). For the past 30 years educational researchers have presented an alternative understanding of assessment, one emphasizing the correlation between assessment practices and learning behaviours (Entwistle *et al.*, 1983; Biggs, 1979; Maron *et al.*, 1976; Biggs, 2002). Dunn *et al.* (2004) have succinctly summarized many of the contemporary issues associated with student assessment, including the current landscape in higher education institutions.

Assessment tasks not only determine to a significant extent what students will learn, but also the methods they will employ to retain, reproduce, reconstruct and engage with learnt material (Biggs, 2002). Student responses to perceived, or actual, assessment tasks will often dominate other extrinsic or intrinsic motivators that initially drive learning behaviour. The motivational factors associated with student behaviour towards assessment may be quite different from those associated with learning itself, yet the assessment outcome is often the lasting legacy that a student from an educational institution will take with them into the future. The ability of teachers to facilitate higher-level learning through purposely designed content and group interactivity, coupled with inspirational delivery methods, may be reduced significantly if the assessment tasks are not aligned closely to the articulated learning outcomes (Elwood *et al.*, 2002). Biggs (2002) has emphasized that *assessment for learning* is just as important as *assessment of learning*: 'A thorough analysis of a well-planned assessment may impact more on future learning outcomes than curriculum design or delivery.'

The epistemologies underlying current assessment practices are being questioned because of changing views of human cognition, and the shift from a behaviourist view of human learning towards a more constructivist view (Nichols, 1994). However, these changes are still dependent upon the psychometric paradigm, and the validation of an assessment will still frequently follow scientific methodologies (Wiliam, 1994). There appears to be a strong dependency in the assessment literature on quantitative methodologies to justify the validity and reliability of assessment practices.

Biggs (2002) has been one of the leading proponents of the concept that assessment drives student learning (or at least approaches to learning) and that teachers should take a strategic and integrated approach to curriculum design so that assessment for learning is clearly distinguished from assessment of learning. Assessment of learning has a valid function for accountability and reporting purposes, whereas assessment for learning acknowledges that systematic feedback from the teacher to the student informs the learning and teaching process itself. In order for assessment to be effective in influencing the teaching process, criterion referencing can be used. Criterion referencing involves the comparison of a student's response against a set of established criteria, not against other students. Individuals can improve their own learning outcomes by using ipsative referencing, where a student compares their own performance over a period of time, or in different assessment tasks. This is often used to achieve personal best performances, and allows students to achieve their own goals, independent of their overall level of performance.

Criterion referencing is often used for competency-based assessment and for benchmarking standards for certification and licensing. The assessor establishes an acceptable standard for setting the pass grade. If someone passes this test, they are deemed to be qualified. This process is contrasted with a norm-referenced assessment, where the pass standard will be dependent on the performance of the other students in the group.

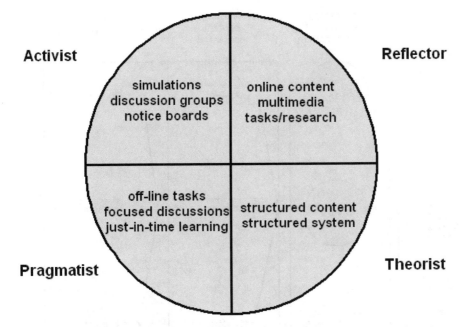

Figure 1.1 Adaptation of the Honey and Mumford learning styles for online learning environment by Palmer *et al.* (2004)

1.2.2 Learning styles

Honey *et al.* (1992) developed their learning styles questionnaire as a diagnostic tool to assist students and teachers adapt their respective approaches to allow for a more productive alignment between learning, teaching and assessment. Their questionnaire was based on the preferred styles of learning resulting from personality models and Kolb's experientially grounded 'Four Stage Model of Learning', namely concrete experience, reflective observation, abstract conceptualization and active experimentation (Kolb, 1984). Honey and Mumford described students as predominantly *activists* (preferring to do something practical), *pragmatists* (preferring to do something related to the real world), *reflectors* (preferring to read and take time to consider alternatives) or *theorists* (preferring to read and analyse the implications). Figure 1.1 illustrates how the Honey and Mumford learning styles could be applied to an online learning environment (Palmer *et al.*, 2004). Activists could be engaged through the use of simulation tools, or game-type activity and the communication tools that facilitate extensive discussion and discourse. Reflectors could find the extensive online content and associated multimedia a rich source of interaction, as they explored issues in depth. Pragmatists would likely be focused on the assessment tasks and their learning would be strategically directed towards the articulated learning objectives that were being assessed. Theorists would be comfortable with a structured virtual learning environment, where consistency in format and well-defined activities were expected.

Palmer *et al.* (2004) have adapted this learning styles approach and investigated how online learning objects (the individual units of learning, or activity) might be presented to students in different ways, depending on the results of a diagnostic learning styles evaluation. The student's learning style is identified by the completion of the diagnostic evaluation, the learning content is then presented to the student in a format compatible with their particular learning style, and an adaptive assessment format is used to maximize efficiency and minimize the number of items presented during the assessment. Figure 1.2 shows an adaptation of the methodology proposed by Palmer *et al.* (2004). A dominant and secondary learning style is identified using this approach, so that corrections may be applied if the students' adaptive assessment results indicate a mismatch between the content presented and the anticipated assessment performance.

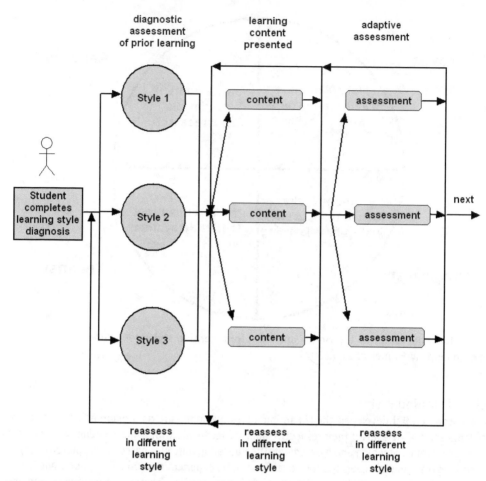

Figure 1.2 Adaptation of the Learning Style Diagnosis methodology proposed by Palmer *et al.* (2004)

1.3 Types of assessment

Assessment tasks may be divided broadly into two types, one requiring responses of a convergent type, in which one correct answer is expected, and the other requiring divergent responses, in which the answer depends on opinion or analysis (Torrance *et al.*, 2001). Examples of convergent assessment responses may include factual knowledge, such as how to determine the slope of a straight line from a graph, or the electron configuration of a particular element from the Periodic Table. Examples of divergent assessment responses may include artistic or literary criticism, medical diagnosis or architectural constructions.

Convergent assessment has its origins in mastery-learning models and involves assessment of the student by the master-teacher, whereas divergent assessment is often associated with a constructivist view of learning, where the teacher and student engage collaboratively within Vygotsky's (1986) zone of proximal development. Assessment tasks are not necessarily limited to either convergent or divergent types, there is a continuum between the two extremes, and it is helpful to the student if the teacher describes where the assessment activity is situated on this continuum. Teachers will often use a teaching methodology that is consistent with their preferred assessment position on the continuum. Thus, teachers may concentrate on knowledge transmission and use if convergent assessment is used predominantly, whereas knowledge synthesis and evaluation will be used if divergent assessment methods are preferred.

Core knowledge for a discipline is often assessed by convergent methodologies, because less time is required to make a judgement about the appropriateness of the student response and specific feedback is readily available because the expected response is predetermined. This type of core knowledge and its assessment is often associated with many of the current examples of e-assessment (Bull *et al.*, 2001). Declarative knowledge (knowing what) is often assessed in a decontextualized environment, and is associated with the unistructural or multistructural level of the SOLO hierarchy (Biggs *et al.*, 1982). Declarative knowledge is mostly fixed for significant periods of time and independent of the context in which it is used. Divergent assessment, where alternative responses have equal validity, allows relational or extended abstract knowledge to be applied, often in a contextual framework that adds meaning for both the student and the teacher.

1.4 Assessment and grading

Assessment is a complex activity. Walvoord *et al.* (2002) have accurately described the context-dependent, complex process of grading, which includes:

- evaluation (the act of judgement)
- communication (the transmission of the judgement to stakeholders)
- motivation (the perception of how the judgement will be made and received, and how behaviours will be modified)
- organization (how the judgement affects student progression, admissions, completions).

All grading involves some form of assessment, but not all assessment involves grading. What then is the difference between assessment and grading? If a teacher assesses the students' response, they do not have to place a value on, nor make a judgement of, the outcome as part of their feedback. They may simply report the students' profile of achievement or what the students' responses were to a particular task. Grading an assessment involves a form of evaluation and may use the students' responses to the assessment task to inform the judgement. Assessment processes may use multiple methods, including tasks that are purposely designed to be graded and allow students to demonstrate what they have learnt. Teachers should decide the purpose of the assessment task, and then inform the students, whether it is associated primarily with improving learning, or for grading purposes. Grading involves judgements about the students' performance, and a comparison of students' responses with a set of predetermined standards (McAlpine, 2002a). Individual teachers may have different expectations for the standards associated with assessment tasks and student responses, so the same assessment process may produce different grades. Thus grades themselves are contextual, they have meaning within a particular environment and to particular stakeholders. Walvoord *et al.* (2002) have proposed 12 principles for teachers to use in managing the grading process:

- appreciate the complexity of grading
- use it as a tool for learning
- substitute judgement for objectivity
- distribute time effectively
- be open to change, listen and observe
- communicate and collaborate with students
- integrate grading with other key processes
- seize the teachable moment
- make learning the primary goal
- be a teacher first and a gatekeeper last
- encourage student-centred motivation
- emphasize student involvement.

Biggs (2002) has described how 'declarative knowledge is traded as a commodity, especially if norm-referencing is used to grade students.' Norm-referencing involves comparing a student's performance with their peers, and assumes the same distribution of student performance for different groups. It is frequently used to justify a predetermined standard expected for all students. Cohort referencing is a form of norm-referencing, and assigns the highest grade to the best performing student in the group, and all other students are graded relative to the best performer. An individual's grade is dependent on the performance of others in the group at that time. Grades could therefore change for an individual student; depending on which group they are in. According to Biggs (2002), the student will determine the amount of effort required to accumulate declarative knowledge based on the assessment methods and their expected outcomes. In a contextualized assessment environment, both declarative and functional knowledge (functional knowledge consists of procedural knowledge, 'knowing how', and strategic knowledge, 'knowing when and why') can be assessed, depending on the consequences of the expected outcome. The consequences of the student response to the assessment task may reflect the situation in real life; there may be an impact on real people, beyond the immediate task at hand. This would be the case where the outcome of the assessment task is not just the awarding of a grade, but a requirement for the student to evaluate the consequences of their responses.

A recent emphasis on the desirability for a hermeneutic judgement (Wiliam, 1994) about the whole student performance has resulted from an awareness of the importance of authentic learning environments and authentic, or performance, assessment tasks (Torrance, 1994). Requiring students to demonstrate competency, or capabilities, by actively undertaking a task that has outcome-based consequences, increases the opportunity to appropriately assess functioning knowledge. Should each assessment task be organized around the authentic paradigm? Assessment tasks are fragments of a complex judgement process, and teachers will frequently deconstruct the whole learning experience to make the assessment process more manageable. Teachers will then assemble the individual component tasks, and their associated student responses and grades, to arrive at a hermeneutic judgement about the whole student performance. As part of the deconstruction process, teachers need to decide the proportion of the assessment that will be associated with the products of learning, and those associated with the process of learning.

Section 2 **How will I make an e-assessment?**

2 Guidelines for e-assessment practices

2.1 Professional bodies publishing guidelines on assessment

The National Science Foundation (NSF) in the USA supported the Committee on the Foundations of Assessment in publishing a review on advances in cognitive science and measurement, and their implications for changes in educational assessment (Pellegrino *et al.*, 2001). The review concentrated on school-level assessment, but is applicable across all educational levels and emphasized the need for classroom and large-scale assessments that would assist students to learn by clearly articulating their accomplishments and the various stages in their developmental progress. Every assessment was seen to:

> rest on three pillars: a model of how students represent knowledge and develop compe-
> tence in the subject domain, tasks or situations that allow one to observe students'
> performance, an interpretation method for drawing inferences from the performance
> evidence thus obtained. (Pellegrino *et al.*, 2001)

The report presents three elements that form the sides of the 'assessment triangle' – cognition, observation and interpretation. The proposed framework for cognition revolves around students using their working or short-term memory, which has limited storage capacity, and long-term memory, which is capable of storing significant quantities of knowledge. Drawing on the knowledge stored in long-term memory, and using it to solve current problems, can improve students' performances in an assessment task. An understanding of how students organize information in long-term memory, rather than improving the working memory capacity, is therefore likely to be more effective at improving performance in assessment. Conceptual models of cognition and learning should form the basis for the appropriate design and implementation of assessment tasks and practices. Cognitive science has well-established methodologies for the design, observation and analysis of students' behaviour and responses when undertaking tasks, and subsequently defining the processes a student has used to achieve the observed result. Such methodologies have the potential to be applied to the systematic design of effective educational assessment tasks.

Many professional educational organizations have published guidelines on general assessment practices. The American Association for Higher Education (AAHE) has developed the following nine principles for assessment activity:

- the assessment of student learning begins with educational values
- assessment is most effective when it reflects an understanding of learning as multidimensional, integrated and revealed in performance over time
- assessment works best when the programmes it seeks to improve have clear, explicitly stated purposes
- assessment requires attention to outcomes but also and equally to the experiences that lead to those outcomes
- assessment works best when it is ongoing, not episodic
- assessment fosters wider improvement when representatives from across the educational community are involved
- assessment makes a difference when it begins with issues of use and illuminates questions that people really care about

- assessment is most likely to lead to improvement when it is part of a larger set of conditions that promote change
- through assessment, educators meet responsibilities to students and to the public.

In the UK, the Higher Education Academy (HEA) has published guidelines for the use of formative assessment feedback to improve student learning, including a conceptual model that highlights the importance of feedback as a means to identify gaps in understanding. Student feedback from an assessment should lead students 'to a re-interpretation of the task or to the adjustment of internal goals or of tactics and strategies' (Juwah *et al.*, 2004). Using feedback encourages the student to be an active participant in the assessment process, and facilitates the use of formative feedback to inform approaches to learning that will lead to improvements in student-identified goals. The Learning and Teaching Support Network (LTSN) series on assessment includes a set of guidelines for lecturers that emphasizes the alignment of assessment with other features of the course, including the aims, clear and realistic outcomes, relevant learning opportunities, well-articulated criteria and consistency of judgement by the teacher (LTSN, 2001). The LTSN has published a series of these guidelines for students, heads of departments and senior managers, as well as a paper on 'Assessing Key Skills by Video or Audio Presentation' (White, 2004) and 'A Briefing on Assessment in Problem-based Learning' (Macdonald *et al.*, 2004).

In Australia, there have been renewed efforts to highlight the link between assessment practices and student behaviour (James *et al.*, 2002). As educational environments become more flexible, students look for guidance on appropriate ways to develop generic skills, such as those associated with communication, group work and critical thinking. The ability of teachers to develop methods for the assessment of these generic skills is seen as an important component of the Australian educational scene. There has been an emerging appreciation of new technological possibilities for assessment, including the potential to integrate assessment in new ways with learning. The recent report from the Centre for Study of Higher Education (CSHE), highlighted five contemporary assessment issues in higher education, including capturing the potential of e-assessment, designing efficient and effective assessment for large classes, responding to plagiarism and developing policies to foster academic honesty, using assessment to guide effective group work and recognizing the needs of students unfamiliar with assessment practices at Australian higher education institutions (James *et al.*, 2002).

The British Standard, 'Code of practice for the use of information technology (IT) for the delivery of assessments', BS 7988, introduces guidelines and requirements for any organization that uses computers to create and deliver assessments (BSI, 2002). The standard includes guidelines on the lifecycle of an e-assessment, the verification of online candidates in remote locations, the provision of practice tests, the design of outcomes/assessment methodology, the distribution and delivery of assessment tasks, how responses and feedback should be returned to students, how response analysis should be completed, as well as the appeals and certification processes associated with assessments.

The key national body, the Scottish Qualifications Authority (SQA), has taken an integrated approach to the introduction of e-assessment across all educational sectors in Scotland through the establishment of the SQA guidelines for e-assessment (SQA, 2003). This integrated approach resulted from a realization that there are significant benefits, but also significant challenges, associated with the use of computer technologies in learning and assessment (McAlpine *et al.*, 2003). The guidelines cover definitions for the various terms used in e-assessments and acceptable behaviours in relation to the use of internet-based tools for the creation, storage and delivery of assessments to candidates; the capture, marking, storage and analysis of their responses; and the collation, return and analysis of the associated results. SQA has identified a number of development activities that must take place if e-assessment is to be adopted more widely by Scottish educational institutions. The first was the need for item banks to be created for all forms of assessment. Item banks are discussed in more detail in Chapter 7, and are required for any large-scale adoption of e-assessment. SQA also identified the need for a more widespread use of scanning technology for the marking and quality assurance of paper-based scripts associated with final year school examinations. The universal adoption of electronic portfolios for collating the evidence generated by internal assessment was also seen as a critical factor if e-assessment was to be embedded in Scottish educational practice.

The SQA collaborated with the Scottish Centre for Research into Online Learning and Assessment (SCROLLA), to examine the pedagogical principles underpinning e-assessment and defined five strategic aims designed to improve the Scottish assessment system (http://www.scrolla.ac.uk). These include:

■ increased flexibility in when and where assessments are taken
■ improved access, especially for those candidates for whom special assessment arrangements are required
■ increased cost-effectiveness of internal processes and enhanced practicability
■ greater reliability and validity of the assessment process
■ enhanced possibilities for feedback and reporting on the results of assessment.

The collaborative approach to implementing good practices in e-assessment use and design in Scotland has also seen the publication of the 'Good Practice Guide in Question and Test Design from Pass-it' (PASS-IT). The guide generally assumes that e-assessment is associated with objective tests, and emphasizes that such tests are just one method of assessment. The guide also supports the premise that declarative knowledge, and to a limited extent some forms of functional knowledge, can be assessed using technology, but proposes that objective tests cannot be used to assess creativity, integration of ideas nor the capacity to develop a sustained argument. This is interesting, because the guide concentrates on the use of technology to assess traditional learning, and does not address the issue of students using technology to find solutions to complex tasks based on higher-level functional knowledge.

2.2 Assessment models

Do all forms of assessment, whether they are based on principles derived from applied technology, cognitive science or psychometrics, have a common framework or design architecture? An attempt has been made to describe the common, underlying features of all assessment types, and identify the relationships between the individual assessment components consisting of the delivery mechanism, the scoring process, the decision rules and any associated feedback.

The four-process architecture, proposed by Almond et al. (2002), uses a generic description that should apply to any assessment, and includes activity selection, presentation, response processing and summary scoring, as summarized in Figure 2.1.

The initial step in the sequence, the *activity selection process*, occurs when the teacher (or assessor) selects and sequences tasks from the *task/evidence composite library* (a database of task descriptions, materials, rules and evidence parameters) in order to construct an assessment task. Once this is completed, information is sent to the *presentation process*, which is responsible for presenting the assessment task to the participant (student). Materials may be retrieved from the task library, for example an examination paper; or for e-assessments, material such as images, audio or Java applets. When the student responds to the task, the presentation process will record their response as a *work product*. This could be in the form of a paper examination script, or a computer file. The work product is delivered to the *response processing* section for evaluation, which may consist of a simple scoring process, or a more complex series of judgements about the students' responses. These evaluations are recorded as a series of observations that are passed to the *summary scoring process* that updates the *scoring record*. The scoring record is the summary of the assessor's judgements about the students' knowledge, skills and abilities, based on the evidence presented for all tasks. Separating the response processing step from both the summary scoring and the presentation is vital to an evidence-based focus in assessment design and supports the reuse of the task in multiple contexts. The advantage of

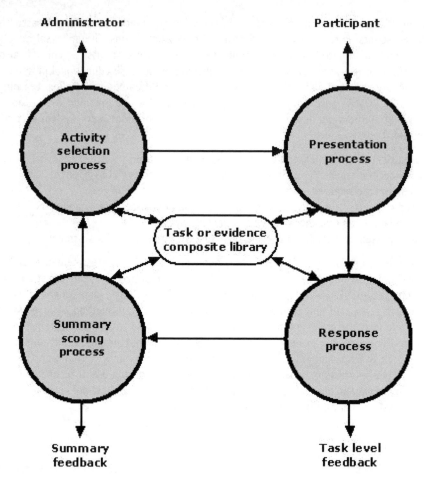

Administrator

Participant

Activity
selection
process

Presentation
process

Task or evidence
composite library

Summary
scoring
process

Response
process

**Summary
feedback**

**Task level
feedback**

Figure 2.1 A four-process architecture for assessment from Almond *et al.* (2002)

viewing an assessment as a modular process is that complex tasks can be undertaken with a clear view of the relationships between the design framework and the operational processes.

A particularly useful approach to categorizing and organizing the entities and activities associated with assessments in e-learning in a visual framework has been proposed in the form of FREMA (Framework Reference Model for Assessment, http://www.frema.ecs.soton.ac.uk). The visualization of the reference model uses a concept map approach and attempts to draw together the disparate service descriptions, software offerings and case studies associated with e-assessments (Millard *et al.*, 2005). The FREMA website provides a number of useful interactive Flash® objects for exploring the complexity of e-assessments, as illustrated in Figures 2.2 and 2.3.

2.3 e-Assessment practices and their relationship to learning

The use of technology will not, by itself, necessarily improve student outcomes with respect to assessment. In order to achieve demonstrable improvements in assessment outcomes a design process that connects the three elements of the 'assessment triangle', the theory of cognition, the observations and the interpretation process, should work together to support the intended outcomes (Pellegrino *et al.*, 2001).

Online learning and e-assessment are sometimes portrayed as universal panaceas for improving the general level of skills and capabilities for the wider group of students now partici-pating in formal education in society (Bennett, 2002). Shifting from what might be regarded as

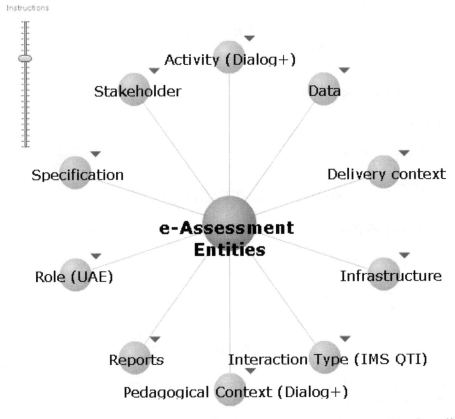

Instructions

Activity (Dialog+)

Stakeholder

Data

Specification

Delivery context

e-Assessment Entities

Role (UAE)

Infrastructure

Reports

Interaction Type (IMS QTI)

Pedagogical Context (Dialog+)

Figure 2.2 Framework Reference Model for Assessment, e-assessment entities (http://www. frema.ecs.soton.ac.uk)

traditional approaches to learning and assessment towards more innovative and technologically enhanced approaches is seen by some as inevitable and inexorable. In North America, there has already been a significant shift to the use of e-assessment by many professional and educational testing organizations.

e-Assessment has often been associated with the presentation of surface assessment tasks that tended to focus on declarative knowledge, and this has influenced some of the decisions associated with curriculum design in online education programmes (Northcote, 2003). Surface assessment tasks requiring students to provide predetermined responses based on declarative knowledge have been linked to multiple-choice (MCQ) and short-answer questions. Deep assessment tasks require students to provide open-ended responses that are based more on functional knowledge rather than just facts. In terms of online instructional design principles, this apparent dichotomy between surface and deep approaches could be better represented as a continuum between an instructivist and a constructivist approach (Herrington *et al.*, 1999). Tam (2000, p. 58) has outlined the consequences of teaching in an online environment as being able to:

> replace the determinist, teacher-controlled model of distance education with contextualised work environments, thinking tools and a conversation media that support the knowledge construction process in different settings.

There are clear distinctions that can be drawn between the cognitive effects of technology on students, and the cognitive effects of learning with technology (Quellmalz *et al.*, 2003). Students may use technology to prepare an essay, but it may have minimal impact on the cognitive

Figure 2.3 Framework Reference Model for Assessment, e-assessment processes (http://www.frema.ecs.soton.ac.uk)

processes they use to mentally construct the components of the essay. In contrast, when students adapt the capabilities of the technology to develop new approaches to problem-solving, they are using cognitive processes that are different from those used without the technology. Appropriate alignment of learning and teaching enables the strategic use of technology in the educational setting. Appropriate learning environments allow students to choose how to integrate technologies into problem-solving activities; including planning how to:

- approach a task
- access and organize information
- manipulate, analyse, interpret and transform data
- evaluate the relevance and reliability of information
- communicate their results and argument
- collaborate with others to solve complex tasks:

(Quellmalz *et al.*, 2003)

Some teachers see e-assessment as a 'risky' activity (Zakrzewski *et al.*, 2000). Teachers are often uncertain of the pedagogic value of objective tests, apprehensive about the level of technical support required in order to maintain the integrity and security of the online delivery system and suspicious of the level of administrative staff required for the operational procedures of complex technical systems. A successful model for implementing e-assessment across an institution should aim to minimize as many risks as possible, as outlined by Stephens *et al.* (1998) in their suggested guidelines:

- establish a coordinated e-assessment management policy for the appropriate central unit and each discipline on campus
- establish a central unit responsible for e-assessment

- appoint discipline coordinators within departments/schools
- establish e-assessment discipline groups/committees
- provide adequate funding
- organize staff development programmes
- establish appropriate evaluation procedures
- identify technical issues and operational procedures to deal with them.

The Computer-assisted Assessment (CAA) Centre in the UK operated between 1998 and 2001, and made a significant contribution to higher education assessment practice with strategic advice on the implementation of e-assessment, the production of staff development and training material and an annual international conference on computer-based assessment. The CAA annual conference continues and is an excellent source of information, case studies and good practice examples in e-assessment. One of the highlights from the work of the Centre has been the CAA Blueprint, which discusses the reasons why an increase in the use of e-assessment would benefit teachers, students and educational institutions (Bull *et al.*, 2003). These reasons include their belief that an increase in the frequency of appropriate e-assessment tasks will lead to an improvement in student learning, that a broader range of topics can be covered in e-assessment tasks, that staff workload in terms of marking can be reduced and that automated feedback will benefit students.

The CAA Blueprint commented that increasing the frequency of high stakes assessment will have a positive impact on students if it is coupled to appropriate learning activities, and not perceived as simply an additional burden. Teachers can facilitate higher-level learning by designing the curriculum around authentic learning and authentic assessment activities. Simply transferring face-to-face classroom assessment tasks to an online environment will not allow for authentic, performance-based assessments. Such assessments require the student to interact with real world tools and to contemplate the real world consequences of their responses. Authentic assessment attempts to measure the process of generating the responses, as well as the response itself.

3 Types of e-assessment items

3.1 Types of e-assessment

e-Assessment involves the use of any computer- or web-based method that allows systematic inferences and judgements to be made about the students' skills, knowledge and capabilities. e-Assessment formats and tools vary widely, and may include activities ranging from non-authenticated, formative quizzes or tests where students can take the assessment as many times as they wish, through to formally invigilated, summative examinations. For an assessment to take place online, three components are normally involved, namely the creation, storage and delivery of an assessment to students; the capture, marking, storage and analysis of student responses; and the collation, return and analysis of the results (SQA, 2003).

Formal examinations are usually summative in nature and are used to verify a student's level of knowledge or skill in a specific discipline. This is often a high-stake assessment, since the results will often be used to determine whether the student is allowed to progress to the next level of the programme. Alternatively, the assessment may be used to verify completion requirements for a programme and the potential employment opportunities for the student may be dependent on the outcomes. Open access quizzes or tests may be diagnostic or formative, and are usually low stakes, since the results will not normally prevent a student from continuing in their current programme. As with other forms of assessment, those carried out online may be either criterion-referenced or norm-referenced. For the criterion-referenced, or mastery learning approach, teachers will predetermine the acceptable standard that must be reached by the student. A benchmark for acceptability will be established and it is irrelevant what one student achieves in relation to another from the same cohort. In contrast, a norm-referenced assessment will compare the performance of students against others in the cohort, and the relative ranking of individual students is important.

The broad categories of e-assessments are summarized in Table 3.1 and may be described as either:

- diagnostic, where an assessment task is used to identify the current knowledge and skill level of students so that learning activities can match student requirements
- formative, where an assessment task provides practice for students on their learning in the current course and possible development activities they could undertake in order to improve their level of understanding
- summative, where assessment task responses are designed to grade and judge a student's level of understanding and skill development for progression or certification.

Table 3.1 Summary of assessment types

Assessment type	Assessment stakes	Authentication of student	Effect on learning
Diagnostic	Low	Not required	Learning can be improved
Formative	Low, Medium	Not required	Learning can be improved
Summative	Medium, High	Required	Learning not usually improved

Diagnostic assessments are undertaken before learning has occurred in the current course. Typical examples would include a skills gap analysis in industry or in an introductory mathematics class where the teacher wishes to make a decision about where to start the first class to ensure that the majority of students will be able to engage with the new material. Students may wish to undertake diagnostic tests to determine if their prior knowledge is adequate to attempt a new course. Foreign language teachers may use diagnostic tests to determine the general level of fluency of the class with respect to grammar and vocabulary. Formative assessment is invaluable during the learning process, since it provides a low stakes benchmark for students and teachers, and provides a suitable method for providing useful feedback to individual students at a critical point in the learning process. For example, if students complete an online quiz designed to assess their understanding of a particular concept enunciated during a didactic presentation, the teacher, on viewing the response files, may discover that a significant proportion of the class has not responded appropriately to a particular question or set of questions. The next time the teacher interacts with the class they may then address the gaps in the class. Both teachers and students may use the results of a formative assessment to strategically map out future learning approaches. As Biggs (1999, p. 142) states:

> Formative assessment is inseparable from teaching. Indeed the effectiveness of different teaching methods is directly related to their ability to provide formative feedback.

Summative assessments usually occur after the learning process, and provide a judgement or summary of the overall knowledge, skills and capabilities developed by the student. They are most often taken at a stage when no further learning is possible for the course being assessed, and are usually taken very seriously by the teacher and student. If diagnostic and formative assessment tasks are used appropriately, and in a timely manner, the summative assessment process should not be particularly stressful, since the content of the summative assessment would build on the tasks used for the diagnostic and formative assessments. As diagnostic and formative assessments are low to medium stake activities, strict invigilation and individual student authentication are not usually critical. The purpose of these assessments is to improve learning and provide feedback to the student, not to rank or grade individuals. Collaboration and cooperation among students during formative assessment would be beneficial since it would encourage engagement with the course content, and a sharing of ideas and experiences. Online formats are highly suited to the design and delivery of diagnostic and formative assessments, where the validity and reliability of the assessment responses are related to their ability to lead to improvements in learning. This contrasts with summative assessments, where a psychometric analysis of participant responses and grade distribution is often conducted because of the high stakes of the assessment results to the individual student and the reputation of the institution. Online formats are also suitable for summative assessments, but more attention will be required for the authentication of individual students, technical support and the validity and reliability of the assessment responses.

A model for diagnostic, formative and summative assessment tasks linked to learning activities is shown in Figure 3.1. An integrated learning-assessment model allows for both intrinsic and extrinsic reward factors for both students and teachers, and the provision of appropriate feedback to students becomes the critical component that links the assessment to the learning. Online activities can provide teachers with appropriate opportunities to provide useful feedback to students in large classes, a task that is difficult in terms of face-to-face sessions. In the online environment, multimedia and helper applications may be incorporated into both the question and student responses. The additional time invested in designing appropriate questions and the associated feedback is often compensated for by less time spent on marking, or providing individual feedback to students. The use of e-assessment will not necessarily reduce expenditure on assessment, nor the time teachers must allocate to the entire assessment process, but it does provide an opportunity for students and teachers to reallocate their resources more efficiently in order to improve the quality of the learning experience and its outcomes.

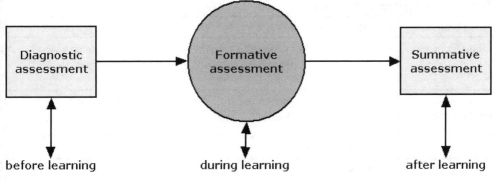

before learning · during learning · after learning

Figure 3.1 Relationship between diagnostic, formative and summative assessment

Different types of e-assessment employ different functionality, ranging from the simple assessment tools embedded in virtual learning environments through to sophisticated, purpose-built applications. Technically, objective question types are relatively simple to incorporate into computer databases, and so this question type has tended to dominate the current use of e-assessment in virtual learning environment. Objective questions are defined as those that have a predetermined correct answer and require the student to respond by:

- selecting a response from a set of choices (MCQ, true-false, matching, multiple response)
- identifying an object or position on the computer screen (graphical hotspot)
- supplying short text responses (text input, word or phrase matching)
- entering numeric responses or mathematical formula (number input or algebraic comparison).

The primary characteristic of the technology that is being used for objective tests is the ability to provide automated marking, grading and feedback in a non-subjective manner, since no teacher judgement is required at the time of marking. However, subjectivity may have been incorporated into the assessment when the teacher provided the marking scheme and predetermined which responses were acceptable. Teachers make professional interpretations and judgements when constructing and marking assessments, and in creating rubrics. In order to make sense of the students' response, teachers must also make sense of their own judgements and assumptions (McMillan, 2000). One issue that frequently arises when online objective assessment tasks are marked is that of relative or comparative equivalence in different student responses. Short-text entry responses are difficult to mark automatically as the teacher must decide which set of responses will be acceptable, including alternative spellings, the use of upper and lower-case text and the use of abbreviations. For online mathematical responses, two different but equivalent responses may be provided by two different students, yet both must be interpreted by the technology as equivalent.

Objective tests do provide a number of practical advantages to both the student and teacher, including the provision of automatic feedback (scores, hints and directions for further learning) and the statistical analysis of class results and individual question responses. The most common concern with objective tests is the assumption that they cannot assess learning beyond basic comprehension. When using a computer for assessment, appropriately constructed questions and web-based tools do allow students to manipulate information or data, and to demonstrate problem-solving capabilities. Objective tests can enable a relatively large number of questions to be included in one assessment, thus allowing a wide coverage of the knowledge base for the curriculum. The inclusion of many short questions may result in students not having sufficient time to complete the test, and it is generally found that students take longer to complete traditional questions on a computer, compared to equivalent questions on paper (Thomas et al., 2002).

Table 3.2 e-Assessment item types

Item type	General characteristics
Bulletin boards	Information or discussion topics posted to online board. Students' work may be posted for peer review. Useful for posting exemplars of student work.
Cloze exercise (fill-in-the-blanks)	A passage of text is presented with key words deleted. Students are required to construct meaning from the text. It is a form of cueing where the student is expected to be familiar with the content and to construct meaning while reading.
Collaborative assignments	Set authentic tasks that groups have to investigate and solve. Students use online resources to work collaboratively and share findings. Develops team-building skills.
Email	Use email for receiving and tracking reports, assignments and essays. Return work by email with annotations.
Free text responses or essays	The student enters short or extended text in an open-ended text entry field. Extensive text passages may require manual marking.
Hot spot	Click on the computer screen to identify a specific part of a visual presentation.
Likert scale	A Likert-scale question is a form of MCQ in which the student chooses a degree of agreement or disagreement, usually 3–7 predefined choices.
Matrix or composite multiple choice	The student responds by selecting one response in each row from a matrix of radio buttons. Used for questions that are related and allow contextual alignment of concepts.
Macromedia® Flash™	A Macromedia® Flash™ question is usually interactive and requires the student to click various objects or move objects on the screen.
Multiple choice question (MCQ)	The student responds by selecting a response from a list of two or more choices; may include text, image, audio or movie. Choices can include hotspots or sliders.
Online discussion, discussion board	Discussion through chat rooms, forums and threaded discussion. Tasks may be set for individuals or groups to complete.
Ordering, matching or sequencing	Students select or arrange choices in an ordered sequence based on a predetermined criterion. May be text, graphic, audio or movie format.
Peer review	Students view and judge each other's work. Useful for setting standards.
Portfolios	Allow students to collect evidence of their learning in the form of a range of materials appropriate to the course. Can include essays, web pages, multimedia files.
Pull-down list	Students choose from a predetermined list of choices, similar to MCQ.
Ranking	Requires the student to characterize the available choices in a predetermined order.
Role-play	Students adopt a persona in a simulated activity. Assess consequences to actions.

Item type	General characteristics
Simulations	Students engage with interactive application to generate results and consequences. Interactions can be complicated, and may not have one correct response. Analysis of interactions may be complicated. Authentic assessment environment.
Text match or short answer	Student enters short text in a limited sized text entry field to respond to the question. Type of free text response.
True/False	Type of MCQ where a statement is presented that is factually correct or incorrect.
Type a number (numeric comparison)	Student enters a number in a text entry field, could be response to mathematics question.
Web design or publication	Allow students to self and peer assess web design work of others, or publish their own web pages.
Wiki	Allow students to undertake group project and present a common product.

There is a preconception that all web-based assessment can only assess lower order skills, such as those requiring unistructural responses (Biggs, 2002). This has lead to justifiable criticism of MCQs that focus on unistructural declarative knowledge and do not allow students the opportunity to demonstrate transferable capabilities and understanding. However, there are several examples of the use of e-assessment applications that test higher order capabilities including the Tripartite Interactive Assessment Delivery System, which uses Authorware™ (TRIADS, http://www.derby.ac.uk/assess), Canvas Learning (http://www.canvaslearning.com) and CASE-IT (http://caseit.uwrf.edu/caseit.html). Specific examples of online question types and student responses can be found in Chapter 6.

3.2 Types of e-assessment items

What are the types of assessment questions that can be developed for use on computers or through a web browser? Potentially, any assessment task can be converted into a digital format that would allow a student to respond in a manner that indicates the development of specific knowledge, skills and capabilities. Table 3.2 summarizes many of the common forms of e-assessment item types. Regular online quizzes using MCQs with appropriate feedback provide students with a valuable learning resource. Learning activities that can be assessed through the online environment include threaded discussions; student conferences or chat sessions; email, bulletin boards, wikis and blogs that are used for collaborative assignments; web-based portfolios, which may include a student generated website or software development; and role-plays and simulations where students are immersed in an authentic environment and the consequences of their actions may be tested.

4 Consequences of using an e-assessment

4.1 Risks involved in using e-assessment

In order to ensure quality in e-assessment, teachers and institutions should identify the risks involved and the processes that may be put in place to minimize, or eliminate, the likelihood of those risks occurring (Zakrzewski *et al.*, 2000). One of the first steps in risk identification is to define the purpose of the assessment, in order to determine whether the consequence to the student from undertaking the task is low, medium or high stakes in nature. For low stakes diagnostic or formative assessments, the adverse consequences that may arise from a major disruption to the assessment process are minimal, whereas for high stakes summative exams the adverse consequences for the individual student and the institution are significant should the delivery system fail or the validity and reliability of the assessment be challenged. The 'Catherine Wheel', describing the spiral nature of the structured approach to e-assessment design and implementation (Zakrzewski *et al.*, 2000), is a convenient model that may be used for risk mitigation and for establishing the strategies that can be put in place at the institutional level. The teacher, and the institution, should be aware that there are risks that may result from the use of e-assessment in the pedagogic, operational, technical and financial domains.

Institutions are usually faced with an initial decision about which e-assessment software system they will implement. When evaluating software for e-assessment, the following issues have been identified as critical to the decision-making process (Bull *et al.*, 2004):

- interoperability (IMS standards – see Chapter 10 for more details)
- existing systems and integration
- scaleability
- performance levels
- upgrading procedures and limitations
- support and maintenance
- security – particularly where summative assessment is intended
- accessibility.

The ability to resolve the conflicting properties of ease of access from remote computer sites on the one hand, and individual student authentication on the other, continues to limit many high-stake applications for e-assessment. Although students may be issued with individual passwords or encrypted smart cards, and e-assessments may be restricted to particular computers by specifying IP addresses, non-invasive methods that allow a secure level of individual authentication from remote locations are not currently available. The issue of impersonation, with or without the students' permission, is a real impediment to conducting large-scale summative assessments if the student is allowed to access the web from any location. It is possible to use iris or fingerprint authentication, but the technology and culture within educational institutions is not really ready for this degree of security.

Students will require a number of practice sessions in order to be confident and adept at using the assessment system, especially if the software tools have not been used during the learning phase (Clariana *et al.*, 2002). Ideally, students should have used the software for diagnostic and formative assessments prior to undertaking a high stakes summative assessment online. Technical difficulties are still frequently encountered when using the World Wide Web, such as computers not being functional, broken links to Internet service providers or networks, slow data transfer rates across telephone lines, slow processor speeds because of old hardware and software incompatibilities. e-Assessments can be designed to run through a basic web browser, but in order to take advantage of many of the sophisticated features of the web environment so that teachers may assess higher level learning, additional technologies such as Java-enabled browsers or browser plug-ins are likely to be required. Teachers will also need to be aware of the bandwidth requirements for any multimedia additions to their assessment tasks, as students accessing the Internet from home using a standard telephone modem may find it impractical to complete a sophisticated and interactive e-assessment.

There are many technical precautions that can be taken to improve the reliability of the delivery process for an e-assessment, including software features that reduce the chances of the loss of students' responses by the prevention of accidental quitting during the assessment and the saving of partially-completed student responses or the ability to commence partially-completed assessments. Student responses may be encrypted when transferred across the Internet, minimizing the opportunities for interference with the data. Teachers can minimize opportunities for copying and cheating by allowing the assessment software to select items randomly from an item bank, and to shuffle the order of items and the order in which options are presented to the student. Care must be taken, however, when questions are randomized, as the selection and ordering of multiple-choice stems and options may affect student performance (Clariana et al., 2002). Test banks will be discussed in more detail in Section 4, but mathematical studies have highlighted the difficulties that may be encountered when ranking students in a high stakes test based on MCQs while using norm-referencing (Burton, 2001).

Bates (1995) states that new technologies are often applied in a manner that attempts to mimic the traditional classroom teaching paradigms that have been derived from face-to-face teaching, and that technological innovations are usually added as extras within an existing model. e-Assessment is often used in courses where the contact between student and teacher is predominantly face-to-face, so the skills developed during the learning phases of the course may not assist the student who is confronted suddenly with an e-assessment. Since assessment tasks must be aligned with the course pedagogy, as well as the stated aims and objectives, the teacher may need to rethink the overall assessment strategy, if it is to reflect appropriately the aims and methodologies adopted during learning. Students may be disadvantaged when using e-assessments, compared to other forms of assessment, unless care is taken with the student-assessment interface. Evidence suggests that students perform better when they are not required to scroll through the question paper and many find it difficult to read from the computer screen for extended periods of time (Ricketts et al., 2002).

There are still a number of challenges facing the teacher in deciding whether to use e-assessment for certain activities. These include how to assess each student's participation in an online discussion, how to assess individual performances within group assignments, how to authenticate individual students in remote locations and how to detect and prevent plagiarism. Sector-wide studies in Australia (Booth et al., 2003) have highlighted a number of concerns from teachers, including pedagogical and technological issues such as measuring the quality of online contributions between students and between students and teachers; creating methods to ensure assessments carried out online yield evidence that is relevant to the skills being assessed; and evaluating students' readiness for online learning and assessment. Teachers were also concerned with the amount of time and resources required to undertake appropriate e-assessments and the level of online support required for both teachers and students during an e-assessment activity. Future versions of e-assessments will need to address all of these issues, and will clearly be dependent upon advances in information and communication technology in general. These advances will inevitably lead to more sophisticated diagnostic and formative assessment tools and the possibility of customized learning programmes based on an evaluation of specific students' needs.

The widespread use of MCQs and other selected response formats for test items has caused an over-representation of quantitative question types in e-assessments. Teachers would like to use questions that require a more qualitative response, so that relational and extended abstract responses can be assessed. Kendle *et al.* (2000) have proposed ten criteria to guide the design and development of effective qualitative e-assessment tasks:

- assessment tasks should be open-ended
- tasks should have a clear purpose and outcome
- tasks should be authentic in nature
- there should be an emphasis on process over product
- collaboration and communication should be incorporated in tasks
- students should have varying degrees of choice in their assessment tasks
- tasks should be linked to unit or course objectives
- feedback mechanisms should be included in the task design
- tasks should encourage the appropriate, discriminatory use of online resources
- tasks should enable students to examine and present many viewpoints.

The consequence of offering a more open-ended question type is that it may be difficult to automatically mark student responses, and automated feedback to individual student responses is very unlikely. Manual marking may be required, depending on the complexity of the student responses. This is not necessarily a disadvantage; it is a consequence that teachers need to be aware of so that appropriate time can be allowed for marking and feedback. Good assessment designs may require that a variety of quantitative and qualitative item types are offered to students, with some marked automatically by the software and some marked manually by the teacher.

The costs that need to be considered with e-assessment are not simply those associated with the software and hardware, but also those associated with creating or purchasing test banks, the provision of feedback to students, staff development to assist staff to produce appropriate questions, supporting invigilation, as well as technical support for staff and students. Economies of scale may be possible as the use of e-assessment increases, and the availability of item test banks becomes more common. Staff development will not only involve the teaching staff, but also librarians, administrative officers and technical support staff. e-Assessment will become a team activity involving a variety of experts, and the management of successful teams will be a critical factor in the development of a high-quality educational product.

One of the frequently discussed, and controversial, topics in terms of marking e-assessment responses is that of negative marking. The main rationale for the use of negative marking is to reduce the perceived advantage of gaining marks by 'guessing', a definite possibility when using MCQs and true/false questions. Mathematical models have indicated the theoretical effect that guessing may have on multiple-choice question responses (Burton *et al.*, 1999; Burton, 2001). If negative marking is used, if can be applied within a particular question, and so affect the mark for only that question, or it can be applied to the test as a whole. Examples of various negative marking schemes may be found within the CASTLE Toolkit (CASTLE Toolkit). Students may respond to questions using 'informed' guessing and teachers may wish to ensure that credit is given to students who respond to a question with some level of skill, rather than penalizing the student or placing them in a position where they would rather not respond because the negative marking is severe. One option would be to assign $N-1$ marks for a correct answer (the key), where N represents the total number of options for each MCQ and deduct $1/N-1$ for each distracter selected. This system is also suitable for MCQs with more than one correct response. Some applications of negative marking in MCQs use the option 'don't know' in addition to the normal distracters. Partial negative marks are then applied to the 'don't know' option, and higher negative marks are applied to the distracters. It is possible to include a scale of certainty with MCQs, and assign marks, both positive and negative, for both the response and the degree of certainty. Negative marking may be regarded as a special case of partial credit, where part marks are assigned to different choices and allow more discrimination in the marking range (Bush, 2001).

4.2 How is e-assessment currently being used?

Who is using e-assessment and how is it currently being used? There has been a marked increase in the use of the web for assessment purposes in recent years. Surveys conducted in the UK have shown a significant number of higher education institutions using computers for assessment (Bull *et al.*, 2003). This is an accelerating trend, with the use more common in the science-based disciplines such as biomedical and geological sciences, chemistry, mathematics and engineering (Bull *et al.*, 2003). Current e-assessment activity most frequently involves the use of a web-browser to deliver assessments to students across the Internet or a local intranet, and accessed from a PC or laptop computer. Alternative devices that are becoming increasingly popular for portable web access are handheld or pocket PCs and personal digital assistants (PDAs) as well as Smart Phones; such devices are now capable of using a web browser and offer wireless access to the Internet or a local intranet.

The accelerated uptake of the use of the Internet for assessment has not necessarily been translated into new learning and assessment methodologies. Many teachers are attempting to introduce teaching methodologies that are built around constructivist theory, but are still entrenched in instructivist practices, especially in relation to e-learning and e-assessment (Herrington *et al.*, 1999). Traditional assessment formats, such as three-hour examinations, 5000-word essays, and standardized MCQ tests are indicative of the retention of instructivist practices. Many current examples of e-assessment are designed to reward surface learning by posing questions that require students to reproduce predetermined responses based on objectivist knowledge. Such knowledge is essential within the learning framework, but students should be encouraged to progress beyond just objectivist knowledge to more creative knowledge forms. This requires more sophisticated forms of assessment, and in the online environment would include the use of additional software tools as well as collaboration and communication tools.

Constructivist assessment practices would provide students with the opportunity to assemble assessment responses that reflect authentic solutions and the exploration of the consequences of the proposed solution. This socio-cognitive environment would allow qualitative assessment tasks to be set and fulfil the potential of e-assessment to move beyond simply quantitative assessment tasks based on predetermined responses. The development of metacognitive capabilities in students would be a natural consequence of the integrated use of diagnostic, formative and summative assessment modes, and the expectation of student participation in authentic problem-solving. The development of metacognitive skills must then be incorporated into the curriculum otherwise students will not be in a position to benefit from the expanded use of the online learning environment.

In the United States, numerous school districts have incorporated online curricular-outcome testing into elementary and secondary schools with a view to maintaining standards and allowing reporting of educational outcomes across an entire state system (Bennett, 2002). The 'No Child Left Behind Act' of 2001 (NCLB, http://www.ed.gov/nclb/landing.jhtml) requires all states to assess mathematics and reading in grades 3–8, plus one high-school grade, no later than 2006 and has resulted in large-scale, standardized e-assessments being used as integral components of legislated, standards-based educational paradigms. The NCLB legislation requires states to set proficiency levels for each assessment task and holds schools, districts and states accountable for educational standards. Such a mandated form of measuring assessment outcomes has many consequences for the relationship between assessment and learning.

Increasingly, many occupational, professional and educational institutions are using standardized testing for certification and quality assurance purposes. Many of these standardized tests are conducted online because of the economies of scale that can be gained from running very large-scale testing for specific student cohorts. Examples include: the College-Level Examination Program® (CLEP®), Graduate Record Examinations® General Test (GRE®, http://www.gre.org), Graduate Management Admission Test® (GMAT®, http://www.gmac.com/gmac), National Council of State Boards of Nursing Examination (NCLEX®, http://www.ncsbn.org), Test of English as a

Foreign Language® (TOEFL®), United States Medical Licensing Examination (USMLE™) and the college admission tests SAT or ACT. The National Assessment of Educational Progress has been referred to as 'the Nation's Report Card' and reports results from standardized tests in reading, mathematics, science, writing, US history, civics, geography and the arts (http://nces.ed.gov/nationsreportcard). A well-designed standardized test can provide details of students' capabilities in a particular field and also provide aggregated data about large cohorts of students. Although standardized tests are sometimes criticized as inadequate for assessing the real capabilities of a student, those listed above have been subject to psychometric standards as part of their development. The effectiveness of each test item in the assessment has been shown to meet acceptable standards, something not all assessments undertaken in tertiary educational institutions can claim. One of the main advantages of a professionally designed, standardized test is that it is able to provide assessments that are valid and reliable from a psychometric point of view, and are usually replicable.

The Federal Government in Australia has also introduced requirements for standardized testing of students in literacy and numeracy skills at Years 3, 5 and 7 in primary schools. The stated purpose for these standardized tests is to identify students with difficulties, and the subsequent deployment of early intervention strategies for these students. The annual National Report on Schooling in Australia publishes aggregated student achievement against predetermined benchmarks (http://www.dest.gov.au/schools/literacyandnumeracy).

The American Educational Research Association (AERA) has issued a position statement concerning high-stake testing in the pre-K-12 education area (AERA, 2000). AERA have proposed that:

> Performance on a standardized test should not be the sole determinant in any either/or decision about instructional placement, promotion, or graduation. Rather, results should be used as indicators of the need for early intervention, programmatic changes, or more specific evaluation of learning problems. (p. 127)

AERA has emphasized that standardized tests should not discriminate against students with disabilities, or those with limited language proficiency. The issue of appropriate training and development for teachers is highlighted, so that standardized tests may be shown to be valid and reliable for their stated use and are administered appropriately.

4.3 What are the limitations of e-assessments?

All assessment methods have their particular strengths and weaknesses. Essays and assignments are appropriate for assessing a student's ability to present an argument logically and coherently, and write cogently so that others might understand their opinions. Technical skills may be assessed by students undertaking practical work in a laboratory; while oral presentations may be appropriate for assessing communication skills. The e-assessment environment is suitable for testing most student capabilities, but not necessarily easily, and not without the use of sophisticated helper applications. The range of question types available for e-assessments was discussed in Chapter 3.2, although the most common question formats in current use are those based on the objective types of MCQ, true/false or yes/no. It is also the case that the most common use for objective items is to test declarative knowledge at the lower levels of the Bloom or SOLO taxonomies. This is not to imply that knowledge, comprehension and application are not important; quite the contrary. If the student does not have a fundamental understanding of discipline specific content knowledge at these levels, they will find it difficult to progress through to the higher levels of analysis, synthesis and evaluation. Chapter 7 discusses item banks in more detail and provides examples of question types covering all levels of the Bloom or SOLO taxonomies.

The main impediment to the current expansion of the use of e-assessment is the amount of time that is required to develop appropriate questions and feedback. Individual teachers do not have the time, or resources, to devote to the pedagogical, technical, implementation and support issues that are required for a successful e-assessment experience. This problem, however, highlights the need for cooperation and collaboration in the development of test items, and the importance of reusable objective items and tests, at least for the lower levels of the Bloom or SOLO taxonomies. It also suggests that institutions should support efforts to develop and share discipline-specific assessments that have been reviewed and found to be particularly effective. Teachers could then concentrate their efforts on developing the higher-level assessments that may be unique to a particular course or programme, or particular groups of students. Chapter 7 provides details of the issues associated with item and test banks.

There are a number of standards that have been developed for accessibility and the inter-operability of assessments across different operating systems and with different browsers. These include the implementation of World Wide Web Consortium standards (http://w3c.org/consortium); the International Test Commission documentation promoting the development, evaluation and uses of educational and psychological instruments (http://www.intestcom.org); CETIS, the Centre for Educational Technology Interoperability Standards (http://www.cetis.ac.uk); SCORM, the Sharable Content Object Reference Model, that provides a technical architecture for learning objects to be shared across different delivery environments (http://www.adlnet.org); and QTI, which is the IMS Question and Test Interoperability standards, designed to make it easier to transfer information such as questions, tests and results between different software applications (http://www.imsglobal.org). Further details of these important issues are developed in Chapter 10.

Online learning and assessment have frequently been implemented as 'add-ons', they are additional features or tasks (often optional) that have been incorporated into an existing programme, whether face-to-face or distance, with little fundamental change to the prevailing learning paradigms adopted within the programme (ANTA, 2003). Each institution tends to adapt the online environment to its own pedagogical culture, and posits the efficacy of online education from this viewpoint. There is a prevailing attitude in educational institutions that learning materials or assessments developed elsewhere are not readily adaptable to the unique educational experience offered at their institution. This is an approach that is not sustainable into the future, and will be increasingly challenged by students and teachers as more sophisticated assessment resources become commonly available.

The Australian National Training Authority Flexible Learning Framework documents (ANTA, 2002) have summarized the challenges for e-assessment as:

■ whether and how to measure student participation in online discussion and activities
■ how to measure individual performances within group assignments
■ authentication of student work
■ preventing and detecting plagiarism
■ issues of security
■ connecting the assessment to the teaching and learning intent and strategies.

As online learning and assessment continues to pervade the educational environment, more adult students will be confronted with asynchronous delivery methodologies, especially as professional training organizations and private companies incorporate web-based materials in the workplace. Adult students have a number of common characteristics, they are generally continuous students, are autonomous and prefer to manage their own learning, they expect learning to be relevant to their immediate needs, and they are problem-centred rather than content-oriented. The implications for e-assessment are that providers will need to be responsive to adult students by adapting outcomes and assessment tasks to match students' needs and motivation, emphasize problem-solving for tangible outcomes, as well as emphasize experiential and contextual assessment approaches (ANTA, 2003).

5 Choosing the right e-assessment software

5.1 Choosing an appropriate assessment format

The appropriate format for an assessment will depend on its purpose. Chapter 1 discussed the various types of assessment tasks, their purpose and the stakeholders in the assessment process. Assessments may be used for diagnostic, formative or summative purposes; they may assess declarative or relational knowledge and they may be high or low stakes. The stakeholders in the assessment process, summarized as the student, the teacher, the institution and the community, may place different priorities on the relative importance that the purpose of the assessment has in determining its format. Before any comparisons can be made between assessment software systems, there are several issues that must be addressed regarding the purpose of the assessment and its relationship to the curriculum and syllabus, the methodologies employed during the learning phase and the status of the assessment outcome. The institution and teacher will need to determine which form of assessment is most appropriate, given the nature of the students' engagement with the syllabus material and the resources that are available to conduct the assessment. The teacher should be cognizant of the drivers that are determining the choice of assessment format. Are all the stakeholders seeking a quality assessment task, one that allows the student to demonstrate the learning that has taken place and the skills and capabilities developed? The construction of quality assessment tasks can be resource intensive. Are all stakeholders seeking an efficient and cost-effective assessment process, one that minimizes cost? Will the community accept various formats for high stakes assessment that will ultimately lead to professional qualifications or certifications?

What are the factors that must be considered in order to determine which format is appropriate for the assessment of a particular learning experience? Teachers will generally determine the objectives for their assessment as part of the curriculum design process. Since the students' perception of the objectives and format for the assessment task will frequently determine their approach to learning, or at least influence their approach to fulfilling the requirements for the programme, teachers will need to consider where their particular assessment activity resides on the continuum between quantitative and qualitative approaches. Quantitative assessment tasks tend to be associated with objectivist knowledge, whereas qualitative assessment tasks are more often associated with constructivist knowledge. Assessment tasks do not have to reside at the extremities of the continuum; hence the teacher should inform the students of the particular emphasis that is being placed on quantitative and qualitative approaches (Northcote, 2003). All assessments should be valid, reliable and fair; they should provide students with an opportunity to show others what they have learnt. Bloom's taxonomy of educational objectives (Anderson *et al.*, 2001) may be used as a theoretical model from which assessment tasks can be constructed, and teachers will need to decide whether the key objective for the assessment outcome is ranking the students or whether mastery learning is the key driver for student engagement with the material.

Will the introduction of e-assessment be a significant cultural change for the teachers, the students and the institution? Each sector of the educational market has a particular historical culture, and within sectors there is often significant variation in the contextual emphasis placed on assessment and its relationship to learning (ANTA, 2002). Each of the stakeholders will need to recognize who or what is driving the introduction, or adoption, of e-assessment. Is the introduction of e-assessment the result of institutional pressure? If the institution is promoting the adoption of e-assessment as a perceived means of reducing marking time so as to lower staff workload, this will have an effect on the culture within the learning environment. If the institution is seeking to increase the capabilities of students in an online environment as part of a strategic move to increase flexibility or diversity in the curriculum, this will also have an effect on the teacher-student relationship. Leaders within an institution must be aware of the cultural effect the adoption of e-assessment will have on the learning environment, and any consequential changes in the relationship between teacher and student. Will an institutional strategic plan be required for any change in direction in pedagogy, or will it be left to individual teachers to decide on the use of online learning and assessment? If an institution has a history of distance education delivery or alternative forms of assessment, then the adoption of e-assessment may have minimal impact on the learning environment, and teacher and student development programmes may be centred around the use of resources and software, rather than changes in pedagogy. However, institutions with a predominant culture of face-to-face interactions between the teacher and the student may experience significant cultural changes within the learning environment if large-scale e-assessment practices are adopted.

Has the adoption of e-assessment been planned as part of a curriculum redesign and the introduction of innovations to the student experience? In order to maximize the potential benefits for teachers and students, the use of e-assessment must be planned as part of a holistic curriculum redesign process and a reappraisal of the purpose of the learning environment. The student will need to interact with the course content in a manner that is appropriate for e-assessment. The objectives for a course should include how the student will demonstrate skills and capability development in an online environment. Has the student engaged regularly with curriculum content in an online environment? The purpose of e-assessment should be to allow the student to use tools with which they are familiar from the learning environment. The course objectives will need to include the use of the assessment tools themselves; otherwise alternative assessment formats appropriate to the regularly used learning tools should be used.

The relationship between the learning environment and the professional activities that students will engage in after their learning experience needs to be considered. Will the student be required to use certain tools in the workplace? If so, then teachers will need to consider the use of these tools in the learning and assessment environment so that students are able to demonstrate competence in their use. Is the nature of the work environment changing, so that the learning and assessment environments must change to be compatible with the wider community and work environment? Developments in technology are offering new formats for learning; it is inevitable that assessment environments will be influenced by these changes (Winn, 2002). Will technology drive the decision as to the format for the assessment? Just as many educationalists are reflecting on the influence that technology has on the learning environment, so they will also review the drivers for changes in assessment practice (Almond et al., 2002). Although technology will have an influence on the assessment environment, this does not necessarily mean it should singularly determine the assessment format. Teachers and institutions need to be aware of the various drivers for change in learning and assessment, and how they affect the decision-making procedures adopted by institutions in terms of resource allocation. All drivers for changes in assessment format must be considered in context. Change is a natural consequence of a regular evaluation paradigm, and not solely as a result of developments in technology.

Implementing e-assessment can involve a significant increase in staff workload, especially if new skills need to be developed. Are teaching staff capable of designing appropriate e-assessment tasks and the associated feedback for students? e-Assessment activity may reduce the time required for marking an assessment, and this could be a significant saving for very large groups of students undertaking standardized tests, but more time must be allocated to designing and authoring the assessment. Also, if feedback is an important objective for the assessment, then considerable time must be allocated to the design of appropriate and worthwhile feedback. The construction of good MCQs is time-consuming, and often requires significant staff development time (Johnstone, 2004). The development effort required for a diagnostic or formative quiz with

Table 5.1 Summary of decision-making issues for assessment formats

Issues	Low-stakes assessment	Medium-stakes assessment	High-stakes assessment
Purpose of assessment	Improve learning, identify teaching gaps	Improve learning, progression to new concepts	Credentials, gate keeping, progression, certification
Consequences if problems arise	Few with low impact	Some with modest impact	Significant with high impact
Resources required	Often minimal, can use low threshold software	Modest investment in large-scale system	Significant investment in enterprise system
Consequences of cheating	Few	Some	Significant
Authentication of student	Not important	May be important	Very important
Invigilation required	Not usual	Sometimes	Always
Development effort	Minor	Medium	Major
Evaluation of reliability and validity	Not usual, anecdotal feedback from colleagues and students sought	Subject-matter experts provide feedback	Requires professional psychometric analysis

minimum feedback would be less than that required for a high stakes summative assessment or a formative assessment with detailed feedback.

What will be the impact of the costs for staff development associated with the introduction of e-assessment across an institution? Any expected reduction in workload for marking may be offset by increases in staff time allocated to developing new skills and constructing worthwhile feedback for students. The return on investment for e-assessment may be seen as improvements in student learning and staff capabilities, rather than simply reductions in fixed staffing costs. The return on investment could also be a change in the learning environment, moving from one involving mastery of declarative knowledge to one emphasizing authentic learning and assessment.

If high stakes e-assessments are planned, then the costs associated with appropriate invigilation and technical support must also be considered. Will there be space issues with large classes requiring access to sufficient screens; does the institution have the required server capacity for large numbers of concurrent users of websites offering assessments? Will a restricted computer environment be required during the assessment, so that students only have access to particular resources during the assessment? What arrangements will be required for students with special learning needs during an e-assessment? All these questions need to be considered, before any decision on whether to adopt an e-assessment system can be made.

A summary of the issues for low, medium and high stakes e-assessments is shown in Table 5.1.

5.2 How do you want to administer your e-assessments?

Once a decision has been made that the online environment is an appropriate format for assessment, either by the teacher or by the institution, the selection process may commence.

Table 5.2 Summary of e-assessment issues for different groups of stakeholders

Student	Teacher	Institution	Community
Ease of navigation	Copyright	Quality of vendor	Validity
Usability	Staff development	Technical support	Reliability
Help facilities	Candidates' responses	Interoperability	Quality
Accessibility	Help facilities	Security features	
Feedback	Institutional support	Costs	
Plugins	Question banks	Server requirements	
Validity	Plagiarism/cheating	Network access	
	Restricting access to other resources	Updates, patches	
	Content validity	Reliability	
	Plugins	Validity	
	Reliability		
	Validity		

The initial step in this process is to identify the stakeholders in the assessment process. The IMS Global Consortium, an organization proposing standards for question and test interoperability, has specified nine stakeholders of a computer-assisted assessment system: the assessor, scorer, candidate, invigilator/proctor, administrator, administrating authority, tutor, author and psychometrician (Smythe et al., 2000). It is possible to detail the role of each of these individual stakeholders and to document their individual requirements, but it is more convenient to consider a simplified summary of stakeholder requirements. The various stakeholders can be placed into four broad groups, the student (candidate), the teacher (assessor, scorer, invigilator/proctor, administrator, tutor, author or psychometrician), the institution (administrating authority, invigilator/proctor, administrator or psychometrician) and the community. The general community is a stakeholder in the assessments undertaken at educational institutions as public funds are often used to support these institutions and quality assurance agencies have been established in most countries to audit and report on the quality of the educational experience of students. A summary of the e-assessment issues for the four different groups of stakeholders is shown in Table 5.2.

Sclater et al. (2003) have discussed the components required for the 'ultimate' e-assessment engine. They have assumed that individuals and institutions would be interested in a system that is capable of delivering both high and low stakes e-assessments for diagnostic, formative and summative purposes. They have further assumed that secure authentication would be required, that feedback based on student responses would be available and that students should be able to access the assessment from a web browser anywhere in the world. Sclater et al. (2003) have identified up to 21 separate roles in their 'ultimate' e-assessment engine roles relating to system, user and group administration; roles relating to the assessment questions; roles relating to the assessment tasks; roles relating to the vendors of the computer software and hardware; roles relating to a particular assessment session; and roles relating to responses and results.

The technical aspects of using any e-assessment system should be intuitive for both students and teachers and require minimal training. A suitable benchmark for students could be that anyone with a basic working knowledge of how to use a computer, for example, how to open and use a web browser or open and use a basic word processing application, should be able to use the system to undertake an assessment. The assessment tasks should be accessible from any recent, standard, platform-independent web browser. One issue that should be decided early in the selection process is whether or not to cater for older web browsers and operating systems. Older systems have fewer features, and will limit the types of online activity that can be incorporated into assessment tasks. Is this acceptable in pedagogical terms to the student, teacher and institution? A compromise may be required between universal accessibility and appropriate functionality. Students should be using a relatively recent version of any online tool in order to develop skills and capabilities that will be valued in the market place. There is little point in minimizing the functionality required for the assessment if this significantly reduces the opportunities for students to display the skills that have been developed during the learning process. Simple, text-based, objective questions may be delivered using simple, low threshold software, but will predominantly test declarative knowledge. This may be appropriate for some assessment tasks based on convergent responses, but is unlikely to engage students in a pedagogical process that relies on divergent responses, or for responses that are testing informed opinion or analysis.

For e-assessments, additional functionality may be provided by the use of plugins (a small application or piece of software that can be used in another piece of software to add functionality), but students should be provided with opportunities to practise using the plugin as part of their learning. Increasing the functionality available for an assessment often increases the complexity associated with constructing, delivering and performing the assessment. The teacher and the institution will need to consider the importance of accessibility, the needs of particular students in the group and whether particular software or hardware will be required for those with special needs.

Not all assessment tasks will be described using words, some will require graphics, some sound, some movies; while others will require text in the form of mathematical expressions. The more functionality that is required for the assessment, the more resources must be allocated and the more time it will take for teachers to construct and students to complete the assessment. Mathematical equations may be written and displayed in a web browser using the Mathematical Markup Language (MathML, http://www.w3.org/Math), a type of eXtensible Markup Language (XML, http://www.w3.org/XML) created by the World Wide Web Consortium (W3C, http://www.w3.org). In order to view mathematical equations written using MathML, a MathML plugin, such as MathPlayer, is required (http://www.dessci.com/en). This plugin also provides the opportunity for mathematical expressions to be spoken aloud by a suitably equipped computer.

Does the institution prefer to deal with a commercial vendor for an e-assessment system, or is it prepared to invest resources in an open source system? Commercial vendors will offer varying levels of customization for their standard product lines, and the costs associated with patches and upgrades to enterprise level systems that are highly customized may be considerable. Open source systems are usually fully customizable, but the responsibility is on the individual institution to solve any technical problems that may occur. Is this acceptable for high stakes assessment tasks? Will the existing institutional authentication system be linked to the e-assessment system so that students can use their existing username and password, and avoid multiple logon requirements or multiple passwords?

The reliability and security of the e-assessment system is critical for the reputation of the institution. The appropriate assessments must only be available to the predetermined set of designated students; their subsequent responses and results must be secure, but readily accessible to the appropriate teachers and administrators. The institution will need to decide if all data associated with the assessment should be encrypted when being transferred over an intranet, or the Internet, and whether secure socket layers (SSL) should be used. Should teachers (or the assessment authors) be able to modify a live assessment, and should the student responses be recorded as they are entered, or at the completion of the e-assessment session? Should students be able to partly complete an assessment, have the responses recorded, but not marked, and be allowed to resume the assessment at a later time? What administrative data should be collected about the date and time the assessment was undertaken and the IP address (internet protocol address which is unique for each computer processing unit) where the student accessed the assessment?

Do students require access to a synchronous or asynchronous help system during the assessment? If students are undertaking an e-assessment using a dialup telephone modem, will they also require access to a separate phone line in order to seek assistance? It is often useful for teachers and institutions to develop procedures for situations where the student has difficulties during an e-assessment, and for students to be fully aware of these before any medium or high stakes assessment is undertaken. Access to help systems from within an e-assessment will maintain student confidence in the process and minimize concerns of equitable treatment of all students in an assessment situation. What level of administrative access should teachers have to the full range of system controls for the e-assessment engine? Will teachers be expected to administer all enrolment and access issues associated with the assessment, or will these be organized through a centralized facility? Should teachers have access that allows them to add, modify and delete student records and to download or upload such records? Teachers may initially find e-assessment difficult and stressful, so institutions should attempt to minimize the amount of administrative tasks that are required of them.

Any e-assessment system, whether open source or from a commercial vendor, should be scalable and accommodate significant numbers of concurrent users. The number of concurrent users will also determine the hardware requirements that will be needed to support the software system, and load testing software is available to assist institutional technical experts determine appropriate requirements for hardware in order to support the expected demands on the system. e-Assessment systems generate considerable amounts of data, and this needs to be stored, and archived, in an appropriate database format. Some commercial e-assessment systems utilize a propriety database, while others use industry standard systems such as Access, Oracle or SQL. Consideration should usually be given to using an assessment system that is based on the same database used at the institution for other enterprise systems. This allows efficient use of hardware, software and technical expertise, and usually means that support systems are already in place for technical help.

From the technical point of view, institutions need to decide whether the assessment software is catering predominantly for a client-side approach or a server-side approach. If students are likely to take the assessments in an environment where there are slow connections to the server on which the assessment is to be delivered, then conservation of bandwidth may be one of the priorities. Issues such as the local caching of content, or the use of a proxy server, need to be resolved against the need for a secure environment.

For low stakes diagnostic or formative assessments in an environment where students will be using relatively slow dialup modem access to the assessment, client-side approaches using JavaScript may be appropriate. For high stakes assessment in a secure environment requiring student authentication, then server-side approaches will be required. These requirements will have an effect on the bandwidth requirements connecting the server hardware and the student computer environment.

How much staff development will be required for teachers to be able to author assessment tasks? Will teachers be able to share assessment tasks, use test banks, will their questions comply with international interoperability standards (Salter et al., 1999)? The assumption cannot be made that teachers will automatically be able to utilize e-assessment resources, no matter how 'simple' the technology (Sawyers et al., 1998). If e-assessment software is to be introduced at an institution, staff development programmes will be required that highlight any differences between traditional assessment models most frequently adopted by teachers at the institution, and those required in the new online environment. This is particularly important for those teachers who have worked in a traditional face-to-face teaching environment and have adopted traditional assessment practices. Staff development programmes could use the online environment for instruction, the provision of exemplars and for teacher collaboration, allowing good practice models to be presented to teachers. Salter et al. (1999) suggest that staff development programmes require defined deliverable material, such as plans, designs, papers and portfolios; provide an appropriate closure to activities; conduct collaborative projects and actively moderated discussions; include guest speakers, debates, role-plays and surveys and encourage the formation of learning teams.

In order to monitor the quality of e-assessment questions, the system should be capable of some form of statistical analysis of the students' responses, including tools to assist with the monitoring of reliability, validity and the discrimination factor of questions. The discrimination factor measures the ability of a question to discriminate between high-achieving and low-achieving students by comparing the performance of student sub-groups and their overall performance on the assessment. This type of analysis is particularly important for objective-type questions and is used as part of reliability and validity checking.

Stephens et al. (1998) have proposed guidelines for an institutional strategy for the implementation of computer-assisted assessment (CAA). These guidelines assume that the implementation of CAA is being driven, or at least supported, by the senior managers within an institution, and centre on a coordinated CAA management policy, with CAA units and coordinators within each discipline, as well as centralized funding and staff development, and the establishment of appropriate operational and administrative procedures. A modified Value Chain Model, termed 'IT Advantage Assessment Model' has been proposed to assist educational institutions formalize their understanding of the strategic and tactical implications of integrating information technology into the institutional planning framework (Turner et al., 2004). This model identifies the values and drivers within the institution, the various stakeholders, and assesses the cultural, structural and attitudinal impact that technology will have on the business of the institution. The Scottish Further Education Funding Council (SFEFC) has funded a detailed investigation into CAA and this has resulted in the publication of a number of documents, including guidelines for the implementation of CAA in Further Education in Scotland (Herd et al., 2003).

What standards does the institution wish to apply to the use of an online environment for assessment tasks? A relevant British Standard 'Code of Practice for the Use of Information Technology (IT) in the Delivery of Assessments' is a comprehensive document that provides a detailed framework for any institution implementing e-assessment and provides suitable guidelines, and minimum requirements, that institutions could utilize to establish appropriate policies and procedures (BSI, 2002). The standard is particularly useful because it describes the lifecycle of an assessment, which includes: the initial identification of the purpose of the assessment; the design of outcomes/assessment methodologies; the articulation of appropriate methods for preparation and calibration of the assessment process; the pre-registration process for students; the distribution of the assessment; the authentication of candidates; the delivery of the assessment; the return of responses; the scoring, determination of results and the provision of feedback; the return of data; the analysis of student responses and scores; the appeals process and final certification of achievement. Such a detailed description enables all aspects of the assessment to be considered in context, and could be adapted to apply to all forms of assessment, not just those undertaken using computer technology. The Quality Assurance Agency for Higher Education in the UK has published a code of practice for quality assurance in flexible and distributed learning which provides precepts to guide institutions in providing a secure environment for the assessment of students undertaking programmes by flexible delivery methods (CODE, 2004).

How important are assessment item interoperability specifications to the institution? IMS develops and promotes the adoption of open technical specifications for all aspects of the computer-learning environment and the latest version of the IMS Question and Test Interoperability specification (QTI Version 2) was released in June 2006 (QTI, 2006). For institutions using predominantly multiple-choice type questions, QTILite is a simplified version and would be easier for those constructing such question types to use (QTILite, 2002). The latest version of QTI specifications are particularly important for vendors of e-assessment systems, and for publishers of item test banks, as the individual questions are usually designed to be used in a number of different software systems. For the majority of teachers writing their own questions in a commercial or open source learning management or assessment system, there is little requirement to read these specifications in detail. The institution should make the decision to use a system that is compatible with the QTI specifications and that will allow questions constructed by teachers, or item banks purchased from publishers, to be moved seamlessly to future assessment engines. The IMS QTI specification includes a standard XML format for defining question characteristics in a manner that is independent of the computer platform or commercial software in which the question resides. The specification describes a basic structure for the representation of a question and an assessment in data terms as well as the corresponding student responses. XML is used because it allows the widest possible adoption of the specifications between learning and assessment systems. The specifications do not limit commercial vendors or open source systems in their product designs, nor do they impose any particular interfaces, technologies or learning outcomes.

A key component in the decision-making process for an e-assessment system will be the evaluation protocols. How will the system be evaluated once it has been implemented? This issue needs to be resolved at the early stages in the implementation strategy, not after the system has moved from the trial phase into the full adoption phase. Individual institutions will likely have existing evaluation procedures they use to monitor the quality and efficacy of the learning environment and assessment protocols for their programmes. However, evaluation models specific to the use of technology in learning and assessment are required in order to appropriately determine the effect of the technology on the four key stakeholder groups. The Flashlight Triad Evaluation Model divides the relevant issues into the type of technology employed, a specific activity enabled by the technology and the outcomes expected from the activity (http://www.tltgroup.org/programs/flashcsi.html). The Flashlight Handbook, consisting of the Evaluation Handbook and the Current Student Inventory of 500 questions suitable for evaluating the impact of teaching-learning practices and the use of technology to aid those practices, has been developed (Ehrmann, 2002).

The Flashlight Model provides a standardized set of protocols and could be used by various institutions as a benchmarking exercise. Alternative models may be developed using evaluation principles that have been developed in the training and assessment literature. The four levels of evaluation described by Kirkpatrick (1998) for training evaluation, and modifications including those by Brinkerhoff (1987), provide a useful guide as to the approaches that could be used to evaluate an e-assessment system. The four Kirkpatrick levels involve evaluating reaction, evaluating learning, evaluating behaviour and evaluating results. Evaluating teacher and student reaction to using the e-assessment system allows institutions to determine if the primary stakeholders enjoyed the experience, and is a type of customer satisfaction measure. Evaluating learning allows teachers to determine the amount of learning achieved during the course, as evidenced by the assessment responses. An assessment such as a mastery test is required to determine objectively if learning occurred and the development of a fair and valid assessment requires psychometrics expertise. Evaluating behaviour determines the extent that student behaviour may have changed as a result of the learning experience and as evidenced by the assessment responses. It is sometimes difficult to develop assessments that allow evidence to be collected supporting changes in student behaviour. Do students approach problem-solving differently after the learning experience? Can students solve unseen problems using strategies developed as part of the learning process? Evaluating results determines the extent that the student, the teacher, the institution and the community benefited as a result of the learning. This fourth level of evaluation is also difficult, but can be related to the concept of a business return on investment, from the point of view of the institution and the community.

The Kirkpatrick model tends to be linear, and evaluations can often terminate at the first or second stage, before the full benefits of the learning experience have been articulated. The linear model also presents as a hierarchical system, whereas one level is not necessarily dependent, or subservient, to the others. A modified approach may be to use a cyclic Kirkpatrick model, where the evaluation process is continuous and may commence with any of the components. Such an approach would allow feedback from the evaluation to be used in an iterative manner. Brinkerhoff (1987) has described a more detailed evaluation sequence and this may be adapted to the evaluation of the e-assessment activity. An example would be an evaluation of needs and goals (the objectives for the learning), an evaluation of the human resource development design (how effective were staff development programmes for teachers), an evaluation of the operation (how the system functioned, did it perform to specifications), an evaluation of the learning (what skills and capabilities did the student develop), an evaluation of the usage and endurance of learning (the long-term benefits of the learning) and an evaluation of the payoff (return on investment).

5.3 What type of questions do you want to ask?

In order to make an informed decision about which e-assessment system is most appropriate for teachers and students in a particular institution, attention must be given to the question types that are required for the aims of the local learning and teaching environment. Are objective test questions, where responses are selected from a limited set of predetermined alternatives, suitable for testing the skills and capabilities developed by students in a particular program (PASS-IT)? What other question types are available within e-assessment systems and will this range influence teachers when deciding whether to engage with this form of assessment? Will the range of questions available for each system influence the decision to implement at the institutional level?

Traditional MCQs require a student to choose one response from a list of possible alternatives (McKenna *et al.*, 1999). Variations to the traditional MCQ include matching questions, where items from two or more lists are selected so that they are related by a predetermined concept; sorting questions, where items are selected in a particular order from lists; true/false or yes/no questions, where definitive statements are presented and the student must judge their veracity; multiple-response questions, where more than one response is deemed appropriate. Responses for MCQs, and their various alternatives, may be text based, or they may be multimedia files such as audio, graphical objects (two or three dimensional) or movie sequences. Matching questions may be used to allow students to not only show mastery of recall for questions based on definitions, dates and declarative knowledge, but they may also be used to show capabilities in higher skills such as understanding relationships.

Questions requiring text or numerical responses involve using the computer keyboard to enter specific text or numbers, and the student may find that they need to be very specific when entering their responses. Students must be advised whether spelling is important, whether both upper and lower-case entries (or mixtures) are acceptable, whether abbreviations are acceptable, and for responses to mathematical questions whether significant figures are important and how numerical responses should be written (e.g. 1,000 or 1 000 or 1000). Different e-assessment systems may handle these issues differently, and the teacher and the institution should be familiar with the options available and the consequences for students when responses are entered in a particular format. Teachers must give careful consideration to how many different responses will be acceptable, and whether alternative responses must be manually entered into the system for the recognition by the assessment software, as this may take considerable time.

Ranking questions require the student to relate items in one or more columns to one another and may be used to test knowledge of sequences, the order of timed events or some form of gradation. Sequencing questions require the student to position text or graphic objects in a given sequence. Other question types may require students to identify or manipulate graphic objects, plot data in graphical format or use graphical objects to construct a more complex visual response (moving images around the screen). Graphical hotspot questions involve selecting an area of the screen by moving the mouse to a certain position and clicking, or by moving a graphical object or marker to a certain position. Advanced versions of hotspot questions include labelling and building questions.

Combinations of question types, such as MCQ and true/false or yes/no, allow assertion-reason items (the question consists of two statements, an assertion and a reason) to be tested (CAA

Centre, 2002). This allows higher order assessment questions to be presented to students and they must make an initial judgement about the veracity of a statement, and determine the reason for their choice.

An example would be:

Carbon dioxide (CO_2) has no permanent dipole [*assertion*, response would be either true/false] because it is a linear molecule [*reason*, response would be either true/false].

This type of question could appear in the following form with choices presented from a pull-down menu:

Carbon dioxide (CO_2) has no ▼ **permanent dipole because it is a** tetrahedral ▼ **molecule.**

Figure 5.1 Example of pull-down menu question

Some examples of the major types of questions available in e-assessment systems are shown below. This list is not exhaustive, and serves to demonstrate possibilities for teachers to consider. Further examples for specific disciplines can be found in Chapter 6.

Multiple-choice text

(Example adapted from http://www.saltspring.com/capewest/mc.htm)

A 20-year-old student was hiking in Australia when she developed a fever and chest pains. A blood gas analysis showed a pH of 7.41 and a pCO$_2$ of 26 mm Hg. Which explanation might best account for these values?

A. Respiratory acidosis
B. Metabolic acidosis
C. Metabolic alkalosis
D. Both respiratory alkalosis and metabolic acidosis
E. Malfunctioning blood-gas analyser

Multiple-choice hotspot

Listen to 🔊 and click the image that most appropriately corresponds to the word you heard.

Figure 5.2 Example of a hotspot question with attached audio for language test

Multiple–choice slider or numerical slider

Anthracene and ethyl benzoate can be separated using thin layer chromatography.
View the movie  showing the separation of anthracene and ethyl benzoate.
Use the slider below to indicate the approximate R_f value for ethyl benzoate in the movie.

| 0.0 | 0.25 | 0.5 | 0.75 | 1.0 |

Figure 5.3 Example of a numerical slider question with attached movie for chemistry test

Multiple response

Some pure metals may be obtained from their ores using electrolysis.
Which of the following metals can only be obtained from their ores by electrolysis?
Check all that apply.

☐ Mg ☐ Al ☐ Li ☐ K
☐ Na ☐ Fe ☐ Ti ☐ Cr

Figure 5.4 Example of a multiple-response question for chemistry test

Drag and drop, move object or label a diagram

Place the name of each continent on the corresponding portion of the world map below.
Use the mouse to drag each word to the appropriate place.

Australia Antarctica South America North America Africa Europe Asia

Figure 5.5 Example of a drag-and-drop question for geography test

Hotspot (click anywhere)

Which continent on the world map below corresponds to Africa?
Use the mouse to place the cursor arrow over the part of the map you think is Africa and click the mouse.

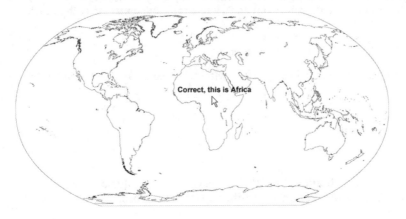

Correct, this is Africa

Figure 5.6 Example of a hotspot question for geography test

Short-answer (string-comparison) or free-text response

How many electrons are in an Fe^{2+} ion?

Figure 5.7 Example of a short free-text entry question for chemistry test

In which country would you find the following structure?

Country name:

Figure 5.8 Example of a short free-text entry question for geography test

For each ion in the table below write the number of valence electrons and the oxidation state in the appropriate space.

ion	Fe^{2+}	Fe^{3+}	Co^{2+}	Co^{3+}	Pt^{2+}
number of valence electrons					
oxidation state					

Figure 5.9 Example of a short free-text entry question in table format for chemistry test

Cloze exercise (fill-in-the-blanks)

Carbon dioxide (CO_2) has [_____] permanent dipole because it is a [_____] molecule.

Figure 5.10 Example of a cloze question for chemistry test

Essay question
Adapted from http://www.clevelandstatecc.edu/Courses

Discuss the ways the Sui, the Tang and the Song Dynasties of China contributed to the economic, political, religious and technological development in East Asia.

Figure 5.11 Example of an extended free-text entry question for history test

Drag to order (sequencing)

Arrange the following names of the planets in the solar system in order of decreasing size. Jupiter is the largest planet.

1. Jupiter
2. [_____] Earth
3. [_____] Neptune
4. [_____] Mercury
5. [_____] Pluto
6. [_____] Saturn
7. [_____] Venus
8. [_____] Uranus
9. [_____] Mars

Figure 5.12 Example of a sequencing question using drag and drop for science test

Draw object

Complete the diagram below the contour map, indicating the relative height and the relative slope of each mountain.

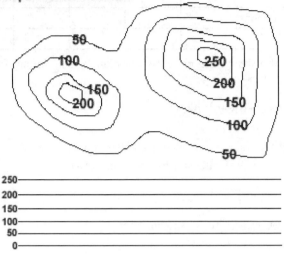

Figure 5.13 Example of a drawing question that uses sequencing for geology test

Plot graph, draw line

The following data were obtained from a first order reaction.
Calculate ln(c) for each data point and plot the data using
ln(c) versus t and determine the first order rate constant (k) for the reaction.

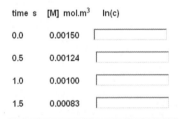

time s	[M] mol.m^3	ln(c)
0.0	0.00150	
0.5	0.00124	
1.0	0.00100	
1.5	0.00083	

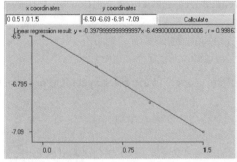

Figure 5.14 Example of a calculation question that uses a plotting tool for chemistry test (Java applet from Bruno Herreros, Department of Chemistry, University of South California, http://chemmacl.usc.edu/bruno/java/linreg.html)

Matrix selection – sequencing

Which of the following names represent Australian Prime Ministers?

- ○ Bill Clinton
- ○ Bill Murray
- ○ John Howard
- ○ Billy McMahon
- ○ John Major
- ○ John Gorton
- ○ Joseph Stalin
- ○ Bob Dole
- ○ George Bush
- ○ John Cleese
- ○ Joseph Lyons
- ○ Bob Hawke

Figure 5.15 Example of a matrix selection question, with 'choose all that apply' options for a history test

Crosswords
Example from http://www.crauswords.com.

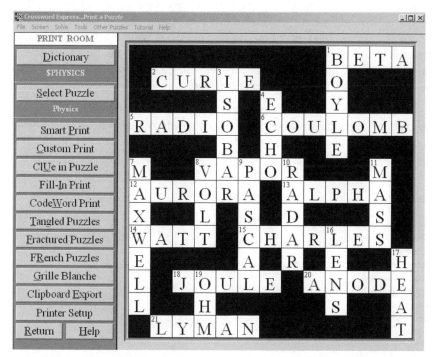

Figure 5.16 Example of a matrix selection question that uses a crossword format for science test

Sore finger questions have been used in language teaching and computer programming, where one word, code or phrase is out of keeping with the rest of a passage. It could be presented as a hotspot or text-input type of question.

German nouns are either masculine, feminine or neuter.
Which noun does not have the appropriate article in the sentence below?

Renate hat *einen* weiße Katze, aber sie möchte einen schwarzen Hund.

Figure 5.17 Example of a sore finger question that uses a hotspot format for language test

Table 5.3 Characteristics of MCQs

Positive characteristics	Negative characteristics
They allow a wide coverage of content	They do not allow students to develop an idea or propose a solution
They are marked efficiently and objectively by the computer	Appropriate distracters take a long time to develop
Statistical data can be collected and analysed readily	Responses may be guessed
Large item banks can be constructed readily	

MCQs are used extensively in e-assessments, and they have been criticized by teachers who posit that they encourage a surface approach to learning by students. Table 5.3 summarizes some of the positive and negative characteristics that are often associated with traditional MCQs.

An alternative format for an MCQ is the extended matching question (EMQ), which retains many of the positive characteristics of an MCQ format, but also allows students to solve a cohesive problem, rather than individual, isolated questions (Wood, 2003). An example of the EMQ format is shown in Figure 5.18; this format is used frequently in the health sciences as it allows a scenario to be presented to students, and judgements made about the likely choices students would have made in the real world situation.

Some e-assessment systems have been purposely constructed for specific discipline-related questions, such as the National University of Singapore which has developed the 'Online Judge', capable of assessing student submissions of computer code (Cheang *et al.*, 2003). This appli-

Theme:Aetiology

Options:

A Alcohol
B Childhood sexual abuse
C Diabetes
D Having given birth 6 months previously
E Impaired hearing
F Loss of mother before age 14
G Peri-natal hypoxia
H Reduced visual acuity
I Regular use of NSAIDs
J Smoking

Lead in: *Which of the above risk factors is most strongly associated with the following:*

33) A young man with mood-incongruent auditory hallucinations, complex delusions and social withdrawal.

34) A young woman with mood-congruent delusions, auditory hallucinations and depressed mood.

35) An older woman with first onset of both somatic and auditory hallucinations and delusions.

36) A cognitively intact older man with visual hallucinations.

Answers:
33 - G
34 - D
35 - E
36 - H

Figure 5.18 Example of an extended matching sets question (EMSQ) (http://www.rcpsych.ac.uk)

cation executes the student submitted computer code and assesses it for correctness, efficiency and maintainability. Another example of such a system is CourseMarker, which is a system for the automatic assessment of student work submitted in the form of computer code (http://www.cs.nott.ac.uk/CourseMarker). CourseMarker also has the ability to administer the student responses and course materials, including the ability to generate reports about potential student plagiarism.

An alternative form of e-assessment is the use of e-portfolios, a format that allows students to present their work and achievements in a holistic manner, instead of the fragmented approach dictated by traditional tests (Mason *et al.*, 2004). An e-portfolio is similar to a curriculum vitae, facilitating the opportunity to present extended pieces of student work that has been refined over time through the process of reflection and adaptation as new skills are developed. e-Portfolios can be continually updated and subject to peer review, they encourage the use of multimedia formats that are more closely aligned with authentic learning and assessment and they can also be used by the student at interviews, unlike the products resulting from traditional assessments.

5.4 Examples of e-assessment software

There are a significant number of commercial and open-source assessment engines available; some are components of integrated learning management systems, whereas others are specialist assessment packages. Table 5.4 summarizes a selection of e-assessment tools and briefly describes their key features and contact details. This list is not exhaustive, but does provide an adequate cover of the main assessment tools currently available, and provides examples of assessment tools from both commercial vendors and open-source groups. The list also provides examples of low-threshold applications that require minimal technical resources, as well as enterprise-level systems designed for large institutions with professional support mechanisms. A number of summaries of e-assessment systems are available on the web (JISC; Brown *et al.*, 1999).

The appropriate assessment environment for a particular institution will be dependent on whether the individual assessment tasks are high or low stakes. The more impact that adverse assessment events have on the student and the institution, the more control the institution may demand and the more stringent the invigilation requirements will become. Professional assessment centres offering high stakes assessments, such as Graduate Records Examinations (GRE), will usually possess dedicated computer systems that have been optimized for high stakes assessments in a controlled environment, whereas most educational institutions will require computer suites that are multipurpose, for both learning activities and assessment.

An example of an assessment engine that highlights some of the issues involved in selecting assessment software is the Canvas Learning Author tool that allows teachers to create assessments that are compliant with the IMS specifications relating to QTI and IMS Content Packaging (Canvas). Question developers who are familiar with authoring in XML, and the details for the QTI specifications, may integrate XML code directly using the built-in editor. However, for teachers who are not experienced in XML, or in using QTI specifications, questions may be entered directly using the Canvas Learning Author interface and the XML code is generated behind the scenes. The Content Packaging specifications relate to the complete collection of assessment materials; including the question and any associated images, sounds, movies and metadata required for the question. Content Packaging allows the questions and the related support materials to be moved from one IMS compliant learning management system to another, without having to reconstruct the question from its constituent parts. In order for a student to undertake an assessment authored by the Canvas Learning product, the readily available Macromedia Flash[R] Player is required and the learning objects compatible with learning management systems such as Blackboard™ and WebCT™. Teachers will come to e-assessment activities with a wide diversity of prior knowledge, and the software system should be able to offer opportunities for both the novice and the experienced practitioner.

Assessment Management System (AMS) is an example of software that may be used in different formats, with assessments able to be delivered through a standard web browser, or as a standalone test on a single computer, or to a local computer suite via a local area network. Such systems may be used within a learning management system, or separately. AMS has a number of useful features, such as the ability to apply metatags to questions so that a search facility may be used to retrieve questions with a certain characteristic from a databank; it also uses a built-in editor for questions that require the Mathematics Markup Language (MathML) or Chemical Markup Language (CML) so that teachers can create algebraic questions and use chemical formulas and structures. Individual questions may also be tagged using Bloom's taxonomy, so that a structured approach to the type of questions offered may be used, and a more cohesive relationship may exist between the learning objectives derived from the different Bloom domains.

Some of the software engines described in Table 5.4 allow a higher level of security for high stakes assessment, for example by restricting the IP (Internet Protocol) address or subnet that is allowed to access the assessment, or by downloading software that restricts some of the normal options available within common web browsers. QuestionMark Secure player enables a modified version of the Internet Explorer browser to operate on the Windows PC platform so that only a predefined URL (uniform resource locator) is available for displaying the e-assessment in a secure environment. The Internet Explorer browser display window is always full screen and cannot be reduced in size, there are no browser menu bars, only those built into the Questionmark Secure player, and none of the web pages visited is stored in Internet Explorer's history listing. This player also prevents students from printing, capturing screens or exiting the assessment screen during the scheduled assessment time.

Blackboard™ and WebCT™ are examples of enterprise-level learning management systems that contain an assessment engine component. Such systems allow an integration of diagnostic, formative and summative assessments with the learning materials for a programme of activity, and can use timed or adaptive release of content and assessments according to a teacher-directed format. Many major publishers of educational textbooks have pre-packaged content and assessment materials that may be readily incorporated into these systems. Online discussion facilities enable threaded, asynchronous discussions that may be sorted and viewed by thread, author, date or subject, and peer collaboration is built around group facilities and group file exchange and viewing. The assessment of discussion forums and group activities is discussed in more detail in Chapter 13 of this book. All of the enterprise-level systems described in Table 5.4 contain some version of a gradebook where leaner responses are recorded, and most allow some form of selected reporting for the teacher and the student, as well as features such as custom grading scales, grade weighting and item analysis. The commercial vendors of these systems allow open application program interface (API) development through open architecture initiatives and public software development kits (based on Java programming). This allows third parties to create new functionality that can be integrated with the commercial system and allows specialist features to be developed.

For assessments delivered by a web browser, the ability to encrypt the data that is being exchanged between the students' computer and the institutional server delivering the assessment is important. Many of the enterprise-level systems in Table 5.4 provide options for the use of secure sockets layer (SSL), a protocol that allows the browser and web server to encrypt their communication.

Features such as scheduling the assessment commencement time and date, as well as the finishing time and date are included in many of the applications described in Table 5.4, as well as how many times an assessment may be attempted. Some assessment engines, such as Questionmark Perception also include an option whereby a monitored assessment cannot be commenced by the student until an invigilator has logged on to formally supervise the assessment. Questionmark

Perception also enables students to synchronize an assessment from their Windows-based PC to the institutional web server so that assessments can be downloaded and completed offline, and once completed uploaded for marking and feedback. Many of these advanced features are specific to a particular operating system, most often the Windows-based platform, and assume that students will be using, or at least have to access to, this particular platform.

The free for non-commercial use Hot Potatoes suite is a set of six authoring tools, created by the University of Victoria Humanities Computing and Media Centre in Canada. The suite enables users to create interactive web-based exercises of six basic types using JavaScript for interactivity and will function equally well on Windows and Macintosh platforms in a number of common browsers. Two of the tools from the suite, JMatch and JMix, can also produce dynamic HTML-based drag-and-drop exercises, but these require a more recent version of the web browser. Hot Potatoes is designed for diagnostic and formative low stakes assessment, and is not suitable for high stakes summative assessments. The authoring tools also enable teachers to use accented characters, so that non-English text, including French and German, may be used.

AiM, CABLE and Maple T. A. are software packages that are specific for the delivery of mathematical assessments via web browsers. The ability to represent and solve questions related to calculus, algebra, vectors and statistics requires the teacher and student to be able to write mathematical expressions in a particular format. For assessments of higher-level mathematics it is critical to be able to compare student responses for mathematical equivalence, and for the software to be able to automatically grade the student response appropriately.

Table 5.4 Summary of software systems for e-assessment

Assessment tool	Summary of key features	Link
AiM	AiM is an e-assessment system for mathematics, able to recognize symbolic representations in mathematics. It is written in the Maple programming language and requires a commercial licence for Maple in order to use. Installation on own server is available, free for non-commercial use, source code available.	http://sourceforge.net/projects/aimmath http://maths.york.ac.uk/moodle/aiminfo
ANGEL	ANGEL is a learning management system that includes e-assessment. Additional features can be added through APIs (application program interfaces). Able to use commercially available 'test banks' from publishers. Installation on own server available, commercial licence. Requires database software.	http://angellearning.com
Assessment Management System	Assessment Management System is an e-assessment system that can be used online, off-line, standalone or via a LAN. Installation on own server available.	http://www.excelindia.com
ATutor	ATutor is a learning content management system. Course server uses HTTP Web Server, PHP and MySQL. Installation on own server available, free for non-commercial use, source code available under GNU General Public License (GPL).	http://www.atutor.ca

Assessment tool	Summary of key features	Link
BOSS	BOSS is a computer program and essay submission system that allows teachers to mark assignments online and use SHERLOCK, a natural language plagiarism detection module.	http://www.dcs.warwick.ac.uk/boss
Blackboard Academic Suite™	The Blackboard Learning System™ is a learning management system that includes e-assessment. Additional features can be added through Building Blocks™ (Java code). Able to use commercially available 'test banks' from publishers. Installation on own server available, commercial licence, annual renewal. Requires database software, such as Oracle.	http://www.blackboard.com
CABLE	CABLE is an e-assessment system for mathematics, using open-source, online algebra systems such as Maxima or Axiom. Free for non-commercial use, source code available. Operating system independent, written in Java.	http://sourceforge.net/projects/cable http://www.cable.bham.ac.uk
Canvas Learning	Canvas Learning Author and Course Builder allow QTI items to be constructed and delivered. Flash™ Player enables integration with learning management systems, such as Blackboard™ or Oracle iLearning®. Users require Shockwave or Flash plugins for Internet browsers. Windows authoring only. Commercial licence, perpetual. IMS QTI compliant.	http://www.the-can.com
CASTLE	The Computer ASsisted Teaching & LEarning (CASTLE) is an e-assessment toolkit for authoring and delivery. Mainly written in Java, with some C programs providing an interface between CGI and Java. Installation on own server available, free for non-commercial use in higher education in the UK.	http://www.le.ac.uk/castle
Claroline	Claroline is a learning management system that includes e-assessment. Installation on own server available, free for non-commercial use, open source software.	http://www.claroline.net/
CQuest	CQuest is an assessment system that can be used online, off-line, standalone or via a LAN. PC Windows program when standalone. Commercial licence.	http://www.cquestsoftware.com

Assessment tool	Summary of key features	Link
Criterion	Criterion is an e-assessment service by Educational Testing Services (ETS) for written assignments, scoring and providing diagnostic feedback. Remotely hosted by ETS, commercial web-based service.	http://www.ets.org/criterion
Desire2Learn	Desire2Learn Learning Platform is a learning management system that includes e-assessment. Commercial licence, perpetual.	http://www.desire2learn.com
Discourse	Discourse is an e-assessment service by ETS for either synchronous interactivity, monitoring keystroke responses in real time, or asynchronous testing. Remotely hosted by ETS, commercial web-based service.	http://www.ets.org/discourse
ETH Lecture Communicator	ETH Lecture Communicator is an in-class, e-assessment and communication system. Operating system independent, written in Java. Installation on own server available, free for non-commercial use, open source software.	http://sourceforge.net/projects/lectcomm http://lectcomm.sourceforge.net
ExamBuilder	ExamBuilder is an e-assessment service remotely hosted by ExamBuilder, commercial web-based service.	http://exambuilder.com
Fast Test Pro	Fast Test Pro is an assessment system that can be used online, off-line, standalone or via a LAN, includes delivery and analysis package, computerized adaptive tests (CAT) possible based on item response theory. Commercial licence.	http://www.assess.com/Software/FTP16Main.htm#InternetTest
Hot Potatoes	Hot Potatoes is an e-assessment system. Installation on own server available, free for non-commercial use for assessments openly available through the Internet.	http://web.uvic.ca/hrd/hotpot
i-Assess	i-Assess is an assessment system that can be used online, off-line, standalone or via a LAN. Windows-based server. Off-line versions are Windows based. Commercial licence.	http://www.iassess.com
IBM Lotus Learning Management System	IBM Lotus Learning Management System is a learning management system that includes e-assessment. Installation on own server available, commercial licence.	http://www.lotus.com/lotus/offering6.nsf/wdocs/homepage
ILIAS	ILIAS is a learning management system that includes e-assessment. Installation on own server available, free for non-commercial use, available as open source software under the GNU General Public License.	http://www.ilias.uni-koeln.de

Assessment tool	Summary of key features	Link
IMS Assesst Designer	IMS Assesst Designer is an assessment system, installation on own server available, requires Windows platform, uses MySQL database, commercial licence, perpetual.	http://www.xdlsoft.com
InterWrite	InterWrite PRS™ (Personal Response System) is an in-class, e-assessment system, using numeric keypads response system. Commercial hardware and licence.	http://www.gtcocalcomp.com/interwriteprs.htm
JExam	JExam is an assessment system written in Java™. Installation on own server available, free for non-commercial use.	http://exams.uga.edu/~jmartin/JExam
Maple T. A.	Maple T. A. is an e-assessment system for mathematics, able to recognize symbolic representations in mathematics and can determine mathematical equivalences, integrates with the Blackboard Learning System™. Installation on own server available, commercial licence, annual renewal.	http://www.maplesoft.com/products/mapleta/
METRIC Maths	METRIC Maths consists of a series of self-tests in maths, based on Java and using client-side marking. Free for non-commercial use, accessed from remotely hosted site.	http://metric.ma.imperial.ac.uk/new/html
Moodle	Moodle is a course management system (CMS) that includes e-assessment. Installation on own server available, free for non-commercial use, available as open-source software under the terms of the GNU General Public License.	http://moodle.org
OASYS	OASYS GPL is an online peer assessment system. Installation on own server available, free for non-commercial use, available as open-source software under the terms of the GNU General Public License.	http://sourceforge.net/projects/oasysgpl http://www.dcs.warwick.ac.uk/~ashley/Research/OASYS
Oracle Learning Management System	Oracle iLearning and Oracle Training Management form part of a learning management system that includes e-assessment. Installation on own server available, commercial licence, annual renewal.	http://www.oracle.com/applications/human_resources/learning.html
Questionmark Perception	Questionmark Perception is an e-assessment system with Windows-based authoring. Can be used online, off-line, standalone or via a LAN. Installation on own server available, commercial licence, annual renewal.	http://www.questionmark.com
Question Tools	Question Tools can be used online or off-line, commercial licence.	http://www.questiontools.com

Assessment tool	Summary of key features	Link
Quia	Quia is an e-assessment service remotely hosted by Quia Web. Subscription licence, annual renewal.	http://www.quia.com
Quiz Factory 2™	Quiz Factory 2™ is a computer-based assessment system requiring a Quiz Factory Player. Can be used as standalone or via a LAN. Commercial licence, perpetual.	http://www.learningware. com/quizfactory
QuizStar	QuizStar is an e-assessment system, hosted remotely by University of Kansas and free for non-commercial use.	http://quizstar.4teachers.org
Respondus®	Respondus® is an e-assessment system that creates assessments for delivery in Blackboard™, eCollege or WebCT™. Respondus is used offline and the assessment uploaded to the learning management system. Commercial licence, annual renewal.	http://www.respondus.com
RIVA	RIVA e·test™ is an e-assessment system. Installation on own server available, or as a hosted service, commercial licence, annual renewal. Requires database system, such as Oracle. IMS QTI compliant.	http://www.riva.com
Samigo, part of Sakai release	Samigo, also known as Quiz and Test, is an online test administering tool, available in Sakai as a Sakai tool.	http://cvs.sakaiproject.org/ release/1.5.0/samigo.html
SPIDER	SPIDER is a learning management system that uses a purpose-built quiz engine SWIMS and uses a Shockwave viewer called SINQ (Shockwave IMS Net Quiz viewer).	https://spider-dev.pharmacy. strath.ac.uk/spiderV
Test Generator	Test Generator (TG) is an e-assessment system that uses Windows-based assessment construction and platform-independent Internet delivery. Can be used as standalone or via a LAN. Commercial licence, perpetual.	http://www.testshop.com
TestPilot	Test Pilot is an e-assessment system. Installation on own server, perpetual commercial licence.	http://www.clearlearning. com
TOIA	Technologies for Online Interoperable Assessment (TOIA) is an e-assessment system. Freely available for installation at all UK higher education and further education institutions.	http://www.toia.ac.uk
TopClass® LCMS	TopClass e-Learning Suite™ is a learning and content management system that includes e-assessment. Commercial licence, annual renewal.	http://www.wbtsystems. com

Assessment tool	Summary of key features	Link
TRIADS	Tripartite Interactive Assessment Delivery System (TRIADS) is an e-assessment system that requires Authorware™ Professional for authoring and the Shockwave plugin for web delivery. Can be used as standalone or via a LAN.	http://www.derby.ac.uk/ciad
WaLLiS	WaLLis is an e-assessment system for mathematics, able to recognize symbolic representations in mathematics and can determine mathematical equivalences. Contact website for availability.	http://www.maths.ed.ac.uk/~wallis
WebAssign	WebAssign is an e-assessment system. WWWAssign host servers are located on the North Carolina State University campus in Raleigh, NC. Subscription licence, annual renewal.	http://www.webassign.net
WebBoard	WebBoard is on online discussion board system. Windows server and a database required. Installation on own server, perpetual commercial licence.	http://www.akiva.com/products/webboard
WebCT™	WebCT Vista™ is a learning management system that includes e-assessment. Additional features can be added through Building Blocks™ (Java code). Able to use commercially available test banks from publishers. Installation on own server available, commercial licence, annual renewal. Requires database system, such as Oracle.	http://www.webct.com
WebMCQ IQS	Interactive Question Server™ (formerly WebMCQ) is an e-assessment system. Commercial licence. IMS QTI compliant.	http://www.mcqi.com.au
WebQuiz XP	WebQuiz XP is an e-assessment system that uses Windows-based assessment construction and platform independent Internet delivery. Can be used as standalone or via a LAN. Commercial licence, perpetual.	http://en.smartlite.it/en2/products/webquiz
WebTest	WebTest is an e-assessment service remotely hosted by a commercial web-based service.	http://www.chariot.com/webtest
xDLS™	xDLS™ uses IMS Assesst Designer, see above. Generates IMS QTI compliant questionnaires. xDLS 2002 SE is a shareware product.	http://www.xdlsoft.com/downloads.html

5.5 Other types in e-assessment software

Not all e-assessment systems offer a range of question types as outlined in Chapter 5.3. Some software packages are designed to offer a specific learning and assessment experience, and may be more appropriate for some discipline areas rather than across an entire institution. For example, IMMEX was originally designed for assessments in the medical discipline, but can be used as a generic tool for recording and assessing problem-solving strategies used by students in many discipline areas (http://www.immex.ucla.edu). IMMEX allows the teacher to propose a scenario and to make information available to the student and then analyse how the student proceeds through the problem-solving stages to arrive at a solution to the task. Students decide which information to access and in what order, and the teacher can assess the pathways that are presented in a graphical format. IMMEX assesses the processes involved in solving a problem, rather than the solution itself, so that the student will place more emphasis on the skills and capabilities developed as part of the journey, rather than the end point.

Personal response systems (PRS) can be used as an alternative form of e-assessment (Penuel et al., 2005; Draper et al., 2002; McCabe et al., 2003). These systems use a hand-held alpha numeric keypad device that allows students to select a response to objective questions, or to provide instant feedback to the teacher on content during classes. PRS are particularly suited to synchronous interactivity and are designed to promote classroom participation, as the student responses are usually accumulated during the face-to-face session so that all students, and the teacher, are able to view the responses. The question types for PRS are traditionally true/false, yes/no, multiple choice or numeric values and may be used for classroom quizzes or to promote discussions. Software that permits student responses to questions proposed in Powerpoint™ slide presentations provide teachers with an opportunity to increase interactivity in the classroom as students may have their accumulated responses displayed on a slide during the class (http://www.socratec.com; http://www.iml.ltd.uk). PRS have been adapted to include a wider variety of question types, including open-ended questions, graphical hotspots and mathematical questions. Teachers may use PRS to construct questions during a synchronous session, or students may review the questions and class responses at a later time (McCabe et al., 2003).

Online peer review systems allow students to develop capabilities in assessing their own written work, by practising on teacher-provided anonymous essays that have been previously graded according to a defined rubric. The advantage of such online systems includes their ability to develop metacognitive capabilities in students and to provide benchmarking opportunities, with a concomitant reduction in teacher marking load for diagnostic or formative assessments. Calibrated Peer Review™, a free web-based service hosted by the University of California, Los Angeles, was originally written to support science programmes by allowing students to write and peer review research proposals (http://cpr.molsci.ucla.edu). This service may be used for all discipline areas, and provides system-stored anonymous assignments at different levels, or teachers may upload their own assignments and marking rubric. The feedback to students is dependent on the teacher providing predefined responses and comments, and the assignments do not have to be written text, but may be graphics, scanned images of paintings or line drawings of equipment. QSIA (Questions Sharing and Interactive Assignments) is an example of a software tool for sharing the authoring and evaluation of assessment items (Rafaeli et al., 2004). Students and teachers are able to rate assessment items, and modify them as appropriate, with peer review and self-assessment key characteristics of the collaborative approach to question bank construction.

A number of software applications are available that allow text essays to be marked by a computer using algorithms that emulate the processes used by human experts to grade student responses (Valenti et al., 2003). Since essays often allow students to engage with the synthesis, integration and analysis areas of Bloom's objectives (Anderson et al., 2001) they are frequently used by teachers, but require considerable time to assess and to provide constructive feedback for students to direct their learning. Essay marking software is the automated assessment of

Table 5.5 Essay marking software

Intelligent Essay Assessor™	Intelligent Essay Assessor™ (IEA) is a web-based service or may be licensed to use within a learning management system. Uses Latent Semantic Analysis (LSA). Requires a large amount of RAM if run on own system.	http://www.knowledge-technologies.com
IntelliMetric™	IntelliMetric uses propriety software CogniSearch™ and Quantum Reasoning™ using a combination of Artificial Intelligence, natural language processing and statistics. Web-based service licensed through MY Access.	http://www.vantage.com/pdfs/intellimetric.pdf http://www.summitintellimetric.com
Criterion™ Online Essay Evaluation Service	The Criterion™ Online Essay Evaluation Service is a web-based system that assesses essay responses through either E-rater® or C-rater™. E-rater provides a score for an essay, and Critique provides feedback to the student on grammar, and style using natural language processing.	http://www.ets.org/research/erater.html

free text responses and relies on the underlying theoretical models based on semantic network theory and latent semantic analysis (Williams, 2001). The teacher must 'train' the software to understand the priorities that humans place on predefined characteristics for student responses, and to apply marks or points for the presence or absence of these characteristics. These systems can be very useful for diagnostic and formative assessments, as feedback is an integral part of the teacher's objective for improving student outcomes. Although computer based assessment of free text entries may be shown to be technically consistent, there is still some variation in teacher perceptions of the consistency in assessing style, intellectual input and holistic merit of a piece of written work. There are also divided guidelines on how many examples are required in order to train the software to emulate common human assessment results (Leacock *et al.*, 2003). Table 5.5 summarizes some of the available software for the automated assessment of free text responses.

5.6 Adaptive assessment software

Adaptive assessments typically use MCQ type questions from an item bank to make a judgement about the ability level of the student and so present questions that match their level of performance. A convergence occurs as the student responds to each question and a slightly more challenging item is presented after each successful response until the student matches a predetermined competency level. In adaptive assessment the student does not have to complete all questions, rather they continue to respond to questions until the predetermined competency level is reached. Constructing adaptive assessment questions takes a significant amount of time as a hierarchy must be established for sets of questions, and an item bank must be prepared with partial marks assigned to each distracter and the correct option assigned a higher mark. As the questions become more difficult, the correct option is assigned higher marks again and the distracters are assigned higher partial marks. The mark obtained from such an assessment will represent a unidimensional variable whereby a student's performance may be ranked with respect to others taking the same assessment. The psychometric models upon which such adaptive assessments are based include the Rasch model and item response theory (McAlpine, 2002b). Item response theory assumes that each question is administered to a large group of students so that an appropriate response function may be determined for validity checking.

Although there are significant advantages for students in taking adaptive assessments, such as fewer questions being answered, more focused questions for a particular level of ability and a predetermined competency level; there are also some disadvantages, including potential inequities caused by different questions being presented to different students and unfamiliarity with the test environment.

The most common use for online adaptive assessment is for large-scale standardized admission tests such as the Graduate Record Examinations (GRE®), computer-based testing for the Test of English as a Foreign Language (TOEFL®), the Graduate Management Admission Test (GMAT®), and the National Council Licensure Examination (NCLEX) for nurses. For these adaptive tests, the score a student obtains is not related to the number of correct versus incorrect responses, but rather the level of difficulty of the questions answered correctly.

Section 3 What does an e-assessment look like?

6 e-Assessment examples by discipline

6.1 General sources of e-assessment questions

By far the most extensive source of e-assessment questions will be found from commercial sources in the form of item banks from textbook publishers or discipline specific professional organizations. It is quite common for standard textbooks aimed at the tertiary education market, especially those designed for large introductory classes, to include an instructor CD or instructor access to a website containing objective assessment items for each chapter of the text. Many of the publishers will provide such questions in a format suitable for importing directly into assessment modules in learning management systems such as WebCT™, Blackboard™ and ANGEL, or into e-assessment applications such as QuestionMark Perception or Respondus® (see Table 5.4 (p. 82) for web contact details for these products).

The commercial vendor for the e-assessment software Quia (http://www.quia.com) offers an extensive collection of shared e-assessment items, particularly for the K–12 category, but also some higher education examples. The Quia website offers a subscription service for access to a range of content covering most discipline areas, including templates for e-assessment activities such as flashcards, games such as memory, word searches, battleship, hangman and scavenger hunts as well as jumbled words and cloze exercises.

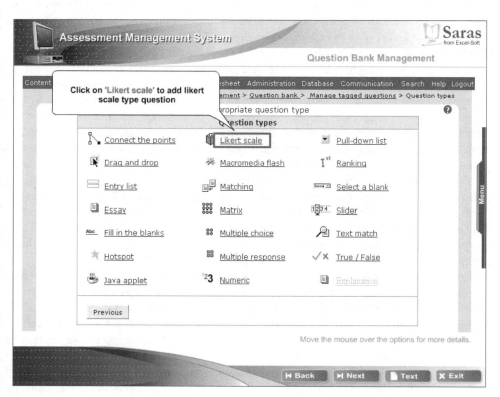

Figure 6.1 Example of e-assessment question types for AMS from Excel-Soft (http://www.excelindia.com)

Many of the learning management systems and e-assessment software tools described in Table 5.4 will enable item pools or test banks to be constructed or imported. Most discipline areas are able to make effective use of e-assessment items by choosing an appropriate format for questions. A good example of the type of questions that can be constructed for use in item banks is shown in Figure 6.1, for the AMS system from the vendor Excel-Soft (http://www.excelindia.com). This software is also the basis for the TOIA project in the UK (http://www.toia.ac.uk).

The Item Banks Infrastructure Study (IBIS, http://www.toia.ac.uk/ibis; Sclater, 2004) was a project funded by JISC under the Exchange for Learning (X4L, http://www.x4l.org) programme. The IBIS report proposed the development of a distributed item bank service for further and higher education in the UK. The proposal recommended the establishment of a commercial brokering system for the storage, validation and distribution of e-assessment items. IBIS proposed a validation process for items before they could be incorporated into item pools and that items in the pools would be subjected to psychometric analysis over time, thus ensuring a degree of quality control of the items in the system.

Test bank items may be used for diagnostic, formative or summative purposes, and Gibbs *et al.* (2004) have provided a succinct summary of the conditions under which assessment will support learning. Educators may use this summary to reflect on their use of e-assessment items for these various purposes, and in particular the role that feedback plays in influencing student behaviour and future approaches to learning. This is important when considering e-assessment items, since the feedback component of the item will be crucial in influencing future learning patterns. Thus teachers will need to carefully review the feedback associated with test items in item banks, especially if the item is to be used for diagnostic and formative purposes.

6.2 Accounting, commerce and economics

The Higher Education Academy (HEA) in the UK supports a number of subject networks that provide useful resources for staff at further and higher educational institutions. The economics network provides an assessment bank of economics questions, in MCQ and essay format, that are free for UK education institutions, but not freely available for organizations outside of the UK (http://www.economicsnetwork.ac.uk/qnbank). An online text on e-assessment for teachers of economics (Chalmers *et al.*, 2002) is also available from this website, and provides additional information on all forms of assessment that is useful for teachers of economics. The economics network website provides useful links to over 40 interactive quizzes, some of which are available from commercial vendors while others are freely available (http://www.economicsnetwork.ac.uk/teaching/quizzes.htm). For teachers who would like to construct their own items the site also contains Javascript tools, including generators for multiple-choice, multiple-response, gap-fill and online maths items.

WinEcon, managed by the University of Bristol and developed as part of the TLTP (Teaching and Learning Technology Programme) funded consortium of eight UK economics departments provides a commercial subscription service with access to texts and software, including numerous e-assessment examples for micro- and macroeconomics, as well as mathematics for economics courses (http://www.winecon.com). WinEcon item banks can be integrated with the assessment tools in WebCT™ and Blackboard™ learning management systems.

Biz/ed (http://www.bized.ac.uk), also at the University of Bristol, provides a free online service for educators in business, economics, accounting and tourism and makes available an extensive question bank of economics test items as well as hosting MCQs on topics in introductory economics, accounting, finance and marketing. Interactive spreadsheets are important tools for teaching economics and accounting and the Biz/ed website contains suggestions on how to incorporate these learning tools into assessments (http://www.bized.ac.uk/educators/he/spreadsheet/section_6.htm). Ferl (Further Education Resources for Learning) is an online information service managed by Becta (http://ferl.becta.org.uk) and their website provides useful examples of interactive spreadsheets that can be incorporated into e-assessments; examples are shown in Figures 6.2 and 6.3.

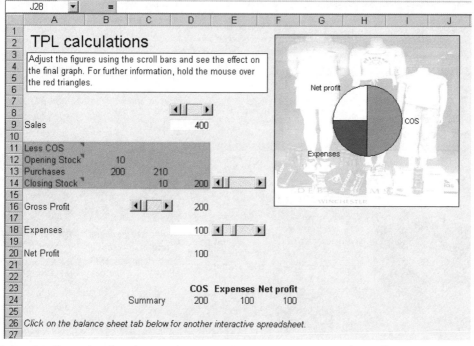

Figure 6.2 Example of an interactive spreadsheet by Colin Vickers (http://www.qmc.ac.uk, http://ferl.becta.org.uk/display.cfm?page=432)

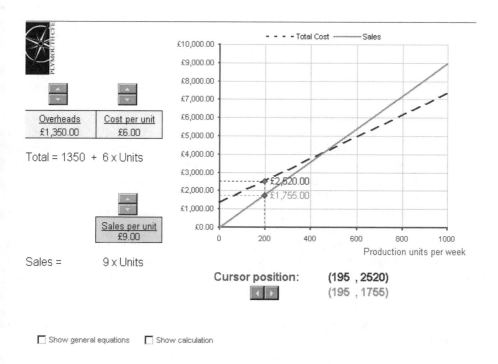

Figure 6.3 Example of an interactive spreadsheet by Brian Watson (http://ferl.becta.org.uk/ display.cfm?resID=2453, http://tech.plym.ac.uk.Research/mathematics_education/people/ brian_watson.htm)

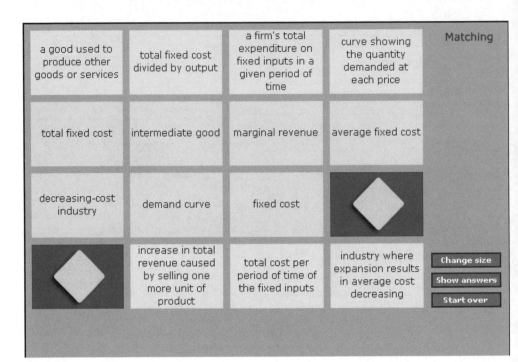

Figure 6.4 Quia quiz example by Mitchell C (mitchc45@aol.com, http://www.quia.com)

The Ferl website contains numerous examples of economics and business formative assessments using Hot Potatoes (http://ferl.becta.org.uk/display.cfm?page=432). Hot Potatoes (http://hotpot. uvic.ca) is an assessment tool that enables teachers to construct interactive, multiple-choice, short-answer, jumbled-sentence, crossword, matching or ordering and gap-fill e-assessment items using a combination of XHMTL, CSS and Javascript templates. Hot Potatoes is free of charge for teachers working for publicly funded, non-profit educational institutions, and teachers must make their assessments or activities made with the software freely available online. It is possible to purchase a licence for Hot Potatoes for other purposes.

The commercial vendor Quia (http://www.quia.com) provides examples of diagnostic and formative quizzes in economics and accounting, such as the matching game outlined in Figure 6.4. Such games are useful for students since they enable benchmarking of key concepts and can be coupled to feedback so that students are directed to specific resources when their current level of understanding is not sufficient to progress to the next topic or level in a course.

JeLSIM (Java e-Learning SIMulations; http://www.jelsim.org) is an open-source tool that allows teachers to construct online simulations and run them as Java applets. Java applets may be incorporated into e-assessments as discussed in more detail in Chapter 14. The JeLSIM Builder toolkit is written in the Java programming language and allows teachers or instructional designers to create Java applets that are delivered through a web browser. The JeLSIM Builder requires some time to master, but does not require any programming skills. An example of a Java applet for a trading forecast exercise is illustrated in Figure 6.5.

An extensive array of accounting questions in e-assessment format may be found at http://www.uwm.edu/People/ceil/systems/aisexam1.html, a website hosted by the University of Wisconsin, Milwaukee. An example of an MCQ from this website, using some of the features of a multiple-response question is shown in Figure 6.6.

For each possible error and irregularity presented in the list below, select one internal control procedure from the answer list that most likely could assist in preventing or detecting the error or irregularity.

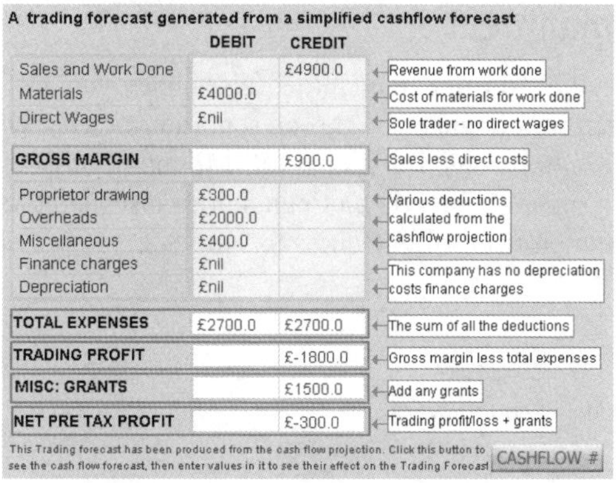

A trading forecast generated from a simplified cashflow forecast

	DEBIT	CREDIT	
Sales and Work Done		£4900.0	← Revenue from work done
Materials	£4000.0		← Cost of materials for work done
Direct Wages	£nil		← Sole trader - no direct wages
GROSS MARGIN		£900.0	← Sales less direct costs
Proprietor drawing	£300.0		← Various deductions
Overheads	£2000.0		← calculated from the
Miscellaneous	£400.0		← cashflow projection
Finance charges	£nil		← This company has no depreciation
Depreciation	£nil		← costs finance charges
TOTAL EXPENSES	£2700.0	£2700.0	← The sum of all the deductions
TRADING PROFIT		£-1800.0	← Gross margin less total expenses
MISC: GRANTS		£1500.0	← Add any grants
NET PRE TAX PROFIT		£-300.0	← Trading profit/loss + grants

This Trading forecast has been produced from the cash flow projection. Click this button to see the cash flow forecast, then enter values in it to see their effect on the Trading Forecast [CASHFLOW #]

Figure 6.5 Trading forecast Java applet constructed using the JelSim toolkit (http://www.jelsim.org/content/applets/bizstartup)

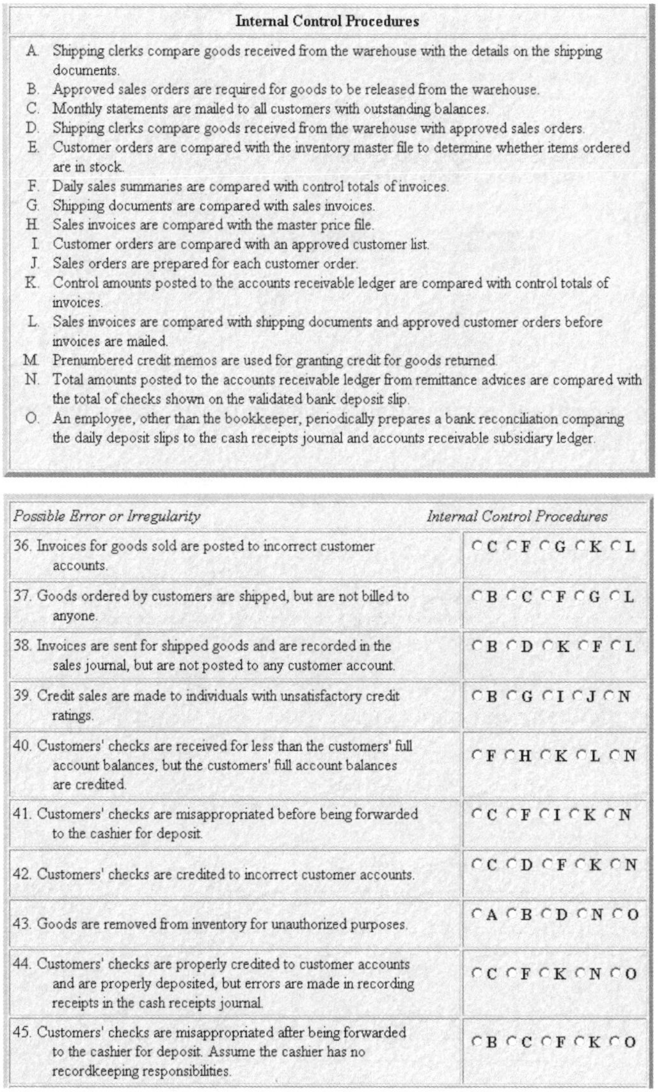

Internal Control Procedures

A. Shipping clerks compare goods received from the warehouse with the details on the shipping documents.
B. Approved sales orders are required for goods to be released from the warehouse.
C. Monthly statements are mailed to all customers with outstanding balances.
D. Shipping clerks compare goods received from the warehouse with approved sales orders.
E. Customer orders are compared with the inventory master file to determine whether items ordered are in stock.
F. Daily sales summaries are compared with control totals of invoices.
G. Shipping documents are compared with sales invoices.
H. Sales invoices are compared with the master price file.
I. Customer orders are compared with an approved customer list.
J. Sales orders are prepared for each customer order.
K. Control amounts posted to the accounts receivable ledger are compared with control totals of invoices.
L. Sales invoices are compared with shipping documents and approved customer orders before invoices are mailed.
M. Prenumbered credit memos are used for granting credit for goods returned.
N. Total amounts posted to the accounts receivable ledger from remittance advices are compared with the total of checks shown on the validated bank deposit slip.
O. An employee, other than the bookkeeper, periodically prepares a bank reconciliation comparing the daily deposit slips to the cash receipts journal and accounts receivable subsidiary ledger.

Possible Error or Irregularity	Internal Control Procedures
36. Invoices for goods sold are posted to incorrect customer accounts.	⊂C ⊂C ⊂F ⊂G ⊂K ⊂L
37. Goods ordered by customers are shipped, but are not billed to anyone.	⊂B ⊂C ⊂C ⊂F ⊂G ⊂L
38. Invoices are sent for shipped goods and are recorded in the sales journal, but are not posted to any customer account.	⊂B ⊂D ⊂K ⊂F ⊂L
39. Credit sales are made to individuals with unsatisfactory credit ratings.	⊂B ⊂G ⊂I ⊂J ⊂N
40. Customers' checks are received for less than the customers' full account balances, but the customers' full account balances are credited.	⊂F ⊂H ⊂K ⊂L ⊂N
41. Customers' checks are misappropriated before being forwarded to the cashier for deposit.	⊂C ⊂F ⊂I ⊂K ⊂N
42. Customers' checks are credited to incorrect customer accounts.	⊂C ⊂D ⊂F ⊂K ⊂N
43. Goods are removed from inventory for unauthorized purposes.	⊂A ⊂B ⊂D ⊂N ⊂O
44. Customers' checks are properly credited to customer accounts and are properly deposited, but errors are made in recording receipts in the cash receipts journal.	⊂C ⊂F ⊂K ⊂N ⊂O
45. Customers' checks are misappropriated after being forwarded to the cashier for deposit. Assume the cashier has no recordkeeping responsibilities.	⊂B ⊂C ⊂C ⊂F ⊂K ⊂O

Figure 6.6 Questions by Ceil Pillsbury at the University of Wisconsin, Milwaukee (http://www.uwm.edu/People/ceil/systems/aisexam1.html)

6.3 Arts and humanities

Assessment formats for the arts and humanities disciplines can be quite varied; they may range from music, drama performances or the presentation of creative works of art, through to standard essays and examinations. Traditional MCQ format assessments may be used to test declarative knowledge in most of the arts and humanities disciplines, as illustrated by the two formative assessment examples shown in Figures 6.7 and 6.8.

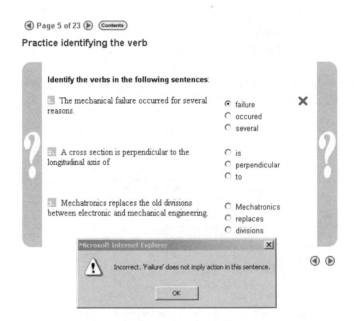

Figure 6.7 Improving written communication skills quiz using radio buttons from the University of Adelaide

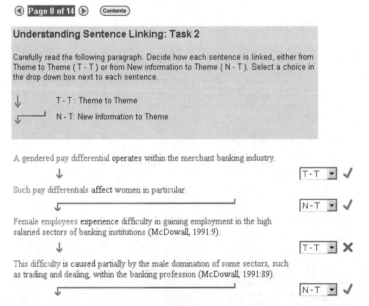

Figure 6.8 Improving written communication skills quiz using drop-down boxes from the University of Adelaide

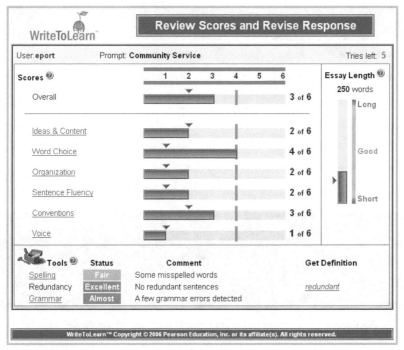

Figure 6.9 Demonstration of the report from a computer marked essay by Intelligent Essay Assessor™ (http://www.knowledge-technologies.com)

Since essays often form a significant component of the summative assessment for the humanities discipline, there has been considerable interest and effort in improving the automatic marking of written text responses. The issues associated with automatic essay marking have been discussed previously in some detail in Chapter 5.5, and some of the software available for this task summarized in Table 5.5. It is possible to achieve acceptable levels of validity and reliability for computer-based marking of essays in many cases, and a variety of approaches have been discussed in the literature, including those based on the analysis of the superficial features of the text, latent semantic analysis and natural language processing (Cohen *et al.*, 2003). Recent approaches to the automatic assessment of digital essays include the use of cue phrases, semantics and argumentation patterns so that a genre analysis of the written text is possible (Moreale *et al.*, 2003). An example of a report from a commercial vendor, Intelligent Essay Assessor™, that automatically marks a submitted text essay and provides some feedback to students, is shown in Figure 6.9.

Plagiarism issues continue to be of concern to further and higher education institutions, in particular where essays are used for a significant component of the summative assessment (http://www.jiscpas.ac.uk). Many institutions are now using online plagiarism detection systems, such as Turnitin (http://www.turnitin.com), for the automatic comparison of submitted work against digital sources on the Internet or in digital repositories. E-assessment may be used to develop skills in essay writing, such as appropriate paraphrasing, citing and referencing, as illustrated in the formative example outlined in Figure 6.10.

The use of e-assessment in the discipline of English was reviewed recently in the UK with the view to aligning learning and assessment practices in the discipline (Whetton, 2005). The use of e-portfolios to support assessment for learning was emphasized, as was the need for a mixture of computer-based and human assessor activities. The report described a clear requirement for formative assessment to improve student learning, and how e-assessment can play an important role in providing appropriate feedback for large classes. The report also described the possible

e-Assessment examples by discipline

Example 1
Read the example of a student's use of source material and answer the question below.

Student's use of material:

Because it was owned by the Government, loans made by the State Bank of South Australia were guaranteed by the S.A. government. Its close ties to the government led to huge public losses in the REMM-Myer Complex. When the REMM-Myer Complex was completed in 1991, the total liability to the bank was over $900 million. In 1996 the Myer Complex was sold for $152 million which meant that the loss was over $750 million for taxpayers. (McCarthy 2002) .

Original Source Material:

When the REMM-Myer Complex was completed in 1991, the total liability to the bank was over $900 million. In 1996 the Myer Complex was sold for $152 million which meant that the loss was over $750 million for taxpayers. The SBSA's largest loss was brought about by a board being prepared to make an ill-judged decision to support a dangerous proposal from the management for an open-ended guarantee to build a prominent shopping centre.

Bibliography:
Greg McCarthy Things Fall Apart: A history of the State Bank of South Australia (Melbourne: Australian Scholarly Publishing, 2002), pp. 203.

Question: Is this an example of plagiarism?
- No.
- Yes, because it quotes another person's actual words, either oral or written; and it is not appropriately acknowledged.
- Yes, because it paraphrases another person's words, either oral or written; and it is not appropriately acknowledged .
- Yes, because it uses another person's idea, opinion, or theory; and it is not properly acknowledged.
- Yes, because it borrows facts, statistics, or other illustrative material, unless the information is common knowledge; and it is not properly acknowledged.

Figure 6.10 Plagiarism prevention quiz from the University of Adelaide

assessment of reading skills which would include test items requiring students to respond using computer-entered text and the recording of spoken language responses; both types of responses should be able to be marked by an appropriate online application. The nature of literacy was discussed in the document and the need to incorporate voice recognition into formative e-assessment.

The ability to incorporate multimedia into e-assessment questions is illustrated in the music example in Figure 6.11. In this particular example the sounds are stored as MIDI files and the overall assessment is played using an appropriate Shockwave™ plugin for the web browser. Students would require access to a computer with a sound card and in a group situation may also require headphones so as not to disturb other students. The development of interactive activities such as that shown in Figure 6.11 requires considerable time and specialized software, and so for most teachers obtaining such activities from commercial sources and incorporating them into their own e-assessments will be more convenient. These learning objects then become important tools for both learning and assessment, and the same object can be repurposed for a variety of uses. By using such learning objects strategically, teachers will be able to reduce the amount of time required to produce quality learning and assessment experiences for their students.

6.4 Biological and health sciences

An extensive manual by Case *et al.* (2002) on the construction of objective questions for teachers in the biological and health sciences is freely available. The manual provides detailed information on question types, how to construct high-quality items, how to undertake a statistical analysis of test results, as well as many tips to assist teachers write valid and reliable questions. A summary of the keys points for objective question items from this document includes the following points:

- they should focus on an important concept, be authentic and not ask trivial details; the wording should be precise and not overly convoluted
- they should assess application, not recall of knowledge; item stems may be relatively long, but the options should be short

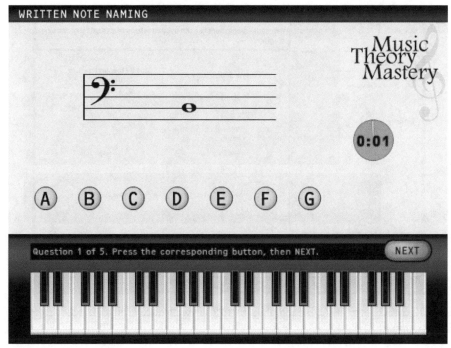

Figure 6.11 Example of online music theory assessment (http://www.hansenb.pdx.edu/mtm.html)

- the stem of the item must pose a concise question that could be answered without the options being present
- all distracters should belong to the same category as the key; they should all describe the same area of the curriculum and all be related to the same concept.

The OLAAF (Online Assessment and Feedback) project provides a set of discipline examples based on the TRIAD Authorware™ format (http://www.bbk.ac.uk/olaaf/triads_demos/bso_conf/bso_demo.htm). Figure 6.12 illustrates a particular MCQ item for use in anatomy. This type of MCQ matching questions may exhibit high levels of dependencies, since an incorrect response to the first part of the question may consequentially lead to an incorrect response to the second part, although the student response to the second part of the question may follow logically from their incorrect response to the first part. This is still a valid format for questions, and teachers will need to consider the consequences of such dependencies so that MCQ matching questions are used in an appropriate manner.

The Strathclyde Personal Interactive Development and Educational Resource (SPIDER) system uses a Shockwave™ IMS (SWIMS) question generator for the construction of MCQ, true/false, drag-and-drop or numeric question types and a Shockwave™ InterNet Quiz viewer (SINQ) for students to complete the assessment (https://spider-dev.pharmacy.strath.ac.uk/spiderV). An example of a matching type question from health science is shown in Figure 6.13. Again, teachers will need to reflect on the consequences of using this format for questions, since the software may allow each option to be used only once, especially if the software requires that the options be moved to a specific location on the screen to align with the appropriate stem. A consequence of one wrong choice will automatically lead to two incorrect responses in this case, and it may be more appropriate to allow students to use a particular option more than once. The decision whether to allow students to reuse options should be a pedagogical one, and not one determined by the software.

IMMEX (Interactive Multi-Media Exercises) offers a web-based platform for students to undertake complex problem-solving exercises that test procedural knowledge in addition to

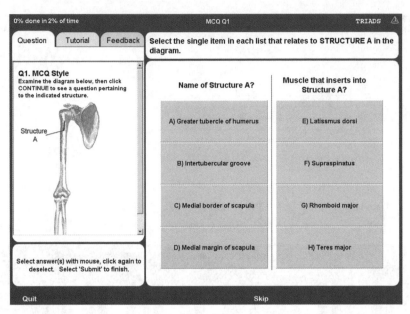

Figure 6.12 MCQ from TRIADS exemplars (http://www.bbk.ac.uk/olaaf/triads_demos/bso_conf/bso_demo.htm)

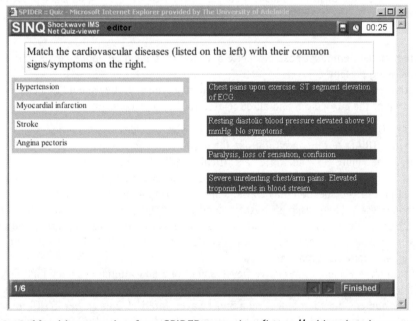

Figure 6.13 Matching question from SPIDER exemplars (https://spider–dev.pharmacy.strath.ac.uk/spiderV/index.php)

declarative knowledge (http://www.immex.ucla.edu). IMMEX has been discussed in more detail in Chapter 5.5. Teachers design a problem using the IMMEX protocols, and schedule session times for students to access and complete the problem online. The IMMEX software tracks how students attempt to solve the problem; it records all the keystrokes and sources of online information used by the student in order to propose a solution to the problem. An example of an IMMEX problem in the biological sciences is 'True Roots', shown in Figure 6.14, which assesses an understanding

CLICK ON ANY OF THE TESTS TO BEGIN. USE THE MENU
WHEN YOU WANT TO SOLVE THE CASE OR ARE READY TO LEAVE.

You are asked to evaluate a 6 month old child who was diagnosed with Pneumocystis carinii pneumonitis at 3 months of age. Since the time of diagnosis, the patient has been on intravenous IgG. When you see the patient in clinic, you find a sickly looking child who is below average on both the height and weight growth charts. The patient has low levels of immunoglobulins and lymphocytes, except for IgG levels, which are in the low normal range.

Furthermore, DTH testing had been performed 1 month ago and PPD, mumps, candida, and tetanus antigen resulted in no skin reaction at the skin test site.

What is wrong with the infant?

You've requested to see:
TYROSINE KINASE mRNA BLOT

Your current score is **100** Points.
Viewing this item will cost you 50 Points.
Do you wish to continue?

YES   NO

NITRIC OXIDE PRODUCTION

Adherent cells were isolated from normal and patient PBLs and were incubated with LPS (bacterial lipopolysaccharide — which is endotoxin), gamma IFN, or a combination of both. After 24 hours, the levels of nitric oxide produced were assayed using the Griess reagent to measure nitrite generated from nitric oxide.

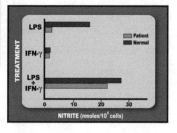

Figure 6.14 IMMEX problem–solving example (http://www.immex.ucla.edu)

of a number of key principles and processes used in genetics (Stevens *et al.*, 2003). 'True Roots' involves a hypothetical case of 'baby swapping' at birth and engages the student in a genetic investigation of parenthood. Students may request various tests for blood type, DNA restriction mapping, karyotype, fingerprints and pedigree charts as they adopt the persona for one of the hypothetical players presented in the problem set. Since IMMEX is tracking all resources used as part of the exercise, teachers may allocate marks for efficiency, and reward students for effective problem-solving strategies. In practice, IMMEX reduces the score allocated by subtracting marks for each piece of teacher supplied online information available to the student. This methodology is meant to encourage the student to be judicious about the amount of information required to solve a problem, and teachers should be clear about this criterion when setting objectives for the course and the assessments. If the teacher has not been explicit about the objective of efficiency, then students may be frustrated when they are 'penalised' for using information provided by the teacher to solve the problem.

An example of an extended matching item (EMI) question is shown in Figure 6.15 (http://www.bris.ac.uk/omr/EMI). EMI questions are growing in popularity, particularly in biological and health sciences, since they may be used to test both declarative and procedural knowledge, and the various levels of either the Bloom or SOLO taxonomies. EMI questions use a scenario or dataset to describe the context and limit of the problem, and an extended set of options compared to a typical MCQ. The EMI format frequently reduces some of the disadvantages of MCQs such as the impact of guessing, or the ability to easily remove unlikely options, while still retaining some of the advantages of MCQs, such as ease of marking, and the ability to construct extensive item banks.

Two chambers ('reference' and 'test') are separated by a selectively permeable membrane. A voltmeter records the electrical potential difference (p.d.) between the chambers (see diagram). The reference ('ref') chamber always contains the same concentration of KCl. The concentrations of KCl in the other ('test') chamber are given in the table (below). The average value of the electrical p.d. (in mV) that is recorded at each concentration of KCl is also given in the table. The measurements were made at room temperature (22–25°C). By convention, the p.d. (= voltage) is reported as the value for the potential in the 'test' chamber relative to the 'ref' chamber (i.e. the ref is taken to be zero at all times and so a positive potential difference means that the test chamber has a positive potential difference, compared to the reference chamber). Nernst equation (note, constant appropriate for 25°C).

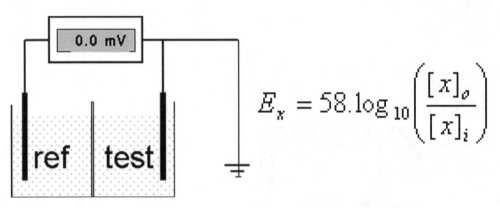

$$E_x = 58.\log_{10}\left(\frac{[x]_o}{[x]_i}\right)$$

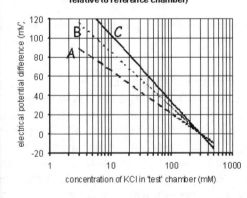

Measured potential difference (test chamber relative to reference chamber)

Concentration in test chamber (mM)	Electrical p.d. (mV)	'Expected' electrical p.d. (mV) for perfectly selective membrane
3	90	X
10	66	–
30	45	Y
100	21	–
200	8	–
300	0	Z
500	-10	–

p.d. = potential difference

Options for the questions below. Please insert the letter that corresponds to the most appropriate answer. Answers may be used as many times as required, or not at all.

A	B	C	D	E	F	G	H	I	
0	58	61	116	-58	122	300	140	5	
J	K	L	M	N	O	P	Q	V	
mV	mM	True	False	Nernst	Goldmann Hodgkin Katz	Boltzmann	Ideal Nernstian slope	Anions	
R	S	T	U	V	W	X	Z		
Permeability	Reversal potential	Divalent ions	Cations	Anions	A	B	Electro-chemical gradient		

1. What is the expected potential difference (voltage) labelled X in the above Table? ▾

2. What is the expected potential difference labelled Y in the above Table? ▾

3. What is the expected potential difference labelled Z in the above Table? ▾

4. The data in the table are plotted as line ▾?

5. The line labelled 'A' shows the relationship between membrane potential and external potassium concentration for a perfectly selective membrane. Is this statement true or false? ▾

6. The equation that relates the concentration gradient of a specific ion and the expected membrane potential is the ▾ equation.

7. The value returned by the Nernst equation has the units ▾?

8. From the table (and the graph) it is clear that the concentration of potassium on the 'reference' side of the membrane is ▾ mM.

9. When ions move passively through a membrane, they always move in accordance with the ▾

10. The line labelled C is consistent with data obtained from a perfectly selective membrane at a temperature of 37°C. Is this statement true or false? ▾

11. In electrophysiology, the Nernst potential (at which there is no net ion movement) is frequently called the ▾, because the direction of electrical current flow changes sign either side of this p.d.

12. The data in the table is consistent with the membrane being most permeable to ▾

13. At room temperature, a perfectly selective membrane will show a ▾ mV change in the potential difference for a 10-fold change in the concentration of the permeant mono-valent ion.

14. The line labelled ▾ shows results expected from a membrane that exhibits 'ideal' ion-selectivity.

15. If a selectively permeable membrane is replaced by a membrane that is totally impermeable to ions (e.g. plastic), the membrane potential difference would always be ▾ mV?

16. A membrane that is said to exhibit perfectly selectivity is shown to have a membrane potential that changes by approximately 29 mV when the concentration gradient of an unknown ion changes by 10-fold. This is explicable if the membrane is permeable to ▾

17. For a mammalian cell membrane that is perfectly selective for potassium ions, what is the intracellular concentration of ions if the membrane potential at 37°C is -88 mV and the extracellular concentration of potassium is 5 mM? ▾

Figure 6.15 Example of an extended matching item (EMI) question (http://www.bris.ac.uk/omr/EMI)

EMI questions in health science tend to follow a standard template as shown by Figure 6.16 (Wood, 2003) consisting of:

■ the item stem (patient vignette which describes a patient with a problem)
■ the lead-in (such as a biological defect which is most likely to be present and results in the particular patient problem presented)
■ the options (which usually comprise of a list of structures and/or processes that may be associated with the particular biological defect).

For the health science discipline, patient scenarios often provide an appropriate stem, and lead-ins will usually commence with a statement about the patient or the description of the patient's symptoms. The questions will generally seek a response to specific aspects of the diagnosis, or the processes used to arrive at the diagnosis. The example shown in Figure 6.17 uses a short video sequence as the lead-in, and uses a multiple-response format for the options.

Figure 6.18 illustrates an alternative approach to matching type questions. In this example a dependent sequence is portrayed, and students have access to the overall relationships between the separate components of the question. This type of question allows multistructural responses from students and may reduce one of the disadvantages of matching type questions discussed

Theme: Absorption and processing of carbohydrates

Directions ("Lead-in"): For each of the following select the correct carbohydrate. (Each option may be used once, more than once, or not at all.)

Question 1. An individual of Afro-Caribbean origin experiences indigestion, gas and bloat after consuming milk products. Avoiding milk products completely cures this problem which is caused by the individual's inability to digest which of these carbohydrates? [A. Deoxyribose ▼]

Question 2. In addition to glucose, an infant on a normal milk diet obtains approx. 50% of its carbohydrate energy from which of the above carbohydrates? [A. Deoxyribose ▼]

Question 3. In normal individuals starch in the diet is hydrolysed in the intestine to produce which of the above carbohydrates? [A. Deoxyribose ▼]

Question 4. Infants with the rare genetic disorder galactosaemia lack the enzyme necessary for dealing with which if these carbohydrates? [A. Deoxyribose ▼]

Question 5. Glycogen in liver can be broken down to produce which of these carbohydrates? [A. Deoxyribose ▼]

Figure 6.16 EMI question type for health science (Wood, 2003)

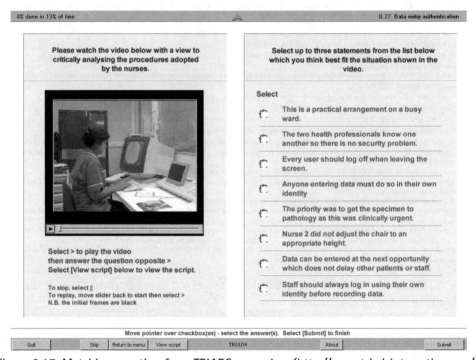

Figure 6.17 Matching question from TRIADS exemplars (http://www.triadsinteractive.com/ Assessment/triads2demo)

above, namely the cumulative effect of one incorrect response. With formats such as that illustrated in Figure 6.18, students may commence at different points, some will work forwards from a particular point in the question while others may work backwards. This type of question will cater for the variety of ways in which students have constructed their knowledge and understanding, and is less dependent on a particular pattern of recall. Teachers may also provide hints (which can be provided at a 'cost' in terms of the marks allocated for a question) in multicomponent questions so as not to disadvantage students who are missing only a specific piece of knowledge, and so provides an opportunity for students to demonstrate what they can do.

An extensive series of simple objective questions related to biological and health sciences can be found at http://www.mrcophth.com/MRCOphth/mcqbank.html. This site covers areas such as anatomy, biochemistry, physiology, pathology, ophthalmology and microbiology. The School of Medicine at the University of Birmingham in the UK hosts the MedWeb site also containing an

Identify the number of chromosomes and the ploidy of the ancestors of wheat.

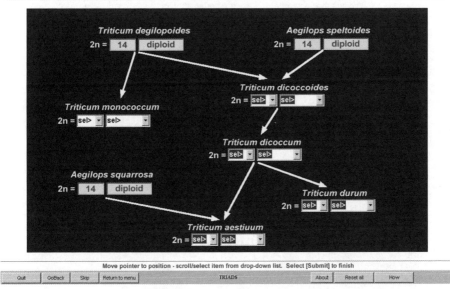

Figure 6.18 TRIADS exemplar from Paul Lynch, University of Derby (http://www.triadsinteractive.com/Assessment/triads2demo)

extensive set of objective questions, some publicly available while access to others is restricted to registered users (http://medweb.bham.ac.uk/caa/mcq).

6.5 Chemical sciences

Simple MCQs, such as those shown in Figure 6.19, allow declarative and procedural knowledge to be readily assessed in chemistry. Item banks of publicly available MCQs in chemistry can be accessed at http://www.tal.bris.ac.uk/Chem.htm and http://mc2.cchem.berkeley.edu/Organic. As with most discipline areas, extensive test banks in chemistry tend to be provided on a commercial basis, either as ancillary material for standard textbooks or from professional associations, for example the American Chemical Society (http://www4.uwm.edu/chemexams/materials/test_items.cfm).

IMMEX examples for chemistry problems may be viewed at http://www.immex.ucla.edu, and an example is shown in Figure 6.20. In this particular problem, students are asked to identify an organic substance, and they may view particular properties associated with the unknown sample. The advantage of presenting this standard structure determination problem in this format is that the IMMEX software tracks the route students take to solve the problem, and this allows a far richer set of criteria to be set for marking the assessment. Credit can be assigned to students who use the minimum number of steps, or view the minimum number of data sets required to solve the problem. IMMEX uses the hypothetical-deductive learning model of scientific inquiry and so is well suited to problem-solving in all the science disciplines (Stevens *et al.*, 2004).

One of the key skills in organic chemistry that students must master is the ability to draw chemical structures using the symbolism illustrated in Figure 6.21. This particular example highlights an alternative question form to MCQs and resembles the format for items in a standard paper-based test. In Figure 6.21, the student is required to draw the structure of the product from the reaction indicated, and then use the associated SMILE notation (a text string automatically generated by the Java applet uniquely describing the particular structure drawn; http://www.

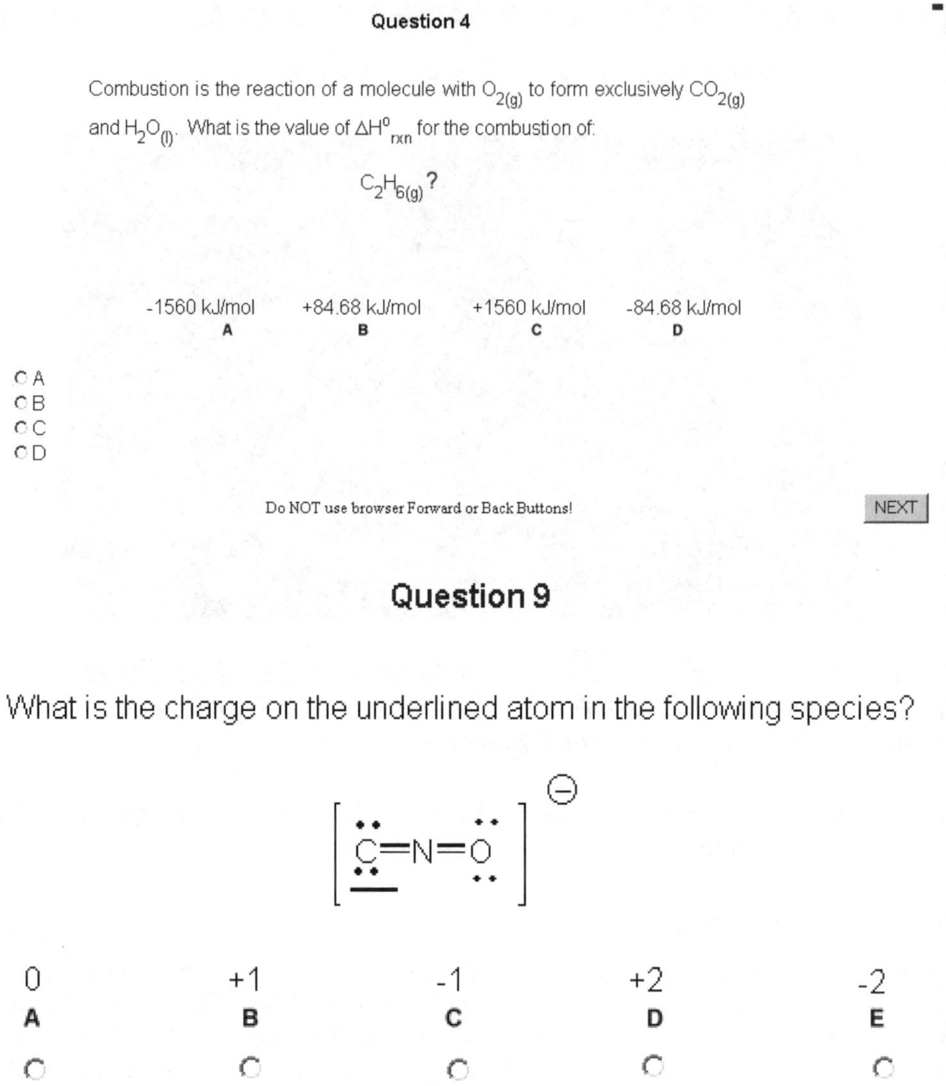

Question 4

Combustion is the reaction of a molecule with $O_{2(g)}$ to form exclusively $CO_{2(g)}$ and $H_2O_{(l)}$. What is the value of ΔH°_{rxn} for the combustion of:

$$C_2H_{6(g)}?$$

-1560 kJ/mol	+84.68 kJ/mol	+1560 kJ/mol	-84.68 kJ/mol
A	**B**	**C**	**D**

○ A
○ B
○ C
○ D

Do NOT use browser Forward or Back Buttons! [NEXT]

Question 9

What is the charge on the underlined atom in the following species?

0	+1	-1	+2	-2
A	**B**	**C**	**D**	**E**
○	○	○	○	○

Figure 6.19 Chemistry MCQs from University of Adelaide

daylight.com/smiles) to enter an answer into a text box. The teacher would have previously entered the correct SMILE string for each question into the assessment software and so the program is able to compare the students' answer with that expected. This type of question is suitable to the development of an extensive item bank, and reduces the chances of guessing associated with MCQs. Numerous Java applets for drawing chemical structures via a web browser are freely available, including JME Molecular Editor (http://www.molinspiration.com/jme), ACD/Structure Drawing Applet (http://www.acdlabs.com/products/java/sda), Marvin (http://www.chemaxon.com/marvin) and JmolDraw (http://jmoldraw.chemit.at). In order to use Java applets in e-assessments teachers will need to use some very simple HTML to call the applet within the appropriate e-assessment application:

```
<applet code=Chemis3D.class archive="Chemis3D.jar"
codebase="Models" width=256 height=256>
```

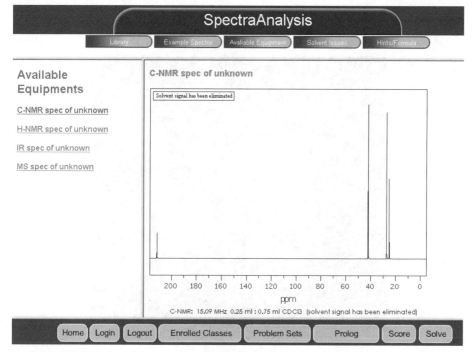

Figure 6.20 IMMEX chemistry example (http://www.immex.ucla.edu)

```
<param name="model" value="Models/Arg.mol">
<param name="format" value="x-mol">
<param name="display" value="ball-stick">
</applet>
```

Question 6
Draw the structure of the major organic product from the following reaction.

Use the Help Instructions if you do not know how to draw the structure and then press the yellow smiley face in the top left corner of the drawing box. This opens a window with a text string. Copy the text string using the mouse (like in a Word document) and paste the text string into the answer box below. If a structure already appears in the window from a previous question then delete it using the CLR tool next to the smiley face.

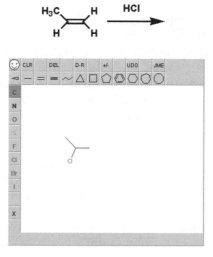

Figure 6.21 Use of JME structure drawing Java applet in chemistry questions from the University of Adelaide (http://www.molinspiration.com/jme)

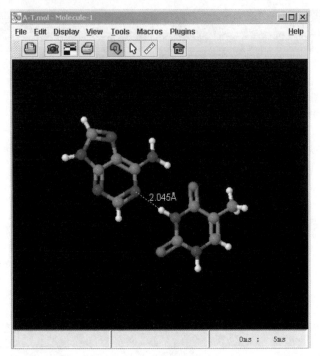

Figure 6.22 Use of 3D structure display Java applet in chemistry using Jmol (http://jmol.sourceforge.net)

Figure 6.22 illustrates an example of a 3D-structure presentation applet that incorporates additional features such as the ability to measure bond lengths, bond angles and torsion angles. In this particular example students are asked to determine the relevant hydrogen bonding distances between the purine and pyrimidine bases shown. Teachers are able to use this type of Java applet effectively in assessments by allowing students to explore the 3D features of molecules, thus enabling questions that are multistructural and relational in the SOLO taxonomy. By providing interactive tools for students to use during an assessment that are capable of generating authentic data, teachers are able to replicate a more authentic learning and assessment environment.

Canvas Learning constructs interactive assessments in Macromedia Director™ or Flash™ format and these can be played over the web using a suitable Flash™ browser plugin (http://www.the-can.com). Players suitable for Canvas Learning objects are distributed in the educational market via partner LMS vendors, and an annual licence to corporate and government organizations. An example detailing the principles of gas chromatography is shown in Figure 6.23. This type of learning or assessment object allows detailed information to be provided to students in multimedia format, and the responses may be in the form of MCQs, text entries, numeric sliders, drag and drop or drag to order, as well as hotspots.

For diagnostic and formative assessments there is little necessity to record student responses or marks, except for the purpose of improving the efficacy of the items. For these types of assessments, teachers may use simple Javascript examples for question items, as illustrated in Figure 6.24. By viewing the source code for the HTML pages used to deliver this test, students would be able to read the text contained in the Javascript, including the correct responses, so this particular method would not be suitable for high-stake summative assessments. However, the purpose of diagnostic and formative assessment is to provide adequate feedback to students to enable them to improve their learning, so the use of simple Javascript works well for this purpose.

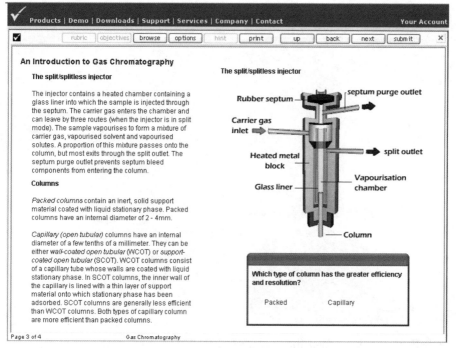

Figure 6.23 Canvas Learning object (http://www.the-can.com)

Nomenclature of Simple Compounds-Formulas to Names

This is a basic exercise in naming simple compounds. Since its effective use requires analysis of text input there are some basic rules:

- This page does not contain any transition elements and,thus, Stock notation is not used.
- Spelling matters very much. No effort has been made to analyze input against possible spelling errors, so double check before entering a name.
- Capitalization does not matter.
- For those combinations for which prefixes are not needed,e.g. $CaCl_2$, their use will result in an error.

Operation:

1.The user should refer to periodic tables or other sources for spelling of elements and ions.
2. Pressing "New Compound" will display a formula to the right of the table.
3. Enter the name of the compound in the answer cell and press "Check Answer."
4. Detailed results and score appear in the table on the top page.
5. If you get all or part of the name incorrect, you may go back and correct your answer and resubmit it.

- Pressing the "Show Answer" will cause the correct answer to appear and you will no longer be able to submit an answer for that problem.

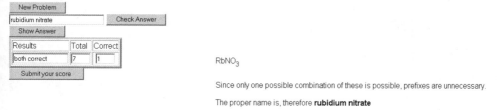

$RbNO_3$

Since only one possible combination of these is possible, prefixes are unnecessary.

The proper name is, therefore **rubidium nitrate**

Figure 6.24 Example of JavaScript used for diagnostic or formative assessment (http://proton.csudh.edu/homework/hwintro.html)

The IrYdium Project (http://iry.chem.cmu.edu/irproject) at Carnegie Mellon University is sponsored by the National Science Foundation and provides numerous educational resources for teaching chemistry in higher education. One of the icon products from the project is the Virtual Lab applet consisting of various simulated experiments that students may undertake using a web browser (http://www.chemcollective.org/applets/vlab.php). The example illustrated

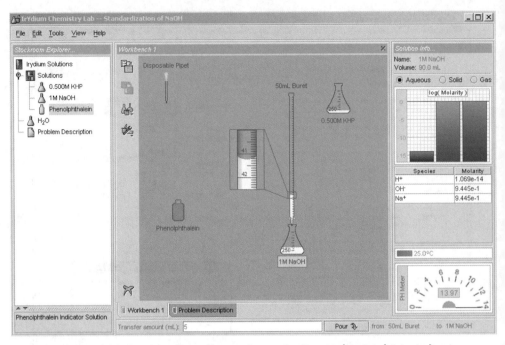

Figure 6.25 Virtual Lab applet (http://www.chemcollective.org/applets/vlab.php)

in Figure 6.25 shows the standardization of a sodium hydroxide solution, a very common experiment in secondary school or introductory university chemistry programmes. The teacher could incorporate the use of this applet into diagnostic, formative or summative assessments by using numerous concentrations of sodium hydroxide and/or hydrochloric acid, and asking the student to perform the simulated experiment in order to respond to specific questions that could be in MCQ, text entry or EMI format. Students may also be required to interpret data from graphs, accurately make readings from the use of simulated experimental equipment or manipulate glassware to construct a specific experimental sequence.

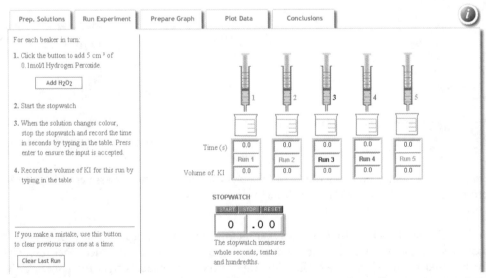

Figure 6.26 JelSim example of a kinetics experiment simulation (http://www.jelsim.org/ourwork.html)

An example of a simulated kinetics experiment using the JeLSim software (http://www.jelsim.org) is shown in Figure 6.26. These simulations allow the teacher to combine the theoretical concepts from the textbook and the classroom presentations with the practical experiential learning of the laboratory into an e-assessment exercise. It is relatively straightforward for the teacher to combine standalone Java applets such as those arising from the IrYdium or JeLSim projects with e-assessment software to provide an integrated learning and assessment environment for students. The feedback in such an environment can be quite detailed, and direct the future learning path for students. These types of simulations are providing useful examples of reusable learning and assessment objects, since the one application may be used for a variety of purposes.

6.6 Earth and environmental sciences

An example of a test bank of diagnostic or formative assessment items in physical geology can be found at http://www.uwgb.edu/dutchs/Exams/202qindx.htm. The purpose of these assessment items is to improve student learning, and so the feedback component is particularly important, and the format for the assessments uses simple HTML. The Higher Education Academy discipline group Geography, Earth and Environmental Sciences (GEES; http://www.gees.ac.uk) has published a guide on assessment in earth and environmental sciences (Hughes *et al.*, 2005). The guide is particularly useful for teachers of earth and environmental sciences since it contains details of many case studies with further links and contacts for particular approaches to assessment.

The TRIAD project uses the Authorware™ application to construct learning and assessment objects that can be delivered through a web browser via the freely available Authorware Player plugin (http://www.derby.ac.uk/ciad). A geological assessment item using the TRIAD software is illustrated in Figure 6.27 and shows how the computer mouse may be used to draw an arrow on a diagram to indicate a particular feature, and is an example of the use of hotspots on an interactive graphic. The Authorware™ file may be incorporated into web pages or called from within an e-assessment application using simple HTML:

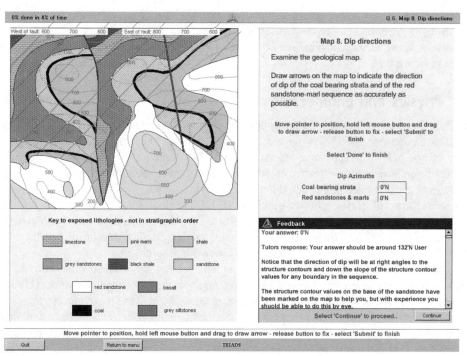

Figure 6.27 Example of the use of a hotspot question type (http://www.triadsinteractive.com/Assessment/triads2demo)

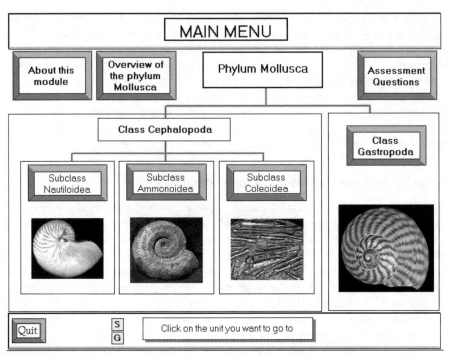

Figure 6.28 Authorware™ example from UK Earth Science Courseware Consortium (http://www.ukescc.co.uk/)

```
<EMBED WIDTH="640" HEIGHT="480" ALIGN="CENTER"
window="onTopminimize" SRC="geology.aam" PALETTE="background"
TYPE="application/x-authorware-map" </EMBED>
```

The UK Earth Science Courseware Consortium provides commercial products for learning and assessment activities in geological sciences and an example using an Authorware™ file is illustrated in Figure 6.28.

6.7 Physics and engineering

Phil Race has produced a useful synopsis of assessment methods for the physical sciences (Race, 2003). Although not specifically on e-assessment, many of the design principles within the guide can be applied directly to e-assessment. Alex Johnstone has also produced an excellent publication on how to write effective objective questions; the guide contains numerous examples from the physical science disciplines (Johnstone, 2004).

A wide array of classic physics problems in MCQ format for diagnostic and formative assessment purposes can be found at the University of Loughborough's Department of Mechanical Engineering website, http://www.lboro.ac.uk/faculty/eng/engtlsc/Eng_Mech/tutorials/tut_index.htm. An example from the extensive selection is shown in Figure 6.29.

A number of Java applets for physics and engineering are available as learning and assessment objects. The Electrical and Electronic Engineering Assessment Network (EEEAN) in the UK offers, free of charge, a large database of assessment items covering concepts from signal processing, circuit theory, digital and microelectronics, electromagnetism and maths for engineers (http://www.e3an.ac.uk/database/download). Further websites that are useful for teachers interested in interactive e-assessments for engineering and physics include http://www.walter-fendt.de, http://webphysics.davidson.edu/Applets/Applets.html and http://www.phy.ntnu.edu.tw/ntnujava. These websites offer numerous Java applets and teachers will need to

If the angular velocity of wheel A is w_A = 2 rad/s, determine the speed of point P located on the rim of wheel B. No slipping occurs between the wheels.

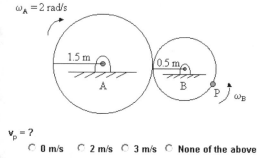

v_p = ?

○ 0 m/s   ○ 2 m/s   ○ 3 m/s   ○ None of the above

Figure 6.29 Example of MCQ in physics (http://www.lboro.ac.uk/faculty/eng/engtlsc/Eng_Mech/tutorials/tut_index.htm)

contact the authors of the Java applets for permission to use them in their own assessments or negotiate appropriate licensing arrangements. Java applets themselves are learning objects, but may be readily incorporated into assessments by constructing appropriate questions that require students to use the applet to generate the response. The applet can reside on a server containing the assessment software at the local institution presenting the assessment, or it may reside on a remote server, with HTML used within the assessment page to call the applet as required. An example of a Java applet in electronics is illustrated in Figure 6.30 and could be used to test students' understanding of the relationship between voltage and amperage when electronic components are placed in series or in parallel in a circuit. This would be an alternative format to testing the same concepts with MCQs.

A series of Java applets from the University of Oregon provide interesting examples of learning objects that may be readily incorporated into e-assessments (http://homework.uoregon.edu). An example for a virtual cannon is illustrated in Figure 6.31 and could be used to test students' understanding of projectile motion.

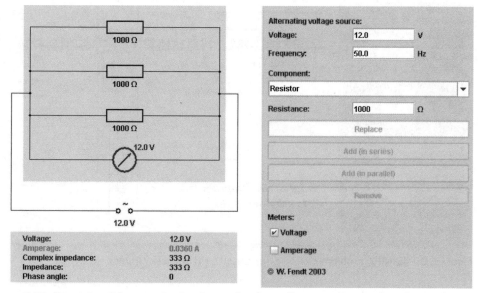

Figure 6.30 Example of Java applet in electronics (http://www.walter-fendt.de/ph14e/combrlc.htm)

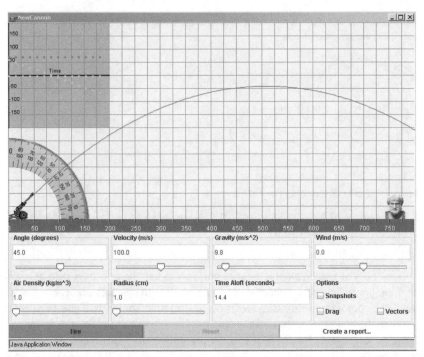

Figure 6.31 Java applet for testing knowledge of projectile motion (http://homework.uoregon.edu:8080/index.jsp)

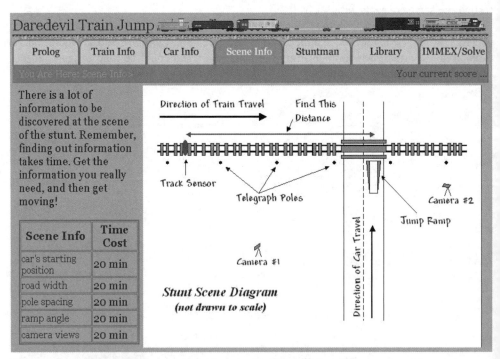

Figure 6.32 IMMEX problem example for physics (http://www.immex.ucla.edu)

In the IMMEX physics problem shown in Figure 6.32 the student is required to imagine that they are a stunt person working on a film and are required to drive a car over a moving train. The stunt requires students to apply mathematical and physics concepts to safely accomplish the task. This type of question format engages students with an interesting problem and allows for group participation as well as individual contributions.

6.8 Mathematics

The Mathematics, Statistics and Operational Research Network (MSOR) of the HEA in the UK is an excellent starting point for teachers in higher education wishing to use e-assessment in mathematics (http://www.mathstore.ac.uk). The Maths CAA Series newsletters contain detailed descriptions of the major issues associated with e-assessment in mathematics, including the requirement to write and interpret equivalent mathematical equations and algebraic expressions; the requirement to use variables in equations; the ability to draw and interpret graphs and the ability to award part marks for complex problems. A specific assessment guide for teachers of mathematics provides relevant case studies on current assessment issues and potential solutions from a number of UK higher education institutions (Challis et al., 2004).

Specialized software is available to perform mathematics teaching and assessment online, such as Maple T. A. (http://www.maplesoft.com). This application may be incorporated into learning management systems, such as Blackboard™, through the use of the Maple T. A. Building Block™, or used to construct standalone assessments that are delivered via a web browser using MapleNet. Maple T. A. possesses a question bank editor that enables teachers to import questions from colleagues, or from item banks such as those available from commercial publishers. Teachers who are familiar with LaTeX (http://www.maths.tcd.ie/~dwilkins/LaTeXPrimer) may convert existing LaTex questions into Maple T. A. format. Maple is also able to determine if two algebraic expressions are mathematically equivalent, thus satisfying one of the important criteria for assessing mathematics questions online.

AIM (Alice Interactive Mathematics) (http://maths.york.ac.uk/moodle/aiminfo) is an open-source application that makes use of Maple and allows assessments to be delivered online without the use of Maple T. A. AIM only requires Maple on the web server, and not on the client desktops, which makes it an attractive option. AIM uses a mixture of Maple and Latex syntax to render the mathematical expressions and for teachers and students who use Maple as a core teaching application, the use of AIM for e-assessment is relatively straightforward. Expressions such as $\sin(2\pi x)/(1 + x^3)$ are entered as sin(2*Pi*x)/(1+x^3), a standard notation used by most students studying mathematics courses. An example of a simple mathematics question using AIM is illustrated in Figure 6.33.

AXIOM is an alternative computer algebra system used for rendering mathematical expressions and algorithms in an online environment (http://wiki.axiom-developer.org/FrontPage). The source code for AXIOM is freely available. HTML is not particularly suitable for displaying mathematics on the web and MathML has been developed to solve this problem (http://www.w3.org/Math). Design Science's WebEQ™ Developer's Suite is a commercial product that enables interactive mathematics to be presented online through the use of Java and MathML (http://www.desssci.com/en/products/webeq). The product uses templates and a toolbar that allows

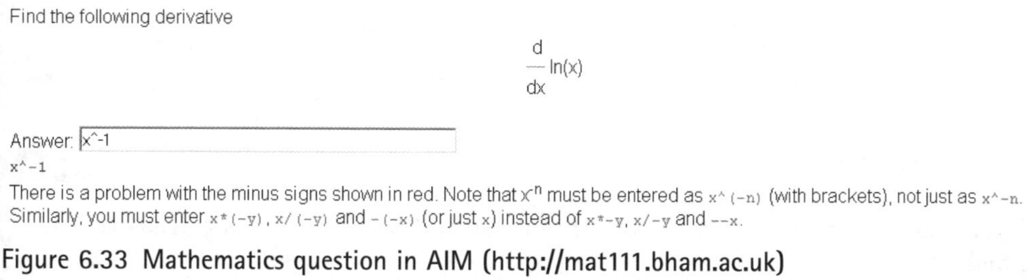

Find the following derivative

$$\frac{d}{dx}\ln(x)$$

Answer: x^-1

x^-1

There is a problem with the minus signs shown in red. Note that x^n must be entered as x^(-n) (with brackets), not just as x^-n. Similarly, you must enter x*(-y), x/(-y) and -(-x) (or just x) instead of x*-y, x/-y and --x.

Figure 6.33 Mathematics question in AIM (http://mat111.bham.ac.uk)

teachers to quickly construct mathematical expressions and equations, while the appropriate MathML is being constructed by the application in the background. A range of standard mathematical and scientific symbols may be used. An example of a simple algebraic expression and the corresponding MathML is shown below.

```
y = x²
<math display = 'block' xmlns='http://www.
w3.org/1998/Math/MathML'>
<mrow>
<mi>y</mi>
<mtext> </mtext>
<mo>=</mo>
<msup>
<mi>x</mi>
<mn>2</mn>
</msup>
</mrow>
</math>
```

Figure 6.34 Example of MathML

The CALM (Computer Aided Learning in Mathematics) assessment system from the Pass-IT project in Scotland provides diagnostic and formative items in trigonometry, basic algebra, analytic geometry, differentiation and elementary probability (http://www.calm.hw.ac.uk). The particular example illustrated in Figure 6.35 using the CUE assessment software shows how partial credit might be assigned for online mathematics questions and how students who cannot proceed may sacrifice some part marks in order to obtain help (Reveal) and potentially proceed the problem and so gain some additional marks.

Metric, based at Imperial College, provides online diagnostic and formative exercises in A-level and introductory undergraduate level mathematics using a Java application on a remote server (http://metric.ma.imperial.ac.uk/new/html). An example is shown in Figure 6.36 and includes the working to assist students who are either experiencing difficulty with the concept, or simply require confirmation that their reasoning was correct.

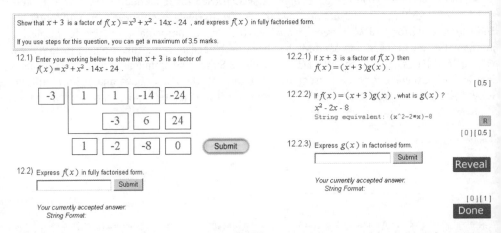

Figure 6.35 Example from CUE e-assessment system (http://www.calm.hw.ac.uk/pass-it. html)

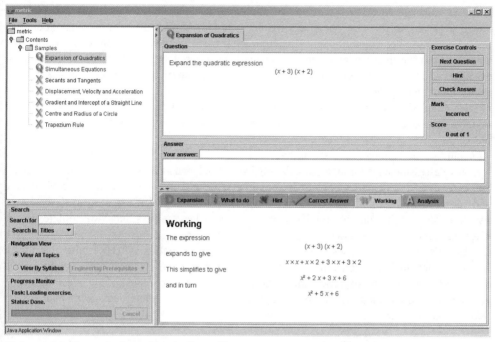

Figure 6.36 Example from Metric (http://metric.ma.ic.ac.uk/new/html)

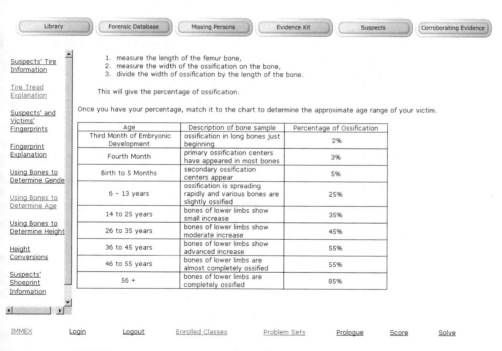

Figure 6.37 IMMEX mathematics problem (http://www.immex.ucla.edu)

An example of an IMMEX problem in mathematics is shown in Figure 6.37 (http://www. immex.ucla.edu). In this case the student is involved in a simulated forensic investigation of a fire and must use bone measurements to determine the age, gender and height of the victim. The mathematics used in this example is relatively straightforward, but the format serves as a good example of how standard mathematics can be tested in imaginative ways that encourage student engagement and highlight the consequences of incorrect calculations. In forensic cases examples of false conclusions about guilt or innocence may result from poor application of scientific or mathematical concepts, and this will highlight for the student the necessity for accuracy and precision.

A number of commercial systems have been developed specifically for diagnostic and/or formative assessments in mathematics. CALMAT was developed at Glasgow Caledonian University and consists of mathematics content lessons in a self-contained online system and diagnostic and formative questions in MCQ format (http://www.calmat.gcal.ac.uk). WALLIS (Web-based Assistant for Learning on-Line Intelligent System) uses Java applets and Javascript to deliver diagnostic and formative assessments in mathematics, and also includes extensive feedback for students on their responses (http://www.maths.ed.ac.uk/~wallis). WALLIS is also able to use Maple to mark algebraic expressions and is capable of taking into account mistakes that students make in one part of their response, that is propagated in subsequent parts of the question, and so is able to mark predominantly on the correctness of the working and not just on the final answer (Mavrikis *et al.*, 2003).

Section 4 **What are the practical issues when doing an e-assessment?**

7 Item and test bank use

7.1 Constructing item and test banks

e-Assessment currently relies heavily on the use of objective questions, also referred to as selected response items since the student must select a response from the choices offered. The term 'objective', in this context, is referring to the manner in which the assessor (computer) judges the student response, not to the question itself. Questions that are marked by an objective process may have been constructed in either an objective or subjective manner. When an assessment uses selected response items the student is often expected to recall specific content information that has been previously presented as part of the learning process, although this does not have to be the case, and examples of selected responses requiring application or problem-solving ability are readily constructed. Selected response items are often in the form of multiple-choice, true or false, matching or fill-in-the-blank type questions and may require students to use cognitive skills ranging from relatively simple knowledge recall or comprehension through to combinations of synthesis, application and evaluation.

In contrast, constructed response questions are short-answer or open-ended questions or tasks that require students to assemble a response generally involving cognitive skills using synthesis, application and evaluation, in addition to basic knowledge and comprehension. Constructed responses may also include worked solutions to a mathematics or physics problem, labelling or drawing diagrams or psychomotor applications such as a music or drama performance or a laboratory practical. For students, constructed response questions may appear to be more aligned to 'authentic task' requirements and individual student responses may not necessarily match those of other students in the assessment cohort. Students may obtain similar marks from quite disparate responses to constructed response questions, whereas students' marks for selected response questions will usually reflect a similar pattern of expected and standard answers. There will be minimum variation expected in assessor marking schemes for selected response questions, but significantly more variation expected with constructed response questions, even when an assessment rubric is used. Consistency in marking in computer-assisted assessment is, therefore, technically straightforward for selected response questions, but more difficult for constructed response questions such as essays that allow students to assemble responses at the relational and extended abstract level of the SOLO taxonomy (Structure of Observed Learning Outcomes; Biggs *et al.*, 1982). Although essay questions may be marked using computers, many expert graded examples are required before a satisfactory level of consistency is obtained. Constructed responses often require the assessor to take a holistic approach to grading the assessment, a process that is often made difficult by the fragmentation of student responses into individual components for analysis, as is often required for e-assessments.

The construction of a test bank is a formal approach to cataloguing and describing questions that may be selected for use in an assessment. Items in a test bank may be classified by the discipline content they cover, their difficulty level or the rules relating to how they might be selected for inclusion in an assessment task. The construction of an item or test bank for an assessment begins with a consideration of the purpose of the assessment and its relationship to the curriculum and the learning activities undertaken. A useful starting point is to use one of the educational frameworks for describing the cognitive domains of learning and assessment. Table 7.1 summarizes the comparative terminology used in four of the more commonly used cognitive domain taxonomies, SOLO, Bloom, modified Bloom (Anderson *et al.*, 2001) and RECAP (REcall, Comprehension, Application, Problem-solving; Imrie, 1995). Each of these taxonomies

Table 7.1 Cognitive domains associated with hierarchical items in assessment

SOLO	Bloom	Modified Bloom	RECAP
Unistructural	*Knowledge*	*Remember*	*Recall*
Response requires recall of one correct item of information Surface passive	Response requires recall of one correct item of information		
	Test item asks who, what, why, when, where, which, choose, find, how, define, label, show, spell, list, match, name, relate, tell, recall, select		
Multistructural	*Comprehension*	*Understand*	*Comprehension*
Response requires recall of more than one correct item of information, may involve a number of unconnected items Surface active	Response requires recall of more than one correct item of information, may involve a number of unconnected items		
	Test item asks to compare, contrast, demonstrate, interpret, explain, extend, illustrate, infer, outline, relate, rephrase, translate, summarize, show, classify		
Relational	*Application*	*Apply*	*Application*
Response relates knowledge and consequences together to make a case or logical argument Deep passive	Student discusses knowledge and consequences, but does not relate evidence to conclusion		
	Test item asks to apply, build, choose, construct, develop, interview, make use of, organize, experiment with, plan, select, solve, utilize, model, identify		
	Analysis	*Analyse*	*Problem-solving*
	Student correlates and differentiates, is able to distinguish between options		
	Test item asks to discriminate, infer, outline, separate		
Extended abstract	*Synthesis*	*Evaluate*	*Problem-solving*
Response relates knowledge and consequences together to make a case and a connection to a related area of knowledge beyond the explicit demand of the question Deep active	Student discusses knowledge and consequences, and relates evidence to conclusion		
	Test item asks to build, choose, combine, compile, compose, construct, create, design, develop, estimate, formulate, imagine, invent, make up, originate, plan, predict, propose, solve, suppose, discuss, modify, change, adapt, minimize, maximize, delete, theorize, elaborate, test, change		
	Evaluation	*Create*	*Problem-solving*
	Response relates knowledge and consequences together to make a case and a connection to a related area of knowledge beyond the explicit demand of the question		
	Test item asks to award, choose, conclude, criticize, decide, defend, determine, dispute, evaluate, judge, justify, measure, compare, mark, rate, recommend, rule on, select, agree, interpret, explain, appraise, prioritize, opinion, support, importance, criteria, prove, disprove, assess, influence, perceive, value, estimate, influence, deduct		

describes a hierarchy of cognitive complexity associated with student activity and assessment tasks or responses, and commences with some form of basic engagement by the student with the material, such as memorizing information and recalling it at a later point in time in either the same, or a modified, context.

Assessment questions associated with this first step in any of these taxonomies may be selected response items in the form of multiple-choice, true or false, matching or fill-in-the-blank type questions. Students may then proceed from simply memorizing knowledge to an understanding or comprehension of several pieces of information that are related in some way. As the level of student engagement and skill development increases, so will the complexity of the assessment items, moving from passive surface learning requiring unistructural responses to active surface learning requiring multistructural responses (Biggs *et al.*, 1982). Unistructural responses to questions usually require basic knowledge recall and tend to use only one significant piece of content information. Multiple-choice, true or false, matching or fill-in-the-blank type questions are very suited to testing unistructural responses as the expected answers can be readily defined and described. Multistructural responses require the student to use several pieces of content information, or to use two or more steps to arrive at an answer, but do not require the integration of information or ideas into complex scenarios. Once the student is required to relate disparate ideas or concepts and to assemble a unique scenario based on relationships and interpretation, the questions are relational or extended abstract in nature. Students will then have proceeded to a stage where they are expected to articulate the interrelationships between facts, and the consequences arising from the use of those facts, in a complex environment. Abstract ideas are used to integrate separate pieces of knowledge, so that a unique answer to the question is prepared and predictions may be made about their use in unfamiliar situations.

A traditional MCQ is one in which a student is asked to choose one response from a number of predetermined, fixed alternatives (Figure 7.1). A typical MCQ consists of:

■ a stem – comprising the text (and any associated multimedia) of the question;
■ options – the alternative options provided to match the stem;
■ the key – the correct option that most appropriately matches the stem;
■ distracters – the incorrect options that do not appropriately match the stem.

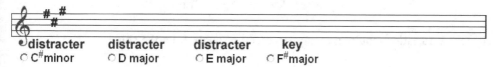

What is the key signature shown in the following diagram? **stem**

distracter **distracter** **distracter** **key**
○ C#minor ○ D major ○ E major ○ F#major

Figure 7.1 Components of a MCQ (multiple–choice question)

This type of multiple-choice format can be used in a test bank in order to generate a large number of alternative questions since the stem is in a generic format and covers a specific concept. The stem also contains a graphic that can be readily modified to correspond to different distracters and an associated key. This type of question is suitable for providing students with different versions of a question based on a specific concept, in order to minimize collusion between students and question exposure. One of the consequences of using classical MCQs is that the teacher does not really have reliable evidence of the reasoning behind why the student chose a particular option, be it correct or incorrect for that particular stem. In order to accommodate the issue of guessing a correct response, various alternatives have been proposed, including an increase in the number of options, the use of negative marking or assigning marks for student confidence levels. Increasing the number of options is feasible for some questions, but it can be difficult for the teacher to provide large numbers of feasible distracters based on the course concepts and common student misunderstandings. Negative marking may be controversial with the student and teacher, and assigning confidence marks to each question in an assessment may be seen as skewing the purpose of the assessment.

An example of a *unistructural* response question requiring simple recall of knowledge is shown in Figure 7.2, where the student is expected to have memorized the definition of a chiral carbon (the simple definition is that it contains four different groups around an sp^3 carbon). The stem 'How many different groups must an sp^3 carbon atom have to be chiral?' may be worded slightly differently, but it does not allow many options for constructing a set of similar questions in a test bank. It is possible to change the order of the options to generate a number of alternatives, but the change is trivial and would be unlikely to have an impact on the students' ability to distinguish the key from the distracters.

How many different groups must an sp^3 carbon atom have to be chiral?

○ 1   ○ 2   ○ 3   ○ 4

Figure 7.2 Question requiring a unistructural response from the student

A *multistructural* question based on the student identifying a chiral carbon atom in a specific structure, such as shown in Figure 7.3, requires the student to recall that a chiral carbon has four different groups around it, as well as understanding the consequences of drawing a three-dimensional representation of a chemical structure. This type of question is amenable to a large number of variations since a common stem may be used with many hundreds of variations in the four types of atoms surrounding the central carbon. This type of question is suitable for an item in a test bank.

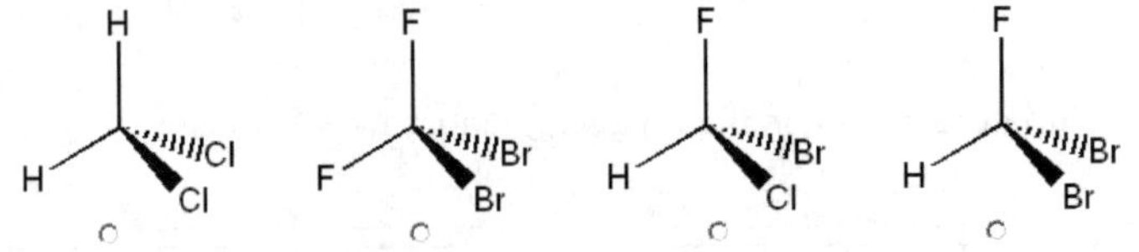

Figure 7.3 Question requiring a multistructural response from the student

A *relational* question based on the student identifying a chiral carbon atom in a specific structure, such as shown in Figure 7.4, requires the student to recall that a chiral carbon has four different groups around it, to understand the consequences of drawing a three-dimensional representation of a chemical structure, and to be able to conceptually rotate chemical structures in order to determine if two structures, drawn differently, are the same or mirror images of each other. This type of question is again amenable to a large number of variations since a common stem may be used with many hundreds of variations in the four types of atoms surrounding the central carbon. This type of question is also suitable for an item in a test bank.

An alternative version of this *relational* question is shown in Figure 7.5, where the student is expected to again recall that a chiral carbon has four different groups around it, to understand the consequences of drawing a three-dimensional representation of a chemical structure, and to be able to conceptually rotate chemical structures in order to determine if two structures, drawn differently, are the same or mirror images of each other. The difference between the questions

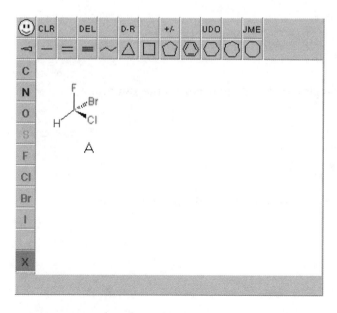

Which one of the following structures is identical to A?

Figure 7.4 Question requiring a relational response from the student

posed in Figures 7.4 and 7.5 is that students are required to actually draw the structure of their response in Figure 7.5, and this adds another degree of complexity to the question. Additional skills and capabilities are being tested for this question. This type of question is again amenable to a large number of variations since a common stem may be used with many hundreds of variations in the four types of atoms surrounding the central carbon.

For the examples shown in Figures 7.1 to 7.5, the stem consists of a simple direct question that tries to minimize any ambiguity about what the student is being asked to do. The main concept being presented is in the stem, not in the options, so that the student is immediately aware of the purpose of the question. The stem, therefore, should not contain large tracts of information that are irrelevant to the purpose of the question. Contextualizing a question may add interest, but too much unnecessary detail may also introduce confusion for the student if it distracts their attention from the purpose of the question. Students will find it easier to understand the purpose of the

Figure 7.5 Question requiring a relational response from the student

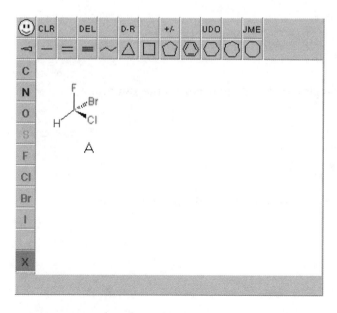

question if the stem is written from a positive frame of reference rather than a negative frame, and the use of the double negative wording of questions should be avoided, as should options such as 'all of the above' and 'none of the above', unless there is a specific pedagogical reason for using these options. Although MCQs frequently appear with four options, this does not have to be a fixed pattern, and any combination of questions with three to six options could be used. The use of only three options will necessarily increase the success of students being able to guess the correct response (key), and more than six options will increase the amount of content that students must assimilate while differentiating between the distracters and the key. There are significant resources available to teachers on constructing good-quality MCQs (Johnstone 2004; Higgins *et al.*, 2003; Carneson *et al.*, 2002; McKenna *et al.*, 1999; Case *et al.*, 2002; Jacobsen *et al.*, 2003).

In order to increase the pedagogical value of an item in a test bank, each item should have features that enable it to be identified, stored, catalogued and retrieved (McAlpine, 2002c). Just as learning objects have metadata tags, items in a test bank may be assigned identifiers to describe subject area, degree of difficulty, any multimedia files associated with the item, cognitive level and any associated marking scheme. For diagnostic and formative assessment, the test bank item may also contain metadata about the feedback that will be presented to the student for both correct and incorrect responses. Indeed, learning objects themselves could also function as items in a test bank since they will have defined characteristics. Items in the test bank should be readily available for use within learning or content management systems, as well as e-assessment software. When using a test bank, teachers will need to begin to conceptualize an assessment as a multi-step process that involves assembling discrete components in a particular order, with each component having particular characteristics that can be measured and described in a standard manner. Tests can then be designed with a particular profile by selecting components with known psychometric and pedagogical characteristics that match the required attributes of the predetermined learning and assessment design (Squires, 2003).

Must all test banks consist of items characterized by extensive metadata or could teachers initially use a simplified version? A simple test bank, such as outlined in Figure 7.6, may consist

1. The outermost layer of the sun is called the:
- ○ ionosphere
- ○ chromosphere
- ○ *corona
- ○ megasphere
- ○ photosphere

2. The most explosive events to occur on the sun are:
- ○ granules
- ○ filaments
- ○ *solar flares
- ○ solar winds
- ○ sun spots

3. Which main-sequence stars are the least massive?
- ○ *red
- ○ white
- ○ orange
- ○ blue
- ○ yellow

Figure 7.6 Items in a test bank based on a text document (questions from Dutch, 2003)

```
<P><B>2.1</B> Ammonia is a pungent, colourless gas that is very soluble in
water. In this practical you will use a 0.4 molL<SUP>-1</SUP> aqueous solution
of ammonia. Solutions containing ammonia can be considered hazardous to your
health at concentrations greater than or equal to 3% w/v. Is 0.4M aqueous
ammonia solution considered hazardous? (N.B. X % w/v corresponds to X grams of
ammonia made up to 100 ml with water). The molecular weight of ammonia is 17.
</P>

Yes, 0.4M ammonia solution corresponds to approximately 6.8% w/v ammonia in
water and hence is considered hazardous to one's health <CENTER>Please
review</CENTER> <P>At this concentration (0.4M), the ammonia should not present
any major health risks when used in this practical, nevertheless, please treat
it with the same respect you would treat all chemicals</P>

Yes, 0.4M ammonia solution corresponds to approximately 12% w/v ammonia in water
and hence is considered hazardous to one's health        <CENTER>Please
review</CENTER> <P>At this concentration (0.4M), the ammonia should not present
any major health risks when used in this practical, nevertheless, please treat
it with the same respect you would treat all chemicals</P>

*No, 0.4M ammonia solution corresponds to approximately 0.68% w/v ammonia in
water and hence is not considered hazardous to one's health
<CENTER>Correct</CENTER> <P>At this concentration (0.4M), the ammonia should
not present any major health risks
```

Figure 7.7 Selected response item with HTML tags and feedback for distracters and key

of a text document containing a series of fixed response questions and an indication of the key. The content of such a test bank could be copied into an e-assessment or learning management system for web delivery. For teachers, such a test bank could be readily expanded over time, and the items shared with other discipline colleagues. As the test bank expands, teachers will have a rich source of questions from which to construct an assessment, and the more items that reside in the text bank, the less chance there will be that students will have encountered a specific item and so item exposure can be controlled. Over time, teachers will be able to modify the test bank by retaining items that have proved useful in terms of discrimination and removing items that were inappropriate.

By assigning feedback to each distracter and the key for a selected response question, as illustrated in Figure 7.7, the pedagogical value of the database is further increased. The text format for the question could also contain HTML tags for direct entry into a web page or assessment software system. By incorporating even simple HTML tags, the format of the item will be retained as it is presented by a web browser and the teacher will have confidence that the student will view the question in the style that it was intended (as shown in Figure 7.8). However, neither of these two examples describes the pedagogical or psychometric characteristics of the items; neither describes the subject area, degree of difficulty or discrimination, cognitive level or marking scheme. In order to maximize the pedagogical value of items in the test bank, a more formal approach is required for the standardization of these metadata tags or descriptors.

The IMS Question and Test Interoperability (QTI) Information Model uses formal definitions for the terms associated with items and test banks (IMS QTI, 2005). An item in a test bank is much more than simply a question, since each question may have instructions associated with it about how it is to be presented, how the students' responses will be treated and what feedback will be presented to the student during the test and at its conclusion. An item that is associated with only one interaction may be classed as a 'basic item', whereas a 'composite item' is associated with more than one interaction. Items that can potentially change their format or score relative to a student response are termed 'adaptive items', a term also applied to items that provide hints if the student is having difficulty completing the task. An 'item template' is a framework for an item that can be used to generate large numbers of variations on the basic framework theme,

2.1 Ammonia is a pungent, colourless gas that is very soluble in water. In this practical you will use a 0.4 molL^{-1} aqueous solution of ammonia. Solutions containing ammonia can be considered hazardous to your health at concentrations greater than or equal to 3% w/v. Is 0.4M aqueous ammonia solution considered hazardous? (N.B. X % w/v corresponds to X grams of ammonia made up to 100 ml with water). The molecular weight of ammonia is 17.

○ a. Yes, 0.4M ammonia solution corresponds to approximately 6.8% w/v ammonia in water and hence is considered hazardous to one's health

○ b. Yes, 0.4M ammonia solution corresponds to approximately 12% w/v ammonia in water and hence is considered hazardous to one's health

○ c. No, 0.4M ammonia solution corresponds to approximately 0.68% w/v ammonia in water and hence is not considered hazardous to one's health

○ d. No, 0.4M ammonia solution corresponds to approximately 0.000234% w/v ammonia in water and hence is not considered hazardous to one's health

Feedback

0.0% a. **Please review.**
At this concentration (0.4M), the ammonia should not present any major health risks when used in this practical, nevertheless, please treat it with the same respect you would treat all chemicals

0.0% b. **Please review**
At this concentration (0.4M), the ammonia should not present any major health risks when used in this practical, nevertheless, please treat it with the same respect you would treat all chemicals

100.0% c. **Correct**
At this concentration (0.4M), the ammonia should not present any major health risks when used in this practical, nevertheless, please treat it with the same respect you would treat all chemicals

0.0% d. **Please review.**
At this concentration (0.4M), the ammonia should not present any major health risks when used in this practical, nevertheless, please treat it with the same respect you would treat all chemicals

Figure 7.8 Rendering of test bank item with HTML tags from Figure 7.7 in web browser

such as the examples presented in Figures 7.1, 7.3 and 7.4. Item templates are particularly suited to mathematical questions where the question contains a variable with a specified value range and error limits. A formal 'item variable' records the state of a particular component in an item, for example a mathematical equation variable, so that an individual student response may be recorded and used in the item. The complete list of terms associated with the IMS QTI specifications may be obtained from http://www.imsglobal.org/question/qti_v2p0/imsqti_oviewv2p0.html.

The IMS QTI specifications use XML (eXtensible Markup Language) to support interoperability; this is where items in a test bank can be used in any assessment or learning management system that supports the XML standards. The significant advantage of this approach is that teachers, publishers and test vendors can interchange items from their test banks and not be restricted to one system or software platform for delivery. An example of the XML code generated from a simple hotspot question is shown in Figure 7.9

Which is the diode?

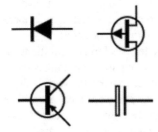

```
<?xml version="1.0" encoding="ISO-8859-1" standalone="no" ?>
<!DOCTYPE questestinterop (View Source for full doctype..)>
<questestinterop>
<item ident="NSFB_xy_hotspot_1" label="NSFB Compliance Set
2(pr1) Item 22" title="NSFB Compliance Set 2(pr1) Item 22">
<presentation>
<response_xy ident="r_xy_id" rcardinality="Single"
rtiming="No">
<render_hotspot showdraw="No">
<material>
<matimage imagtype="image/gif" uri="Image1.gif" width="193"
height="163" embedded="base64" />
</material>
</render_hotspot>
</response_xy>
<material>
<mattext texttype="text/plain" charset="ascii-us" xml:
space="default">Which is the diode?</mattext>
</material>
</presentation>
<resprocessing>
<outcomes>
<decvar varname="SCORE" vartype="Integer" />
</outcomes>
<respcondition continue="No">
<conditionvar>
<varinside respident="r_xy_id"
areatype="Rectangle">8,29,39,81</varinside>
</conditionvar>
<setvar action="Add" varname="SCORE">1</setvar>
<displayfeedback linkrefid="diode" feedbacktype="Response" />
</respcondition>
<respcondition continue="No">
<conditionvar>
<other />
</conditionvar>
<displayfeedback linkrefid="wrong" feedbacktype="Response" />
</respcondition>
</resprocessing>
<itemfeedback ident="diode" view="All">
<material>
<mattext texttype="text/plain" charset="ascii-us" xml:
space="default">Well done.</mattext>
</material>
```

```
</itemfeedback>
<itemfeedback ident="wrong" view="All">
<material>
<mattext texttype="text/plain" charset="ascii-us" xml:
space="default">No, that wasn't it?</mattext>
</material>
</itemfeedback>
</item>
</questestinterop>
```

Figure 7.9 XML code for a simple hotspot question from the e³an database (http://www.e3an.ac.uk)

An example of a test bank with an extensive series of questions in this format is that of the Electrical and Electronic Engineering Assessment Network, which has a large database of peer reviewed items for electrical and electronic engineering (http://www.e3an.ac.uk). Questions may be exported in Microsoft Word, HTML, XML or QuestionMark Perception format, as illustrated in Figure 7.10. The question bank incorporates the ability to add metadata for individual items; this is particularly useful for teachers who are searching the database for questions with particular characteristics (Figure 7.11).

Textbook publishers have included test banks with many of the high volume texts available for common discipline areas, particularly areas with large introductory classes where stand-ardized questions might be deemed appropriate. Teachers must be aware of any copyright issues associated with the use of these commercial test banks, and determine whether they may use the questions if they discontinue use of the particular texts. Attention should also be directed to the format of the items in the test bank. Are they suitable for direct inclusion in learning

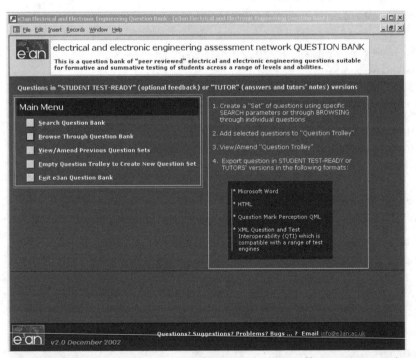

Figure 7.10 Example of test bank from the e³an database (http://www.e3an.ac.uk)

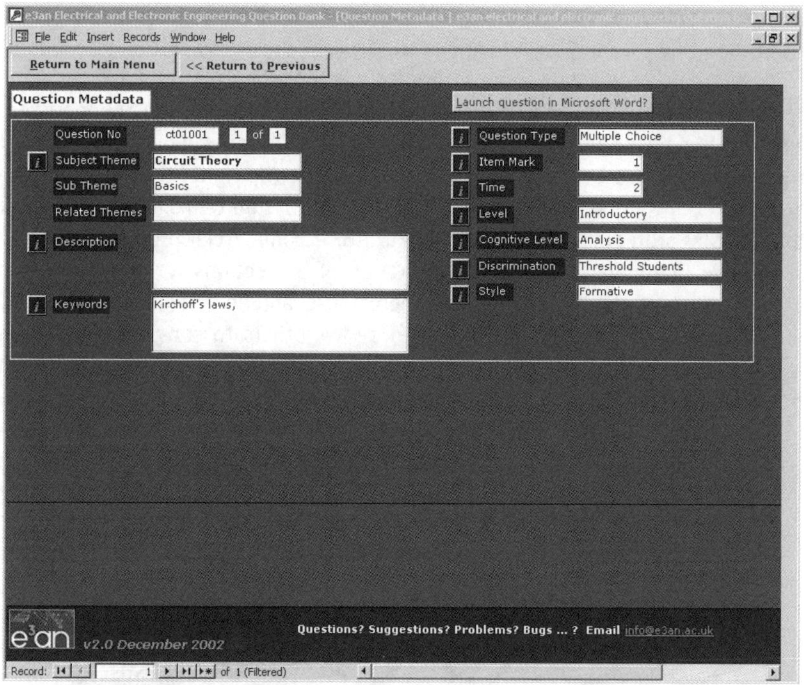

Figure 7.11 Example of test bank search from the e³an database (http://www.e3an.ac.uk)

or content management systems or e-assessment software? Does each item contain specific feedback for the distracters and the key so that the student may be directed to helpful resources or obtain confirmation that their reason for choosing a particular option was appropriate? Can the questions and feedback be changed; can the teacher add new questions to the test bank? Does the publisher insist that students pay a fee to access questions from their server or must they buy the textbook to have a code to access the assessment? Are results available to teachers on their own server, or is the test available only on a remote server?

A summary of practical aspects for teachers to consider when constructing items for a test bank, based on Sevenair (2001) is:

- do the items in the test bank appropriately span the range of topics covered in the curriculum?
- do the items in the test bank appropriately cover the range of responses expected for the different cognitive domains?
- do unistructural questions dominate the items in the test bank, or have items requiring multistructural and relational responses been included?
- have the keys been distributed equally and randomly over As, Bs, Cs, Ds, etc. for multiple-choice questions?
- does the range of items in the test bank reflect the importance or time allocated to specific sections of the curriculum?
- do the items require a sufficient level of understanding specific to the discipline so that those who have not studied the course cannot guess the correct response?
- have items been assigned a facility factor and a discrimination factor?

An alternative approach to commercial test banks is for educational institutions and professional societies to develop test items that are freely available for non-commercial applications. There are several models that may be adopted for this approach, including the Creative Commons initiative (http://creativecommons.org) and the copyleft approach (http://www.gnu.org/copyleft)

of the open source software movement. Copyleft is a general mechanism for making works freely available, but requiring that any modifications to the work must also be freely available. If works are made freely available without some form of copyright, then it is possible for an individual or organization to modify the work and legitimately claim a copyright on the modified work. In order to prevent this possibility, the copyleft approach distributes a work in copyright form but attaches distribution terms to the copyright giving anyone the rights to use, modify and redistribute the work, or any work derived from it, but the distribution terms must be maintained. The work is then legally protected from being turned into a commercial product, but is also freely available. Creative Commons licenses allow a range of protections for the creators of works, based on the concepts of attribution, non-commercial use, and no derivative works or share alike categories (Figure 7.12). The right of attribution allows others to copy, distribute, display and perform copyrighted works and derivatives by explicitly acknowledging the original author. The right of non-commercial use allows others to copy, distribute, display and perform copyrighted works and derivatives for non-commercial purposes only. The right of no derivative works allows others to copy, distribute, display and perform copyrighted works in their original format, but not derivatives. The right of share alike allows others to distribute derivative works only under a licence identical to the original distribution licence.

Figure 7.12 Creative Commons symbols for dealing with copyright issues (http://creative commons.org/)

7.2 Using item and test banks

7.2.1 Non-adaptive test delivery methods

In order to use items from a test bank to construct an assessment, the purpose for the assessment must be clear. Assessments may be used for diagnostic, formative or summative purposes, they may assess declarative or relational knowledge and they may be high or low stakes. All assessments aim to provide evidence that students have learnt something and attempt to quantify the extent and depth of the learning. Thus, the construction of a test from the component items should use a design framework that highlights the alignment of the items with the articulated objectives for the course. The individual items should allow students to show what they have learnt, and the score or grade that an individual student obtains should reflect the depth and extent of learning. The validity of the test should be apparent to all stakeholders including teachers, students, the educational institution involved and the wider community.

When delivering e-assessments, teachers should be aware of the potential variety in hardware and web browsers that students will be using to access the items in the delivered assessment and which may introduce unintended disadvantages for the student. A number of studies on screen size and assessment performance have been reported, with no significant effects found for a mathematics test (Pommerich, 2004) or for reading passages of text involving scrolling (Higgins et al., 2005). When constructing items for the test bank, teachers should think about the amount of space available on a single screen for displaying essential information. This is particularly important for testlets that may use a sizeable stem, or where passages of text or multimedia files are used for the stem and the options appear off the screen.

Once items are viewed as the component units of an assessment, various models for constructing and delivering the assessment are possible. The delivery models may be summarized as shown in Figure 7.13 (Patelis, 2000), where the degree of adaptation is highlighted and ranges from simple linear tests that present all items to the student in a predetermined, sequential manner, through to adaptive tests that use item response theory (IRT) to characterize each item, and the software determines how each new item will be presented to students based on their response to the previous item. Linear tests are designed to appear similar to paper-based examinations and all students receive the same questions in the same order. Linear On the Fly Tests (LOFT) introduce a degree of randomization of the items from the test bank as they are presented to students, so that each student may receive a different version of a set of similar questions, depending on the size of the test bank. This type of approach is common in many content and learning management systems, where the teacher places items in the test bank and instructs the system to select items from the pool in a random manner for presentation to the student. Neither the teacher nor the student is aware of which specific items will be presented to an individual student. The randomization factor assists with reducing item exposure and also reduces the opportunities for cheating and improves security for e-assessments. A testlet is an assembly of question items that is based on a single stem that describes a scenario, and a series of hierarchical questions related to that scenario (Wang et al., 2002). Testlets are suitable for constructing authentic assessments since they can be used to present real world situations and items can be set at different levels to match the appropriate cognitive domains of the students.

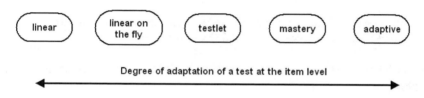

Figure 7.13 Continuum of test delivery models (Patelis, 2000)

A simple example for a testlet is illustrated in Figure 7.14, where 'Question 1' requires the student to interpret a single concept: as planets are situated further from the sun they become colder. Alternatively, a student would simply assume from the diagram and relative position of the planets to the sun, that Pluto was furthermost from the sun. 'Question 2' requires the student to realize that the diagram shows the relative position of all planets, in order, from the sun. 'Question 3' requires the student to understand the relationship between the given information about distance from the sun and planetary temperature. 'Question 4' requires the student to use information from disparate sources to propose a general explanation for the effect the relative position of the earth from the sun has on climate and seasons.

Various models exist for constructing an assessment based on the use of testlets. The overall assessment can be divided into a series of testlets; each covering a specific area of the curriculum, and within each testlet items may be selected using one of the taxonomies described in Table 7.1. One issue that arises from the use of testlets is that of dependencies, the consequence that individual questions are not independent of each other and the scoring of questions should be considered as polytomous rather than dichotomous. In order to discuss dependencies a basic understanding of item response theory (IRT) is required (a more detailed discussion of IRT occurs in Chapter 9). In this chapter we will look at the use of classical test theory (CTT) (McAlpine, 2002c) to define some item parameters that teachers should use.

The acceptable mean (or average) mark across an assessment will depend on the purpose of the assessment and whether it is criterion or norm-referenced, but many teachers would aim for a mean mark across the whole assessment of between 50 and 60 per cent (McAlpine, 2002c). For each item in a test bank it is relatively straightforward to use CTT to determine a facility index (FI); this indicates how many students chose the key compared to those who chose the distracters, expressed as a fraction (Figure 7.15). This value gives the teacher an indication of the

1. Which is the planet furthermost from the sun? **(Unistructural)**

2. Which two planets are closest to Earth? **(Multistructural)**

3. Explain how distance from the sun and temperature are related. **(Relational)**

4. Given the Earth's position relative to the sun, in what ways does this affect the climate and seasons for the Earth? **(Extended abstract)**

Figure 7.14 Simple testlet constructed according to SOLO taxonomy (adapted from Hattie *et al.*, 2004)

level of difficulty for the item and is one type of metadata tag that can be used to characterize an item. This can also be formally expressed as:

$$FI_{Q1} = \frac{\text{mean mark for Q1}}{\text{maximum mark for Q1}}$$

Figure 7.15 Facility index definition

Facility values for items that are above 0.8 indicate that the item was selected by most of the cohort, while facility values below 0.2 indicate that only a few students chose the key compared to the distracters. For Assessment 1 in Table 7.2 below, each question had the key selected by the same number of students, so the distribution of marks across the cohort would be narrow and this assessment would not differentiate higher-achieving students from lower-achieving ones. Assessment 2 has effectively divided the cohort in two with a bimodal distribution, in that students found each question either very easy to answer correctly ($FI = 0.9$) or very difficult to answer correctly ($FI = 0.1$). This type of assessment would not generate a continuum of marks across the cohort, but may serve the purpose of distinguishing students who have prerequisite knowledge or skills from those who do not, in a diagnostic assessment. Assessment 3 is more typical of the pattern a teacher might expect for an assessment that would generate a continuum of marks across the cohort, and assist in distinguishing high and low-achieving students.

It is pointless to add distracters that have very low facility values to an item. The distracters are designed to differentiate those students who have learnt the material well from those who have not, although a continuum of understanding would be expected across a cohort of students. Useful distracters should cover a known misconception experienced by previous students, or factual errors that are familiar to the experienced teacher. Distracters are designed to be strategic and should lead to a *FI* of at least 0.2–0.3 for an item.

Table 7.2 Example of Facility Index (FI) values for an assessment

	Question 1	Question 2	Question 3	Question 4	Question 5
Assessment 1	0.4	0.4	0.4	0.4	0.4
Assessment 2	0.9	0.1	0.9	0.1	0.9
Assessment 3	0.7	0.2	0.4	0.5	0.6

The discrimination index (DI) can also be calculated for each item to give a measure of the ability of the item to differentiate between those students who, on the basis of this assessment, achieved a higher mark compared to those who achieved lower marks. A simple method for calculating the discrimination index for an item is to calculate the number of correct responses to an item by the top (N_H) and bottom (N_L) third of the assessment cohort (ranked according to their overall score on the assessment). The discrimination value is determined by the expression described in Figure 7.16, subtracting N_L from N_H and dividing by the total number of students undertaking the assessment (N_{test}). A description for calculating the DI, based on the Pearson product-moment correlation appears in Chapters 9.2 and 9.3. There are a number of formulae for calculating discrimination, and for selecting the cut-off point for high-achievement and low-achievement marks, with 27.5 per cent mark distribution intervals often recommended on statistical grounds.

$$DI_{Q1} = \frac{N_H - N_L}{N_{test}}$$

Figure 7.16 Discrimination index definition

The DI may range from 1.0 or −1.0, with 1.0 being a perfect correlation for those students selecting the key and also scoring high marks and −1.0 being a perfect correlation for those students who chose a distracter but scored highly overall. Either way the item has discriminated between students, but the expected outcome would be a value that was positive and between 0.3–0.8. In Table 7.3, Assessment 1 uses items that have poor discrimination, since all values are around 0, which means that high-achieving and low-achieving students will answer the questions equally well. Assessment 2 contains items that are highly discriminating (0.8 and 0.9), but items with negative discrimination values indicate that high-achieving students are choosing distracters instead of the key, whereas low-achieving students are able to choose the key. This may indicate that the high-achieving students are misunderstanding the point of the question, or there is an inconsistency between what has been presented during the learning phases of the course and what the teacher is expecting as a correct response to these items. Assessment 3 contains items that would be expected to produce a reasonable continuum of marks across the student cohort and allows good discrimination between high-achieving students and low-achieving students.

An example for a test specification, modified from Johnstone (2004) and McAlpine (2002c) might look like the following:

Table 7.3 Example of Discrimination Index (DI) values for an assessment

	Question 1	Question 2	Question 3	Question 4	Question 5
Assessment 1	0.1	0.2	−0.1	0.0	0.05
Assessment 2	−0.5	−0.2	0.9	0.8	−0.4
Assessment 3	0.45	0.5	0.33	0.6	0.28

- contain 30 questions where 20 multiple-choice or true-false items are allocated one mark each, multiple response, matching or fill-in-the-blank type items are allocated between two and five marks each
- facility values for each item should be close to 0.5, and between 0.3 and 0.8
- discrimination values for each item should be 0.4 or higher (assuming a norm-referenced approach)
- using the SOLO taxonomy, a distribution of unistructural and multistructural response types, with some relational and extended abstract, using an approximate distribution ratio of 4:3:2:1
- between 5–10 per cent of students should choose each distracter for a selected response item.

Whether the e-assessment is delivered in linear, LOFT or testlet format, the administrative aspects of test delivery become increasingly efficient as the number of test takers increases. The online environment offers various opportunities for test delivery, ranging from the familiar invigilated, small-room examination style format to anywhere, anytime testing (Jodoin et al., 2002). Those involved in the administrative aspects of test delivery will need to be aware of the factors that impinge on student access to the e-assessment, the level of security required for the e-assessment and item exposure. The LOFT format allows a simplified version of a unique set of questions for each student, and a subsequent analysis of which particular items were presented allows teachers to reduce item exposure. Most of the delivery formats for e-assessments are capable of generating statistical data that may be subsequently used to characterize the items in the test bank and allow teachers to set the rules relating to the delivery parameters. It is often convenient to use LOFT, rather than adaptive testing, for small-scale tests, because of its simplicity and operational efficiency. Adaptive testing, in which the presentation of items or testlets is dynamically determined, is based on a student's response to each question presented and requires significant item-level analysis, as well as a substantially larger item bank to accommodate all the possible rules relating to selection. e-Assessment delivery formats usually include the ability to vary whether items are presented individually, with one item per page, or clustered together in groups. e-Assessment also allows for multiple windows to appear for the web browser, so that resources might be available to students in addition to the content that is delivered from the items in the test bank. Indeed, the test bank may contain helper applications such as calculators, spreadsheets, word processors and custom software that can be delivered with the item (Pomplu et al., 2004). Test delivery might also allow students to return to questions that have not been answered, or to change their response later in the test, allowing students to respond initially to questions they feel more prepared to answer, and returning later to those that they may have found difficult.

e-Assessments are most often delivered in linear, LOFT, testlet or adaptive format, and are typically based on a norm-referenced approach where a distribution of student scores is expected. An alternative approach is that based on mastery assessment; this is associated with criterion-based and performance assessment and based on a predetermined level of competency or defined standard that the student must match (Yang, 2006). For mastery assessment it is irrelevant how many students are in the cohort, each student must meet the predetermined standard or competency, so it encourages an outcomes-based approach to assessment. Mastery learning normally assumes that time is not the key determinant in achieving competency and it incorporates appropriate and timely feedback to the student, including explicit guidelines on the expected standards and competency levels. It allows teachers to define better what might constitute acceptable responses to test items, and allows the alignment of authentic learning and assessment.

7.2.2 Adaptive test delivery methods

Adaptive assessments (often referred to as computerized adaptive tests or CATs) allow branching with respect to the items presented to the student on the basis of selection rules assigned by the teacher or test administrator. For an adaptive assessment it is possible to either double the accuracy of a student's ability estimate using the same number of items selected from the test bank, or to halve the number of items required to make an accurate ability estimate for a particular student (Eggen *et al.*, 2000). The ability estimate for individual students is used as part of the algorithm for selecting items in an adaptive test, and it is the score the student, with a given ability, would achieve when completing a perfectly reliable assessment. Since all assessments contain errors, including inconsistencies in item sampling and variability in the manner in which tests are administered and presented, the true score for a student is a theoretical concept, whereas the actual score obtained by the student is a combination of their true score for their ability level and the accumulated effects of errors in the assessment measurement.

Adaptive tests attempt to estimate a student's ability by presenting them with an item with well-defined psychometric parameters from the test bank, then interpreting the student response to that item according to an item response model. The algorithm then iteratively modifies the ability estimate for the students. This process continues until the discontinuation parameters for the assessment are satisfied. The administration of a CAT is essentially the repetition of a two-step process. At Step 1, an item is presented to each student based on an estimate of the ability of the student and the difficulty level of the item. At Step 2, a student's response to the presented item is scored, and a student's proficiency estimate is updated. These two steps are then repeated until some discontinuation criterion is met, which is usually either a predetermined number of items or a desired level of measurement precision (Figure 7.17).

The face validity for an adaptive test will depend on the confidence that is placed on the psychometric detail embedded in the item parameters and the item selection process. Adaptive testing has the advantage of efficiency, but the individual items in the test bank must be of a very high quality since the sequence of items presented to the student is assembled dynamically,

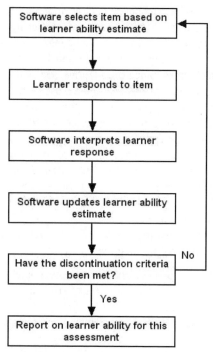

Figure 7.17 Model for adaptive testing

using previous student responses to each item to determine which item to present next. Reducing the time it takes to complete an assessment may not be the primary efficiency driver for an adaptive test, rather the ability to improve content balance and coverage may be considered more important for quality reasons. Reducing the number of items presented in a test has the advantage of reducing item exposure, a situation that arises when items are presented frequently to different groups of students, and so become well known.

Adaptive tests rely on the invariance principle of IRT, which assumes that item parameters are independent of the distribution of student abilities for a particular cohort. This allows test administrators to present different groups of items to different groups of students, yet still use a common scale to report relative ability levels across all cohorts. Rasch and IRT models that provide metadata about individual items in a test bank are discussed in more detail in Chapter 9, but in general, to develop a selection model to use in adaptive tests, items are assigned to classes in some form of hierarchical structure based on a number of dimensions including content, format, cognitive level and discipline. Test construction rules then specify the number of items from each group that will allow for the assessment to have content and construct validity.

How does the adaptive test algorithm choose items from the test bank? The common feature of all algorithms is the use of some type of constrained item selection process (Li *et al.*, 2005). The common constraints put on item selection include content, item exposure and conflicting item constraints. The algorithm for a particular adaptive test will contain the code for commencing, continuing and terminating the assessment, and the particular methodology that is to be used for reporting the students' responses. Thus, item selection models are not based solely on statistical principles or the psychometric parameters derived from Rasch or IRT models, but also include content balancing constraints. The item selection algorithm and the content classification protocol of the item model work cooperatively to achieve an appropriate distribution profile for the exposure of items, especially in high-stake assessments.

Individual items in the test bank that have excellent facility and discrimination values may be chosen frequently in an adaptive test; this requires good models for item selection that minimize overexposure but still allow content balancing. Three models that may be used for content balancing are the constrained, modified constrained or modified multinomial models (Leung *et al.*, 2003). The constrained model selects an (optimal) item from a defined content area of the test bank on the provision that it has been previously selected below a prescribed number of times during the current test. The modified constrained model is similar, but an item may be selected from any content area on the provision that it has been previously selected below a prescribed number of times. Since an adaptive test will terminate when an accurate ability estimate for a particular student has been made, use of the modified constrained model will mean fewer items are overexposed compared to the simple constrained model that selects items sequentially through the content areas. The modified multinomial model can take an item from any content area, up to a predetermined exposure level for that area, and once this level has been reached, will not select items from that content area again for any student in the current cohort. This method tries to make maximum use of each item pool, but assumes that a sufficient number of item pools will exist in the test bank. The three different models result in different levels of item exposure, and much research is still being undertaken to optimize the efficacy and efficiency of large-scale adaptive tests.

Wise *et al.* (2000) have summarized the key issues that should be addressed in order to appropriately maintain a test bank suitable for adaptive assessment:

- ensure a suitable item pool size and control over the psychometric parameters
- verify the dimensionality of an item pool in terms of student responses
- use an appropriate response model
- use appropriate procedures for item addition, removal and revision
- maintain item scale consistency
- for high-stake assessments consider using multiple item pools.

Since content constraints invariably lead to large numbers of items required for the test bank, commercial testing centres frequently have a minimum of 1,000 items in a test bank. Many item response models rely on the fact that student responses will be unidimensional, meaning that one characteristic is responsible for how a student responds, or the assessment measures a single 'latent trait' of the student. The assumption is that all students responding in a certain way to the item will be assumed to have the same latent trait, or reason for responding correctly to a question. Multidimensional responses will mean that there are various characteristics that have caused the response, not just a single trait. Factor analysis, such as a scree plot, may be used to distinguish unidimensional and multidimensional responses. Response models may be based on one-parameter, two-parameter or three-parameter logistic models (see Chapter 9.3 for a more detailed discussion on 1PL, 2PL and 3PL). It is possible to use IRT to obtain an item response curve for an item, and determine if it is suitable for inclusion or retention in the item pool. Over a period of time it will be necessary to recalibrate items from the test bank to ensure that the parameters are still valid and that sampling errors are still within acceptable limits.

8 Grading and marking items from a test bank

8.1 General grading and marking issues

The simplest grading scheme to use for an e-assessment is to assign an unweighted raw mark to each item in a test bank. This approach assumes that each response and each item would be of equal value (though not necessarily equal marks), but this may not always be appropriate. A weighted raw mark for each item may be used to accommodate such issues as the amount of effort and time students were required to allocate in order to gain expertise in a particular component of the curriculum, or to highlight the relative importance of the concepts to the programme. The relative amount of time taken to read, construct and respond to each question may also be taken into account when assigning marks to an item, as it is not productive to assign one mark to a question that requires a significant amount of time to read, analyse and formulate a response if this is out of proportion to other items presented to the student. Selected response questions generally take less time to physically respond to, compared to constructed response items, although considerable time may be required to decide on an appropriate response. Constructed responses require a longer time to answer, as the student must physically write the response, either on paper or by using a computer keyboard. For this reason, it is often seen that constructed responses are allocated more marks per question compared to selected response questions because of the time required to physically construct the response, rather than the time taken to mentally construct the appropriate response.

Equating is a form of scaling that takes into account differences in relative difficulty level and grading schemes used in different tests (Livingston, 2004). This would be important for adaptive tests where different forms of the test are presented to different cohorts, but the results must be presented on a common scale. A simple form of equating would involve adjusting the scores on one test to match the ability estimates for students with the same relative ability level on the other test. Linear equating can involve taking the score on one test and converting it into an adjusted score, using the standard deviations from the mean on both tests to equate scores. Since the mean and standard deviations in both groups will be constant, the mean of the adjusted scores from one test will be equal to the mean of the raw scores from the original test. To take into account the possibility that adjusted scores may fall outside the marks range intended for the test, equipercentile equating allows the adjusted score to be calculated by a non-linear equating method (and usually a form of smoothing based on log-linear smoothing) that retains the relative position of each test taker based on the same percentile rank in the test group.

Even though items in a test bank may have been characterized extensively by psychometric parameters and chosen on the basis of appropriate facility and difficulty values, and the delivery method may be matched to the students' requirements, selected response items may still be responded to by guessing. Burton (2001) has described measures of test unreliability and attempted to quantify issues associated with question selection and guessing, test length and the number of options per question. Clearly the reason for a particular student choosing the key in a MCQ will reside on a continuum from absolute certainty through to arbitrary guessing. This continuum includes 'informed guessing' or partial understanding and judicious identification of distracters. In other words, students may know something is incorrect, rather than being sure that something is correct. One option for improving reliability is to increase the number of items selected from the test bank for all test takers, thus reducing the statistical significance of random guessing. The number of distracters may be increased for a MCQ, but the discrimination factor for the item must be maintained. Another option to reduce the impact of guessing is to use 'negative marking'.

8.2 Negative and confidence level marking of objective items

The marking scheme for items can include negative marks for distracters and a mark of *n* for the key, where *n* is the number of distracters. This approach has the advantage that students can choose which questions to answer based on their level of confidence of the key or which distracters are incorrect. For a typical MCQ with one key and three distracters, not answering the question could result in a mark of 0, choosing the key could result in a mark of 3 and choosing one of the distracters could result in a mark of −1. The main issue with using negative marking in each item is the parity between different types of selected response questions. What marking scheme will be used for multiple-response questions or MCQs with more or less than three distracters, or for true/false questions? An example of post-test correction for guessing has been reported by Harper (2003) and involves the use of a spreadsheet to automate the correction and generate a grade.

Burton (2005) has drawn our attention to 12 myths associated with selected response questions and the fact that guessing is rarely random, and so statistical data based on purely random guessing are not really relevant for most assessments based on selected responses. The impact of guessing on the face and construct validity of the test is most crucial for students whose ability estimate is near the passing grade for the assessment, since guessing may allow students with marginal abilities to be able to gain a passing mark for a high stakes assessment.

Myth 1   With number-right scoring, random guessing generally has little effect on test reliability.

Myth 2   Blind guessing is reduced if the test items are well constructed.

Myth 3   Blind guessing is harder when test items are complicated.

Myth 4   With number-right scoring, the extra score obtained by blind guessing can be exactly calculated from the number of test items guessed blindly (if known) and the number of answer options per item.

Myth 5   Negative marking corrects for guessing. Negative marking is usually used to discourage arbitrary guessing of responses, and may involve a marking scheme that is explained to students before they undertake the test, and allows them to decide how to maximize their score, or it may be applied as part of the analysis and scoring process and used to adjust marks in relation to the pattern of student responses.

Myth 6   Negative marking of true/false tests is necessarily less fair than number-right scoring because people differ in their willingness to gamble on uncertain answers.

Myth 7   Negative marking never works. Should an assessment be testing for the risk taking behaviour of the student? The instructions to students undertaking a test should explain the purpose of the marking scheme, and what is being expected and rewarded with marks. The impact of guessing, or applying partial knowledge, should be explained to test takers, so the validity of the assessment is increased.

Myth 8   Incorrect knowledge has the same effect on number-right scores as does complete ignorance.

Myth 9   True/false tests are limited to testing for factual recall.

Myth 10   Tests of around 60 items generally suffice to sample the facts and ideas taught in a given course, assuming these to be much more numerous.

Myth 11   Reliability coefficients measure test reliability.

Myth 12   Item response theory (including the simplest version, the Rasch model) is superior to classical test theory for analysing items in academic tests.

The Computer-Based Alternative Assessment (CBAA) project has described methods for capturing the confidence level that is associated with student responses to selected response questions (Paul, 1998). Figure 8.1 shows the CBAA Triangle, in which the student moves the cursor across

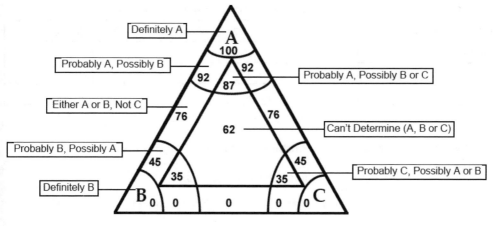

Figure 8.1 CBAA Triangle indicating confidence level and marking scheme (Paul, 1998)

the triangle and chooses the region that corresponds to their level of confidence in their response. The student will see the text portion as indicated by the boxes in Figure 8.1, while the assessment engine uses the percentages indicated in the sections of the triangle to modify the score according to the selection.

For example, if A were the correct response, then a student choosing the portion of the triangle indicating 'definitely A' would receive 100 per cent of the marks for that question. If the student was not absolutely sure that A was the correct response, but thought it was 'probably A, possibly B', then choosing this region of the triangle would result in 92 per cent of the marks for the question, whereas choosing 'probably B, possibly A' would result in only 45 per cent of the marks for this question. This method of assigning partial marks based on the key and confidence level is based on an adaptation to the logarithmic admissible scoring system for three alternatives (A, B or C). Paul (1998) has also described how capturing the confidence level with which the student responds to the question may also be used in feedback to the student about how they might maximize their scores on such selected response tests. By plotting the relationship for each of the recorded confidence values and their relative frequencies, and analysing the fit of the data points to an ideal response pattern, a 'realism function' may be used to predict what score the student could have achieved by maximizing their confidence in answering questions correctly. Similarly, this type of analysis could also advise students if they are overly confident in responding to questions based on limited knowledge, or a limited ability to differentiate the key from distracters.

In the LAPT (London Agreed Protocol for Teaching) system used at University College London, a three-point scale is used to measure confidence levels in answers to selected response questions, 1 = low confidence, 2 = mid-level confidence and 3 = high-level confidence, as illustrated in Table 8.1 and Figure 8.2 (http://www.ucl.ac.uk/lapt). For a true/false question students are required to respond to the question and also indicate their level of confidence in their response. Choosing an incorrect response with a high level of confidence (C = 3) will result in a mark of −6, so students must make a judgement not only on the correct response, but how they might maximize their mark for each question. Such grading schemes are assessing not only the knowledge and skills associated with discipline content, but also meta-attributes related to a student's understanding of their own abilities, and their ability to take risks in order to maximize marks. However, for the LAPT protocol described, a mathematical adjustment can be made to accommodate students who are less inclined to take risks and so may achieve a lower grade than is warranted by the number of correct responses.

Table 8.1 Example of marking scheme from LAPT system (LAPT, 2003)

Confidence level	C = 1	C = 2	C = 3	No reply
Mark if correct	1	2	3	0
Mark if incorrect (T/F)	0	−2	−6	0
Mark if incorrect (MCQ)	0	−1	−4	0

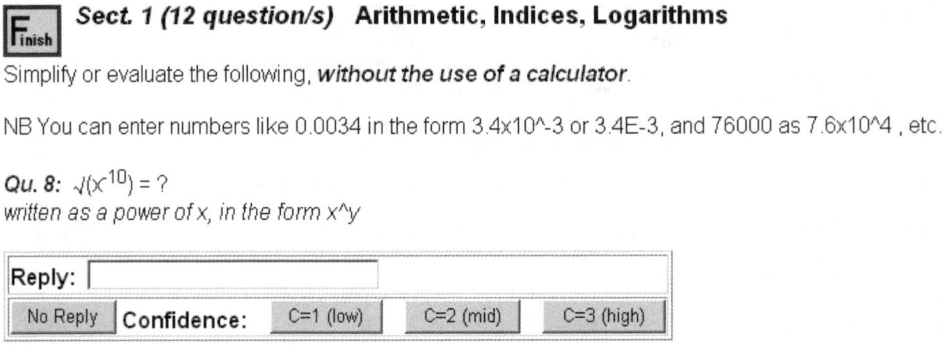

[Finish] **Sect. 1 (12 question/s)   Arithmetic, Indices, Logarithms**

Simplify or evaluate the following, *without the use of a calculator*.

NB You can enter numbers like 0.0034 in the form 3.4x10^-3 or 3.4E-3, and 76000 as 7.6x10^4 , etc.

Qu. 8: $\sqrt{(x^{10})} = ?$
written as a power of x, in the form x^y

Reply: [   ]

[No Reply] **Confidence:**   [C=1 (low)]   [C=2 (mid)]   [C=3 (high)]

Figure 8.2 Example of confidence based marking of questions from LAPT system (http://www.ucl.ac.uk/lapt)

McCabe *et al.* (2003) have discussed an alternative approach to grading selected response questions based on partially constrained responses. A classical MCQ with one key and three distracters delivered in the usual constrained mode means that the number of responses a student is allowed is equal to the number of correct answers and scores a mark of 1 for a correct response and 0 for an incorrect response, or if negative marking is used, 3 for a correct response and −1 for an incorrect response and 0 for no response. For a partially constrained MCQ, the number of choices can be two or three, with a corresponding marking scheme of 2 marks for a correct response if two choices are permitted, or 1 mark for a correct response if three choices are permitted (Table 8.2). This type of grading scheme rewards students who can eliminate incorrect choices, but may not be able to distinguish between the key and the last distracter.

For multiple-response questions, a similar approach may be adopted, using the grading scheme shown in Figure 8.3 where N is the number of options, r is the number of correct responses, a is the mark for a correct response and b is the mark for an incorrect response. However, in this case the score for the question will be independent of whether the question is offered in constrained, partially constrained or unconstrained mode.

Table 8.2 Example of marking scheme for partially or unconstrained responses (McCabe *et al.*, 2003)

Mode	Maximum selections a student can make	Maximum score	Minimum score
constrained	1	3 (1/4)	−1 (3/4)
partially constrained	2	2 (1/2)	−2 (1/2)
partially constrained	3	1 (3/4)	−3 (1/4)
unconstrained	4	0 (1)	0

$$a = -\left(\frac{N-r}{r}\right)b$$

Figure 8.3 Marking scheme for a partially constrained MRQ (McCabe *et al.*, 2003)

For example, in a multiple-response question with five options and two correct responses, $a = 3$ and $b = -2$, with each correct response scoring 3, to give a maximum of 6 marks for two correct responses but using only two choices, whereas for two correct responses and one incorrect response from three choices, a mark of 4 would be obtained. If a student chose all the options then the mark for the question would be 0, as expected. Using this marking scheme, a MCQ is a subset of the multiple-response questions, with $N = 4$, $r = 1$ and $a = 3$ and $b = -1$.

8.3 Marking constructed response items

In developing the items for a test bank, the teacher or test administrator will need to consider whether to include appropriate examples of selected response and constructed response items, and what will be the marks associated with each type of item. The scoring for an assessment overall might be based on the unweighted or weighted raw scores (for example a per cent mark or number correct), or based on the IRT pattern score where a maximum likelihood estimate is reported based on the students' particular pattern of item scores (Schaeffer *et al.*, 2002). For assessments that use both selected response and constructed response items, the use of IRT pattern scoring tends to result in the smallest standard errors, although differences between the three scoring methods reduce as the number of items increases (assuming a proportionate increase in time allocated for students to complete their responses) especially as more constructed response items are included. Different scoring methods may be appropriate at different levels, or when deciding if certain subgroups in the student cohort are advantaged or disadvantaged by the weighting applied to constructed or selected response items.

When considering the construction of an assessment based on one of the taxonomies described in Table 7.1, teachers may wish to include constructed response questions that require students to write an extended piece of text or an essay. The ability to use computers to automatically assess constructed responses has the potential to reduce the significant cost of marking such assessments and to provide specific feedback to individuals in large classes. In order to automatically mark extended text responses or an essay, one requires an appropriate set of meaningful characteristics that are generally accepted as essential or required criteria and are interpretable by a computer, a sufficiently large set of human marked essays as exemplars and an algorithm that matches the two (Landauer *et al.*, 2003).

Many items in a test bank ask the student to state, suggest, describe or explain in response to a particular question by using a few words or a short phrase. Different students may provide slightly different variations to these responses, and so some form of natural language processing (NLP) could be used to mark the responses in a consistent and valid manner (Sukkarieh *et al.*, 2003). Patterns of words have specific meanings in many disciplines, and it is important in text responses to questions that the appropriate language is used. NLP uses the existing patterns of linguistic knowledge such as part-of-speech tags, nouns and verbs. Software that can accommodate paraphrasing and acceptable alternatives is required, and human markers are required to enter these details.

Some of the linguistic characteristics that might be used for automatic essay marking include the frequency and order of certain words or phrases, the length of sentences, spelling and grammar usage, the appropriate application of active and passive voice and characteristics related to discourse and style analysis. A common approach used by software publishers for automatic essay marking to validate the computer-based approach to assessment is to compare regression data for a set of computer-scored and human-scored essays. The more training the software is allowed to undertake by analysing human-marked exemplars, the closer the correlation between computer-scored and human-scored essays. Latent Semantic Analysis (LSA) is a mathematical technique used to represent the relationships between the implied meaning of similar words or phrases used in different contexts (Landauer *et al.*, 1998). LSA uses word co-occurrence statistics based on a development corpus that results in a matrix that can be reduced mathematically to vector items for use in an overall algorithm that compares the students' response to a model response. LSA provides a similar scoring pattern to humans for tests based on standard vocabulary and subject matter, and is able to be used successfully to assess essays based on standardized content knowledge and word usage. LSA is usually one component used for the automatic marking of essays, other components may include human constructed dictionaries of appropriate meanings, grammar usage, semantic networks, natural language processes (NLP) and discipline specific meaning of words and phrases. The technical details of LSA may be further investigated in Landauer *et al.* (1998).

The commercial product, Intelligent Essay Assessor (IEA, http://www.knowledge-technologies.com), arrives at an overall mark for an essay based on content, style and mechanics, as well as validity measures (Landauer *et al.*, 2003). The content component uses LSA to represent the meaning of words in the discipline area of the essay, and samples of human-marked exemplars are used to train the software. Style and mechanics cover aspects of coherence in the meaning of the words used and appropriate spelling and grammar, and validity levels are based on comparisons with human-marked essays on the same, or a similar, topic. An example report is shown in Figure 8.4, illustrating the three reported domains and the overall grade for an essay. The software used to automatically assess essays will often require large quantities of RAM (random access memory), so applications such as IEA are offered as a web-based service.

Automatic essay marking is currently used for the extended response sections of several, large-scale, standardized university admission tests such as the Graduate Management Admissions Test, GMAT® (GMAT, 2007) and the Test of Written English (TWE, http://www.ets.org/toefl), administered through Educational Testing Services (ETS) in the USA using the E-rater® software system

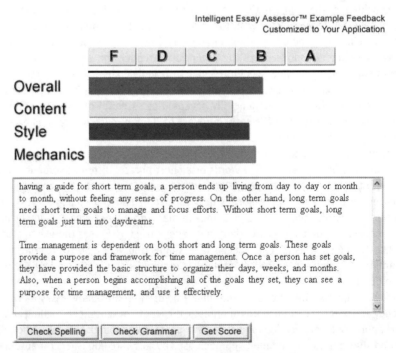

Figure 8.4 Example of Intelligent Essay Assessor™ report (http://www.knowledge-technologies.com)

(ETS, 2007). ETS also offers a commercial service for the automatic marking of essays through the Criterion[SM] Online Essay Evaluation Service. The correlation between automatic marking and human marking is reported to be between 0.8 and 0.9, although this will vary depending on the type of questions being presented to students (Valenti *et al.*, 2003). The E-rater® system uses components of NLP to parse sentences and LSA techniques for statistical purposes, along with human-marked exemplars and discourse features.

The key issue at the present time in developing automatic essay marking is the difficulty in obtaining an appropriately sized corpus of human-marked essays in which subject matter experts agree on the assessment criteria and apply a consistent score. Software must undergo the iterative process of training in order to better reproduce the approach human markers take in applying the assessment criteria, and the opportunity to modify the parameters used in the algorithms to construct the partial and final scores.

8.4 Marking problem-solving items

e-Assessments that attempt to measure problem-solving competence for situational learning or simulation activities will not be able to satisfy the requirements of unidimensionality, since the analytic and dynamic aspects of competence must be distinguished (Wirth *et al.*, 2003). Analytical problem-solving abilities will be related to reasoning competencies, whereas dynamic problem-solving involves an ability to adapt to a changing environment by continuously processing feedback information. IMMEX (Interactive Multi-Media Exercises) is software that allows a teacher or test administrator to track pathways that are used by students during an assessment task involving simulations or problem-solving activities (IMMEX, http://www.immex.ucla.edu). Vendlinski *et al.* (2002) have reported an example of using IMMEX™ and an analysis involving artificial neural networks to identify the most common strategies that a group of secondary-school chemistry students used to respond to a set of qualitative chemistry items. It was then possible to use Markov hidden chain analysis to develop a model that would relate the student strategies to solve these problems to the development of curriculum content and activities that could enhance problem-solving strategies to other problem types. IMMEX™ software records the students' path through their responses to the problem, including which pieces of information they used and how many times they viewed particular content. This particular study concluded that students tend to use the same strategies to solve all problems, irrespective of whether they enabled the student to correctly solve the problem or not. Stevens *et al.* (2005) have undertaken a similar study with 776 university sophomore molecular biology majors analysing the range of strategies used to solve a series of genetics problems.

9 Validity and reliability

9.1 Overview of validity and reliability

How does a teacher know if the items in a test bank are appropriate and which ones should be used for a particular assessment? How does a teacher know if the overall assessment is valid and reliable? A valid assessment is one that measures what it professes to measure, and individual items in a test bank may be valid for one assessment purpose but not another. A reliable assessment is one that would produce similar results over a period of time when used by students of similar ability and in the same circumstances. These are relatively simple definitions for validity and reliability, and it is now appropriate to consider a more detailed description of these two terms and the means by which a teacher or institution can demonstrate that items in a test bank and overall assessments are valid and reliable.

The intention of most teachers in designing an assessment task is to provide students with the opportunity to demonstrate what they have learnt, and to make some form of distinction between the various levels of understanding of the learnt material. The act of translating the teacher's intention into an actual assessment involves operationalizing the assessment construct in a manner that is both valid and reliable. Although there are different definitions for the subclasses of validity, they may be summarized as face validity, content validity and construct validity, where the latter term refers to criterion-based measures such as predictive, concurrent, convergent and discriminant validities (McAlpine, 2002a; Trochim, 2005). Face validity involves the perception of stakeholders in accepting the item, or the assessment, as measuring what it purports to measure. Would experts in the field accept the item or assessment as appropriate to the discipline and the level of achievement expected of the student? Content validity concerns the breadth and depth of the students' skills or competencies that must be used in order to respond appropriately to the test items. Are the items dependent on skills and capabilities outside of the discipline domain or the primary content presented as part of the programme of learning? Most students will require some skills and competencies beyond those developed in the specific discipline domain, and teachers can assume some generic attributes for the expected year level of the student. For e-assessments, one critical issue related to content validity is the dependence of the test item or assessment on the ICT skills of the student. Will test takers with a minimal level of computer competency still be able to satisfactorily undertake tasks presented online? If the purpose of the assessment is to test understanding in a chemistry or history programme for example, will the individual items in the test bank, when presented to students online, also be testing an understanding of keyboard skills or the use of helper applications such as Java applets? Face and content validity may be referred to as subjective judgements, since there are usually no external criteria with which to demonstrate compliance, except that derived from a general agreement of discipline experts.

For the criterion-based measures of construct validity, some form of external validation or standard is used and a prediction can be made about how a student might respond to an item, or what the expected performance of a student with a particular ability level might be on this particular assessment. Concurrent, convergent and discriminant validity are facets of criterion-based construct validity, and refer to the ability of the assessment to quantitatively distinguish between different students, or groups of students, and the degree to which this distinction converges or diverges from other similar or different assessments (Trochim, 2005). Correlation coefficients may be used to show a convergence or divergence between the attributes associated with different assessments or the results from different groups of test takers. Construct validity measures may be applied to the items in the test bank once student response data has been collected and analysed.

Reliability is concerned with consistency, and the different ways in which it might be measured. Reliability theory assumes the existence of a theoretical true score in which the actual score obtained by a student is equal to the true score plus the sum of all errors in the measurement of the actual score (Trochim, 2005). Teachers would be aware of issues of variability in assessor reliability, where different assessors may award different marks for the same response. Even with the use of marking rubrics, there may be variability in human marked responses, and this is a source of error in the score measurement and so contributes to reducing the reliability in the actual score. It is possible to measure the correlations between the results from the same test being given to different (but similar) groups of students, as a measure of test-retest reliability. Correlations may also be measured between the performances of students in the same test, where they are presented with a random selection of items from the test bank, thus providing a measure of parallel forms reliability. The most common measure used for internal consistency within a single test is the correlation between items using Cronbach's Alpha (α) coefficient of reliability for tests containing only compulsory items or Backhouse's P for tests with optional items; 0.70 being the minimum value generally considered acceptable (McAlpine, 2002b).

The more formal treatment of validity and reliability involves a discussion about the assumptions at the core of Classical Test Theory (CTT) and the latent trait models using Item Response Theory (IRT) or Rasch modelling. The items discussed so far, such as the facility and discrimination indices, are examples of the application of CTT, since the characteristics are dependent on the particular group of test takers, and the item parameters are not independent of the student. Latent Trait Models for item analysis are based on characteristics that are substantially independent of the test takers; there is invariance between the test item and the ability level of the test taker (McAlpine, 2002b). Latent trait theory assumes that the assessment is unidimensional, that is, it is measuring only one underlying trait, the ability level of the student.

9.2 Classical Test Theory

We have already discussed two of the important indicators for items in a test bank using CTT, the facility (*FI*) and discrimination (*DI*) indices. These parameters may be assigned to items and the items selected from a test bank on the basis of these values. The calculation of these values can be performed simply using statistical software, or through the use of a spreadsheet with appropriate formulas. An example of the latter is the commercial software LerTap 5, which integrates with Microsoft Excel and allows a wide variety of parameters to be calculated (http://www.assess.com). The output from a standard LerTap analysis of a 25 question MCQ is illustrated in Figure 9.1. This output includes information such as the highest (24) and lowest scores (3), the mean (60.2 per cent) and the reliability ($\alpha = 0.88$).

The standard deviation (*SD*) can also be used to give a measure of the spread of correct and incorrect responses to a particular item. The *SD* is the square root of the sum of the deviations from the means (Σx^2) for the particular item divided by the number of test takers who responded to the item (Figure 9.2). An item with a *SD* of approximately ± 1.0–1.5 units for a normal distribution about the mean and *DI* (discrimination index) in the range 0.3–0.6 would be appropriate. It might be a deliberate strategy to place easy items, *SD*, ± 0.5 and *DI*, 0.3, at the beginning of a test and difficult questions, *SD* ± 1.0–1.5 and *DI* > 0.8, towards the end of the test. Thus, items in a test bank do not have to have a uniform *SD*, *FI* and *DI*, as the teacher may wish to provide a variety of question types (in terms of parameters) in the test.

These parameters apply to the individual items in the test; what of the relationship between the items and the test score for the student? The Pearson point biserial or Pearson biserial correlation coefficient can be calculated and will give an indication of the student response to each item correlated to their score overall (minus this item). The values will be in the range -1.0 to

Summary statistics

number of scores (n):	20	
lowest score found:	3.00	(12.0%)
highest score found:	24.00	(96.0%)
median:	14.00	(56.0%)
mean (or average):	15.05	(60.2%)
standard deviation:	5.81	(23.2%)
standard deviation (as a sample):	5.96	(23.8%)
variance (sample):	35.52	

number of subtest items:	25	
minimum possible score:	0.00	
maximum possible score:	25.00	
reliability (coefficient alpha):	0.88	
index of reliability:	0.94	
standard error of measurement:	2.04	(8.1%)

Figure 9.1 Example of LerTap 5 output for 25-question MCQ test (http://www.assess.com)

$$SD = \sqrt{\frac{\sum x^2}{N}}$$

Figure 9.2 Standard deviation (*SD*) for an item in a test bank

1.0, with negative values implying an inverse correlation between the individual item and the overall score. The usual values expected for this parameter would be 0.4 or greater, and used in conjunction with the *FI* will give an indication of the discrimination for the item. This would be similar to using the *DI*.

Figure 9.3 shows the LerTap analysis of Question 10 in an e-assessment, which was an MCQ with four options, and we can readily see that 65 per cent of the participants chose the key (D) over the distracters. The point biserial correlation (pb(r), a measure of the discrimination value), is small and positive for the key, which means students who scored well overall marginally selected this option over students who did not perform highly overall on the test, and the two options A and B have negative correlations, which means students who scored highly tended not to choose these options.

A typical example of the output from software designed to analyse item responses is shown in Figure 9.4, from ITEMAN (http://www.assess.com/Software/iteman.htm). The third column in Figure 9.4 indicates the proportion of test takers who gave the correct response, 58 per cent of students, so the item is not too easy, nor too difficult. The fourth column is the discrimination index, and a value of 0.62 indicates a reasonable item in terms of discrimination. The fifth column is the point biserial correlation, and indicates the correlation between the correct response for

Q10

option	wt.	n	p	pb(r)	b(r)	avg.	z
A	0.00	3	0.15	-0.15	-0.23	13.00	-0.35
B	0.00	1	0.05	-0.12	-0.25	12.00	-0.53
C	0.00	0	0.00	0.00	0.00	0.00	0.00
D	1.00	13	0.65	0.07	0.09	15.69	0.11
other	0.00	3	0.15	0.02	0.03	15.33	0.05

Figure 9.3 Example of LerTap 5 output for an individual item

		Item Statistics				Alternative Statistics				
Seq. No.	Scale -Item	Prop. Correct	Disc. Index	Point Biser.	Alt.	Prop. Total	Endorsing Low	High	Point Biser.	Key
1	1-1	.58	.62	.54	1	.16	.32	.07	-.31	
					2	.58	.32	.93	.54	*
					3	.08	.00	.00	-.02	
					4	.18	.37	.00	-.38	
					Other	.00	.00	.00		

Figure 9.4 Example of ITEMAN output for an individual item

the item and the total scale score for the test. A positive value means that students who chose the correct response to this item also scored highly on the test overall. The point biserial correlation for each of the options is of interest, since a good item should deliver a positive value above 0.4 for the key, and low or negative values for the distracters. The alternative (option) statistics give the individual parameters for the various options. The asterisk indicates the key and we can see that 93 per cent of high scoring students chose the key, whereas only 32 per cent of low scoring students chose the key.

9.3 Item Response Theory – 1PL, 2PL and 3PL models

Item Response Theory (IRT) relates the characteristics of test items (item parameters) and the characteristics of students (latent traits) to the probability of a correct response being given by the student to a test item. The core characteristic of the student, their ability, is a theoretical construct in IRT, although it can be related to measurable quantities. The previously discussed CTT item parameters were dependent on the particular group from which they were derived, and are useful to teachers and test administrators so long as the different groups of students have common characteristics. For IRT, the item and student parameters are said to be invariant; they are not dependent on each other. This property of invariance means that appropriately characterized items can be removed or added to a test bank, and the overall integrity of the bank can be maintained. These models are also based on the assumption that the items are scored dichotomously, the responses being either correct or incorrect. IRT also allows for predicted outcomes from tests that are administered to students with a particular ability level. These tests are constructed from items in the test bank with known parameters, and are particularly applicable to the assembly of adaptive tests (McAlpine, 2002b).

IRT is used predominantly for large-scale, high stakes, summative assessments in standardized testing environments, where the validity and reliability of each test item must be verified. Many classroom teachers will not use IRT in its complex form, but should be aware of the logic and principles behind its use, especially if items from a test bank are to be used for summative assessments. Teachers should understand the concepts behind the use of item difficulty and discrimination measures, as they can be applied to all assessment situations. It would be advantageous if teachers could be presented with modified, simpler versions of the application of IRT that could be used routinely by non-psychometricians.

The one parameter IRT model (1PL, one parameter logistic model) is similar to the Rasch model that is discussed later in Chapter 9.4. For the 1PL model, the probability of a particular student responding correctly to an item is given by the following equations:

Probability of answering correctly = (ability − difficulty) /
(1 + (ability − difficulty))   Eq1

Probability = exp(ability(θ) − difficulty)/(1+exp(ability(θ) − difficulty))   Eq2

$$P(\theta) = \frac{e^{D(\theta-b)}}{1+e^{D(\theta-b)}}$$ Eq3

Eq1 describes in words what the 1PL model is portraying, that the probability of a student answering a question correctly is related to their ability and the difficulty level of the question. Eq2 expresses this mathematically in words and theta (θ) is used to describe the ability level of the student. Eq3 expresses this mathematically and is in the form of the logistic function and uses the term b to describe the difficulty level of the item. D is a constant that is normally 1.7 and allows the expression to be represented by a logistic ogival function (McAlpine, 2002b). For students with a low ability the probability of responding correctly to an item approaches zero, and for students with a high ability level the probability of a correct response approaches 1. In Figure 9.5, Curve 1 illustrates an easy item, Curve 2 a moderately difficult item and Curve 3 a difficult item. The b parameter defines the location of the inflection point for the curve along the ability (θ) scale. Lower values of b will move the curve to the left whereas higher values will move it to the right.

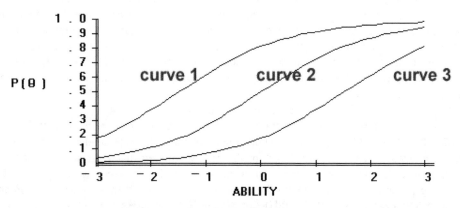

Figure 9.5 Item response function with varying difficulty but constant discrimination (Baker, 2001)

The 2PL (two parameter logistic) model adds an item discrimination parameter a, in addition to the item difficulty parameter b, and can be expressed as:

$$P(\theta) = \frac{e^{a(\theta-b)}}{1+e^{a(\theta-b)}}$$ Eq4

This is shown graphically in Figure 9.6, in which Curve 1 is a straight line representing an item of medium difficulty but no discrimination, Curve 2 an item of medium difficulty with medium discrimination and Curve 3 an item of medium difficulty with high discrimination. The a parameter defines the slope of the curve at the inflection point, and is flatter for lower values of a and steeper for higher values. The steeper the slope, the better the item discriminates between test takers.

For selected response items, it is always possible for a test taker to guess the correct response and so the three parameter model, 3PL, adds a 'guessing' parameter, c, to the item difficulty and item discrimination. This leads to Eq5.

$$P(\theta) = c + (1-c)\frac{e^{a(\theta-b)}}{1+e^{a(\theta-b)}}$$ Eq5

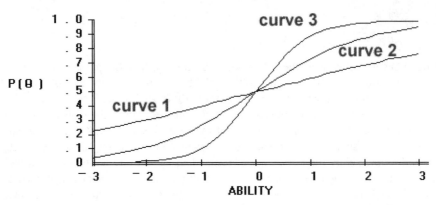

Figure 9.6 Item response function with varying discrimination but constant difficulty (Baker, 2001)

The 'guessing' parameter is considered to be independent of either the ability level of the student, or the difficulty level of the item, although previous discussions in this chapter have highlighted the fact that many responses to items could be regarded as 'informed guessing'. However, for the purposes of 3PL, this is a mathematical description of chance, rather than 'informed guessing'. 2PL and 3PL parameter models are most often used for an analysis of large-scale unidimensional test data, and have been shown to be particularly useful for adaptive tests.

In practice, the IRT models are applied to data sets from actual tests, and psychometricians determine if there is a good statistical fit to the observed assessment data (Downing, 2003). The 2PL and 3PL models often show a good fit for large-scale, unidimensional test data from well-established commercial test banks. The initial item parameters are estimated by conducting calibration tests, where a sufficient number of test takers, with a known ability level, are presented with the items. The student responses are then analysed by appropriate software (for example MULTILOG, BILOG or XCALIBRE from Assessment Systems Corporation) using the Joint Maximum Likelihood Estimation or the Marginal Maximum-Likelihood Estimation (http://www.assess.com). These estimations are based on a Newton-Ralphson multivariate analysis that iteratively determines appropriate item parameters, given the constraints that are applied to the variables by the psychometrician. The item parameters can be updated as more data is collected from test takers and it is possible to obtain items with highly refined parameters. A portion of the output from MiniSteps (http://www.winsteps.com/ministep.htm) is shown in Figure 9.7.

```
    Calculating Fit Statistics
>=====================================<
Standardized Residuals N(0,1)  Mean: .00 S.D.: 1.08
Grouping and Recoding
+---------------------------------------------------------------------+
| PERSONS      32 INPUT     32 MEASURED           INFIT      OUTFIT    |
|            SCORE    COUNT    MEASURE   ERROR   IMNSQ  ZSTD  OMNSQ  ZSTD|
| MEAN       50.5     21.5     -1.16     .39     1.00  -.1    .97   .0|
| S.D.        9.4       .0      1.23     .05      .42  1.3    .40   .9|
| REAL RMSE   .39    ADJ.SD    1.17  SEPARATION  2.98  PERSON RELIABILITY  .90|
|---------------------------------------------------------------------|
| ITEMS       20 INPUT     20 MEASURED           INFIT      OUTFIT    |
| MEAN       75.1     32.0       .00     .34     1.00   .0    .97   .0|
| S.D.       24.4       .0       .81     .11      .27  1.2    .29  1.2|
| REAL RMSE   .35    ADJ.SD     .72  SEPARATION  2.04  ITEM   RELIABILITY  .81|
+---------------------------------------------------------------------+
```

Figure 9.7 Typical output from MiniSteps analysis of test results (http://www.winsteps.com/ministep.htm)

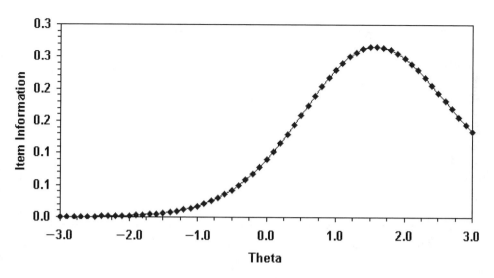

IIF Plot for Item 1

Figure 9.8 Item information function (IIF) for 3PL model (output from WinSteps analysis of test results, http://www.winsteps.com/ministep.htm)

Why spend so much effort on determining item parameters? IRT allows valid and reliable high stakes assessments to be presented to students, and also allows different items to be presented to different students, yet still allows a comparative judgement of their ability. It is possible to rank test takers on their IRT parameters, rather than the test score. The advantage of this is that the rank order is determined by both the difficulty of the question and the ability of the student. It takes into account which questions the marks were gained from and gives higher rankings for students who scored more marks from higher ranked items.

What information from the various IRT models is useful for the teacher? A psychometrician would normally perform a full analysis of a large-scale, high stakes assessment. The data reported for such tests can be quite complex, and would normally not be used routinely by classroom teachers. However, it is useful for teachers to understand a number of the item parameters, and their consequences. For an individual item, IRT can provide an item information function (IIF), and an example is shown in Figure 9.8. The individual points along the curve represent individual responses from students with a particular ability (theta, θ), and the shape of the curve indicates that a reasonably high-ability level is required to answer this item correctly, as the maximum is at approximately 1.5 along the ability axis. This item is useful for discriminating responses from high-achieving students, but contains little information about students with low ability, as shown by the relatively flat region from −1.0 to −3.0.

The test information function (TIF) is the sum of all the IIF curves, and provides an overview of the test responses, as illustrated in Figure 9.9, taken from a WinSteps output. This shows that information about low and high achievers can be obtained from the overall test, as useful data is contained in the region from 2.0 to −2.0 along the theta axis. This information is useful, as it gives a visual check on how much information is being obtained about students at the different ability levels.

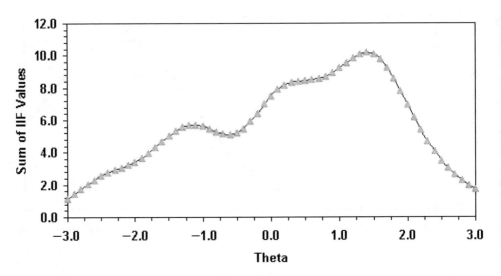

TIF Plot

Figure 9.9 Test information function (TIF) for 3PL model (output from WinSteps analysis of test results, http://www.winsteps.com/ministep.htm)

9.4 Rasch modelling

Rasch models are concerned with a theoretical construct of describing the relationship between the hypothetical student ability and the difficulty of a test item; it is based on predictions about what should happen in a test. In order to derive any benefit from the use of the Rasch model teachers and test administrators must transform this hypothetical model into the reality of a test that conforms to the model. The Rasch model uses the concept of odds and a student's ability is described in units called logits (log-odds unit). A logit is the natural log odds for a student with a particular ability (θ), responding correctly to an item of difficulty b, in the test (Eq 6). By using the logit it is possible to place the ability and difficulty functions on the same scale.

$$P(\theta) = \frac{e^{(\theta-b)}}{1 + e^{(\theta-b)}}$$ Eq 6

Mathematically, Rasch is identical to the basic 1PL IRT model (Eq 3) however there are some practical differences that make its use a more viable prospect for teachers. All the test items measuring a particular trait can be aligned on the same scale with their relative positions being compared to their difficulty. The visual presentation of the ability and difficulty data on the same scale is relatively easy for most teachers to interpret. Once this relationship is known, it is straightforward to use items from the test bank to design a test with an anticipated distribution of responses for students with known abilities. For dichotomous items (the response is scored as correct or incorrect) the Rasch model provides a good correlation between the ability and difficulty parameters and the use of the 'number-right' scoring method. Other unknown parameters do not have to be estimated, all the information from the actual test is used. For a typical test bank, items will generally have logit values between −4 and +4 with a mean of 0 (Burghof, 2001). It is generally found that items with logit values less than 0 tend to be easier, and those above 0 become progressively more difficult.

There are a number of commercial programs that perform Rasch analyses (http://www.rasch-analysis.com), and Figure 9.10 illustrates a typical output from RUMM2020 (Rasch Unidimensional Measurement Model, http://www.rummlab.com.au). The item characteristic

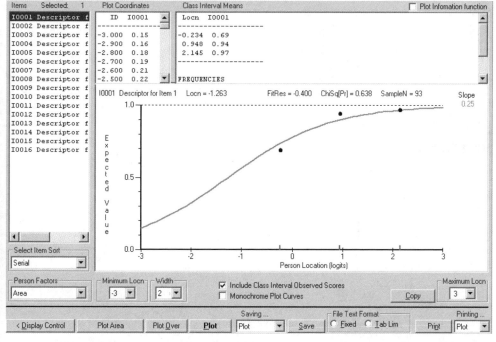

Figure 9.10 RUMM2020 Rasch output in the form of an item characteristic curve for Question 1 from a MCQ

curve (ICC) shown for Question 1 from a standard MCQ test represents the probability of a student answering the question correctly for each possible location of a student's ability on the person location continuum (Figure 9.10). This particular curve shows that Question 1 was very easy, as students with a low ability still had a high probability of answering it correctly.

The ICC for Question 16 from the same test is shown in Figure 9.11. This particular curve shows that Question 16 was more difficult than Question 1, as students with a low ability still had a low probability of answering it correctly. Only students with a high ability would have answered this question correctly.

This type of analysis is particularly useful when data from the use of the same items is accumulated over an extended period of time, since it allows a precise definition for the characteristics of an item. Teachers would then have confidence when assembling an assessment from a disparate group of items from a test bank that the test outcomes will align with its purpose.

A typical item map showing the person/item distributions with the items identified is shown in Figure 9.12. This type of presentation is very useful for the teacher, as it illustrates in a visual manner the correlation between how the students performed overall and if there was a reasonable overlap between the more difficult items and high-achieving students answering them correctly. We can see that there is not a good overlap between the distribution of the items on the right and the student marks on the left, and as the student marks extend higher on the presentation compared to the item locations, this would indicate a rather easy test. Students with average marks are answering the more difficult questions readily. The other useful piece of information from this presentation is that the easiest questions have the lowest number, (0001, etc.), indicating that the order of the questions in the test went approximately from easy to more difficult.

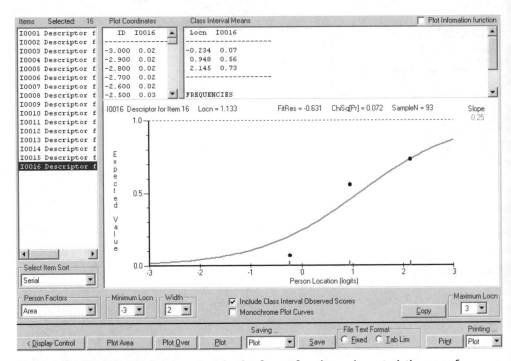

Figure 9.11 RUMM2020 Rasch output in the form of an item characteristic curve for Question 16 from a MCQ

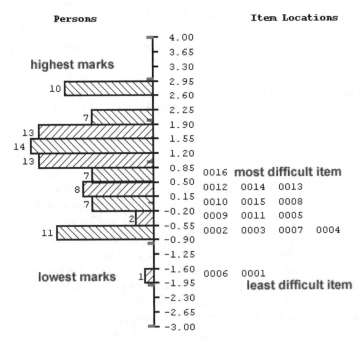

Figure 9.12 RUMM2020 Rasch output in the form of a person/item distribution from a MCQ

9.5 Estimating reliability

How does the teacher or test administrator know if the results from a particular assessment are reliable? It is rare that a teacher would insist that students repeat an identical assessment for a test-retest correlation measurement. One correlation that can be measured is that between different tests taken by the same cohort of students, however this method can be problematic if the different tests have items with varying difficulty levels, or if there is a substantial change in the trait being measured. For tests that are assembled using items from a large test bank, it would be possible to administer multiple tests to the same students such that the different items presented were based on similar concepts. Similarly, a large test bank of similar items can be divided into two or three subtests, and administered to the same student cohort. The degree of correlation between students and scores for the subtests can be used to estimate reliability.

The most common measure of reliability for a single test involves correlations for internal consistency using either Cronbach's alpha, K-R20 or the spilt-half methodology (Cronbach, 2004). The most frequently reported internal consistency estimates are the K-R20 and Cronbach alpha, with the K-R20 method applicable only to test items that are scored dichotomously, whereas Cronbach's alpha can be used for internal correlations with items that are scored dichotomously or through the use of a weighting scheme. It is appropriate to use Cronbach's alpha for norm-referenced assessments, but not for criterion-referenced assessments. The data illustrated in Figure 9.1 shows a Cronbach alpha value of 0.88, which would indicate good internal reliability.

The standard error of measurement (*SEM*) may also be used to assess reliability since it attempts to define the possible difference between the theoretical true score and the actual score obtained (McAlpine, 2002c). *SEM* uses the standard deviation and the estimated reliability for the assessment (Eq 7). For individual scores that are within the range of ± 1 *SEM* units, there is a 68 per cent confidence limit that the actual score reflects the true score, and for individual scores within ± 2 *SEM* units there is a 95 per cent confidence limit.

$$SEM = SD\sqrt{1-r} \hspace{4cm} \text{Eq 7}$$

where *SD* is the standard deviation and *r* is the estimated reliability

9.6 Evaluation of test banks

The evaluation of the overall assessment includes an analysis of the content coverage and balance, the determination of item and person parameters using classical test theory, or item response theory, or the Rasch model, as well as the distribution of items and marks based on one of the pedagogical taxonomies (Zakrzewski et al., 2000). The reporting of data from a statistical analysis of all high stakes assessment should be a mandatory component of assessment reporting, and could be incorporated into good practice guidelines at the local institutional level.

Wang (2004) has reported 12 methods (Table 9.1) that are commonly used to evaluate the performance of test banks used for high stakes assessment. These methods are based on three principles of functionality (what information is obtained?), e-assessment relevance (is the method appropriate to the online environment?) and comparability (can the evaluation of one test bank be compared to another test bank?).

When items are used from a test bank an important consideration, especially for adaptive tests, is the exposure rate for a particular item. If a particular item is used frequently, then students will become familiar with the question, and the validity associated with its use will be diminished. Many of the software applications used to construct adaptive tests allow estimated item exposure rates to be calculated through simulation runs of a hypothetical pool. However, it is still necessary to analyse the actual exposure rates for each item from a test bank, and to determine if the validity of particular items is being compromised. This corresponds to Method 6 described in Table 9.1.

Table 9.1 Methods used to evaluate test banks used for high stakes assessment (Wang, 2004)

Method	Description of method
1	Correlations between measures
2	Pool composition characteristics: item parameters and item distribution across content areas and item types
3	Selected demographics of the examinees
4	Distribution of reported scores
5	Conditional standard errors of measurement and pool reliability estimate
6	Distribution of exposure rates from simulation and observed data
7	Model data fit (difference between an item's expected proportion correct and observed proportion correct)
8	Constraint summary of simulation and observed data
9	Distribution of reported scores for gender and ethnic/racial subgroups.
10	Distribution of section times (in minutes) for gender and ethnic/racial subgroups
11	Distribution of number of items answered for gender and ethnic/racial subgroups
12	Distribution of number of items answered for score level subgroups

One important component of evaluation is concerned with the number of items a student does not respond to because of a lack of time. Did the student respond to all items after considering the item properly, or did they run out of time and guess the response? Method 7 in Table 9.1 is concerned with the type of person and item fit analysis discussed in Chapter 9.4, and allows inferences to be drawn about the actual results compared to the expected results. This type of inference will be more reliable for large-scale standardized tests involving many thousands of participants, than for small-scale tests. For e-assessments it is possible to record how long a student took to respond to a question after it was presented (for one-at-a-time questions, rather than an all-questions-at-once format).

Large-scale, standardized tests undergo extensive psychometric analysis and scrutiny, but for most teachers who prepare classroom tests this is not normally the case. There is still a need to provide a relatively simple way for classroom teachers to be able to use psychometric tools to analyse assessments, but in a convenient and time-efficient manner. The majority of tools described in this chapter are still the domain of professional psychometricians.

10 Standards, specifications and guidelines

10.1 Assessment standards

When assessment standards are discussed by teachers, should they be concerned with the relative or absolute measure of quality against a specified benchmark? Are they also referring to the assessment items themselves and their relationship to the learning objectives for the course or their suitability for a particular group of students? Should we be including the conditions under which the assessment is undertaken, and how it is marked, as well as how it is reported? In practice, each of these issues is relevant to assessment standards, as are the perceptions of the wider community in which the assessments and the reporting of results take place.

10.1.1 National standards

Assessment standards can provide evidence with which to judge the quality of assessment items and practices. Assessment standards are generally guides to the acceptability of particular uses of the assessment. Quality assurance or accrediting agencies for higher education exist in most countries and the majority have explicit or implicit statements on standards of acceptability for assessment practices. The Quality Assurance Agency (QAA) for Higher Education in the UK states that 'We safeguard and help to improve the academic standards and quality of higher education in the UK' (http://www.qaa.ac.uk).

The QAA publishes a code of practice on assessment as one of a series of codes for the assurance of academic quality and standards in higher education (QAA Assessment, 2000). The Australian Universities Quality Agency (AUQA) does not issue codes of practice, but does publish a good practice database promoting exemplars for higher education from the various audits of institutions (http://www.auqa.edu.au). The Association of Universities and Colleges of Canada (AUCC) publishes its principles for institutional quality assurance in Canadian higher education (http://www.aucc.ca/qa/index_e.html) and the Higher Education Quality Committee (HEQC) from South Africa is developing a quality assurance framework and criteria based on the principle of fitness for purpose and a framework that allows differentiation and diversity (http://www.che.ac.za/heqc/heqc.php).

These national standards are not specifically for e-assessments, they apply to all forms of assessment. The British Standards Institute (BSI) published 'BSI7988: a code of practice for the use of information technology in the delivery of assessment' in April 2002 (http://www.bsi-global.com). The standard outlines the minimum requirements in terms of standards for educational institutions and training organizations undertaking computer-based assessments. The Scottish Qualifications Authority (SQA) has produced guidelines specific to e-assessments in further education (SQA, 2003). These are general guidelines, tips and suggestions for good practice and still allow a significant variation in the actual manner in which e-assessments are undertaken.

10.1.2 Professional association standards and guidelines

Professional bodies in most countries also publish documents relating to assessment standards in higher education. In South Africa the HEQC publishes resources on improving teaching and learning, including good practice guidelines on assessment (http://www.che.ac.za/documents/d000087/index.php). The Australian Universities Teaching Committee (AUTC) commissioned a set of guidelines for assessment in higher education (James et al., 2002) and practical examples and resources, including tips for teachers. The recently formed Carrick Institute for Learning and Teaching in Higher Education in Australia has commissioned a number of studies of assessment practices and the development of good practice guidelines in specific disciplines (http://www. carrickinstitute.edu.au). The subject networks of the HEA in the UK publish discipline specific examples and guidelines for assessment practices, and the HEA itself has a number of very useful documents on how to use diagnostic and formative assessment to improve student learning as well as recommended benchmarking practices in assessment (http://www.heacademy.ac.uk).

Many institutions and organizations have published good practice guides for individual teachers and course coordinators to use for the improvement of their assessment activities. A typical example is that available from the HEA Bioscience network in the form of an audit tool that assists in the review of assessment practices (Bioscience, 2005). The document does not propose explicit standards, but is developmental in nature, encouraging teachers to identify areas for improvement and could be used as a benchmarking framework if external appraisal of the completed audit tool is sought. Another useful HEA document is that produced by the Managing Effective Student Assessment (MESA) benchmarking club (MESA, 2005). This document provides a practical tool and case studies on managing assessment at a higher education institution. The HEA also makes available a series of assessment guides for senior managers, heads of departments, lecturers and students (http://www.heacademy.ac.uk/Assessmentoflearning.htm).

The International Test Commission (ITC) has published guidelines on computer-based and online testing (Bartam *et al.*, 2005). The guidelines cover the following items:

1. Give due regard to technological issues in Computer-Based Testing (CBT):
   - Give consideration to hardware and software requirements
   - Take account of the robustness of the CBT/Internet test
   - Consider human factor issues in the presentation of material via computer or the Internet
   - Consider reasonable adjustments to the technical features of the test for candidates with disabilities
   - Provide help, information and practice items within the CBT/Internet test
2. Attend to quality issues in CBT and Internet testing:
   - Ensure knowledge, competence and appropriate use of CBT/Internet testing
   - Consider the psychometric qualities of the CBT/Internet test
   - Where the CBT/Internet test has been developed from a paper and pencil version, ensure that there is evidence of equivalence
   - Score and analyse CBT/Internet testing results accurately
   - Interpret results appropriately and provide appropriate feedback
   - Consider equality of access for all groups
3. Provide appropriate levels of control over CBT and Internet testing:
   - Detail the level of control over the test conditions
   - Detail the appropriate control over the supervision of the testing
   - Give due consideration to controlling prior practice and item exposure
   - Give consideration to control over test taker's authenticity and possible cheating
4. Make appropriate provision for security and safeguarding privacy in CBT and Internet testing:
   - Take account of the security of test materials
   - Consider the security of test taker's data transferred over the Internet
   - Maintain the confidentiality of test-taker's results

The Association of Test Publishers (ATP) in the USA has published guidelines for computer-based testing (ATP, 2002). The ATP guidelines are not a set of explicit instructions or standards, they are intended to foster good practice and cover many of the generally accepted criteria for quality assessments, including aligning assessment items and expected responses with the stated learning outcomes for a course and taking into account the computer literacy levels of the students.

The British Psychological Society has also published specific guidelines around the four activities for the generation, delivery, scoring and storage of e-assessments (BPS, 2002). The guidelines are built on the following principles:

Principle 1	That, as with all psychological assessments, users should be made aware of what constitutes best practice in computer-based assessment (CBA) so that they can make informed evaluations and choices between CBA systems offered to them.
Principle 2	That CBAs should be supported by clear documentation of the rationale behind the assessment and the chosen mode of delivery, appropriateness and exclusions for use and research evidence supporting validity and fairness.
Principle 3	Requirements for administration of the CBA should be clearly documented and should include the knowledge, understanding and skills required for competent administration.
Principle 4	The knowledge, understanding and skills required for interpretation of CBA information and for the provision of such information to a third party should also be clearly stated.

10.1.3 Identifying standards

Assessment standards will inevitably be contextually based, and the purpose of benchmarking is to make some form of comparison between the criteria used to articulate the standards and the manner in which they are applied in a particular context. For standardized assessments, acceptable student performance levels may be determined through the setting of cut points. Students whose performance exceeds a cut point are presumed to have exhibited adequate knowledge or capability and those below the cut point are deemed to be deficient in the required knowledge or capability. The most common method for determining this cut point is to use the Angoff approach (Angoff, 1971), or one of the various modifications to this method (Brandon, 2004). The general class of Angoff procedures provides:

- a framework for describing the expected standard
- a method for estimating the probability that a student will respond correctly to each item in the test at the required level
- a method for summing the item estimates for each assessor
- a method for averaging the scores from assessors that results in the cut point.

An alternative methodology to that based on the traditional Angoff approach is the bookmark method that uses an approach based on item response theory (Beretvas, 2004). In the bookmark method the order of item difficulty, from least difficult to most difficult, is used, but not the number of correct responses to the items. Each assessor places a bookmark in the difficulty order series at a point that is representative of where a student deemed to have met the acceptable minimum standard would likely answer the items correctly, to where they would likely answer the items incorrectly.

The gradual move from traditional forms of assessment, such as end of year examinations and written essays, to more non-traditional forms of assessment, such as e-assessment, has caused a reappraisal of the issues surrounding quality and standards in assessment (Boyle *et al.*, 2003, p. 77). In general terms, for e-assessment considerable effort must be expended during the development stages of the process, and less effort in the physical marking process, whereas for traditional assessment methods the most time-consuming phase is that associated with the marking. For the traditional assessment method standards were associated with an appropriate level for the assessment and consistency in marking, as well as issues around double marking, moderation and external examiners. For e-assessment these issues are still important but the individual question items are subject to more scrutiny. The processes associated with the delivery of e-assessment is also subject to more attention, compared to traditional forms of assessment, as technical issues may influence the ability of students to respond to an item, or even successfully complete the assessment itself. As noted by Boyle *et al.* (2003), 'a poor assessment, delivered appropriately, would conform to BS 7988.' It is important that the psychometric properties of question items be recorded and available for teachers who are considering their use. Thus it is relevant that teachers are aware of the implications of using process standards to validate assessments; process standards are important at the institutional level and teachers will interact more often with them through the various policies and guidelines relevant to their particular institution. However, individual teachers will need to engage with the methodologies associated with validation and reliability of the assessment items they use in their individual assessments (more details are available in Chapter 9).

Boyle *et al.* (2003) have also proposed a set of recommendations that should be followed if the use e-assessment items are to develop characteristics of high quality:

- mandatory training and certification of staff involved in CBA production, preferably via nationally recognized qualifications
- expert panels to review assessments, membership thereof to include assessment development experts
- piloting of new items in assessments (with scores not contributing to grades)
- full evaluation of CBA within institutions, using quantitative and qualitative approaches as appropriate
- subject networks (e.g. LTSN) to discuss methods and arrangements for sharing validated items within national assessment banks
- wider dissemination of QA (quality assurance) procedures within the CBA community.

10.2 Content standards, specifications and guidelines

A new industry has emerged in the area of standards and interoperability with the growth of numerous software providers and the realization that in order to foster a sustainable approach to the use of computers and the web in commercial, financial and educational activity, efficiency and building upon the work of others is essential. This has led to a plethora of acronyms for standards and specifications that are now associated with learning and assessment objects, such as:

AICC (Aviation Industry (Computer-Based Training) Committee; http://www.aicc.org)
CMI (Computer Managed Instruction; http://ltsc.ieee.org/wg11/)
IEEE (Institute of Electrical and Electronics Engineers; http://www.ieee.org)
IMS (Instructional Management System; http://www.imsglobal.org)
LOM (Learning Object Metadata; http://ltsc.ieee.org/wg12)
LTSC (IEEE Learning Technology Standards Committee; http://ieeeltsc.org)
SCORM (Sharable Courseware Object Reference Model; http://www.adlnet.org)

The underlying purpose of this considerable effort is to provide an agreed set of technical specifications for learning and assessment objects so that users can be confident that their content can be moved from one particular software application, either from a commercial vendor or an open-source system, to another system and still have it behave in a predictable manner.

The Advanced Distributed Learning (ADL) Initiative is funded by the Department of Defense in the USA and develops the SCORM specifications (http://www.adlnet.org). SCORM is a set of specifications that have been adapted from various sources so that online content may be developed in a manner that allows interoperability, accessibility and reusability. SCORM 2004 has specifications for a 'Content Aggregation Model' and a 'Run-Time Environment' so that items may be tested in real online systems. SCORM is not an enforceable standard; vendors and content

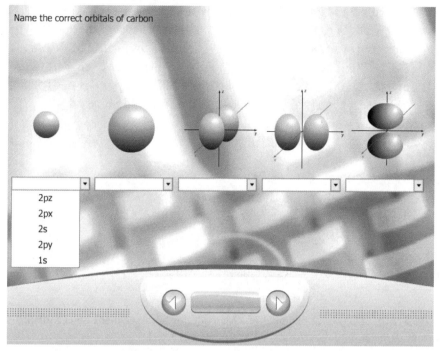

Name the correct orbitals of carbon

2pz
2px
2s
2py
1s

Figure 10.1 Example of e-assessment delivered using a Flash[R] Player plugin (http://www2.warwick.ac.uk/elearning/aboutus/steve/flash/questionwriter)

creators use the SCORM specifications because of demands from clients who wish to ensure that the materials they purchase or incorporate into their current learning or assessment applications can be transferred to another system at some time in the future.

Figures 10.1 and 10.2 show an example of content that has been developed so as to comply with the SCORM specifications. Figure 10.1 shows an assessment item from Steve Carpenter from the University of Warwick that was delivered using a Flash® Player plugin for a standard web browser (http://www2.warwick.ac.uk/elearning/aboutus/steve/flash/questionwriter). The files used to deliver the assessment include Shockwave, Flash, Javascript, XSD, XML and HTML. Figure 10.2 shows part of the XML file that uses the ADL SCORM 1.2 specifications. Teachers do not have to be overly concerned with the details of these specifications, unless they wish to develop and distribute original content. The details within the specifications are of primary interest to software developers, commercial content creators and publishers. Many of the open-source and commercial learning management and assessment systems are SCORM compliant and teachers should check with the vendor or distributor specific details for particular applications. There are also several applications that are available that assist developers generate the required XML files associated with SCORM compliance, including commercial products from the Macromedia suite (http://www.adobe.com/devnet/authorware/articles/compliant_files_print.html), Canvas Learning (http://www.the-can.com), Questionmark™ Perception™ (http://www.questionmark.com); and open-source applications such as ATutor (http://www.atutor.ca) and RELOAD (http://www.reload.ac.uk). These examples are representative and are not an exhaustive list; teachers should consult documentation accompanying specific products for conformance with SCORM specifications.

```
<manifest identifier="CQFaceism" version="1.0" xmlns="http://
www.imsproject.org/xsd/imscp_rootv1p1p2" xmlns:adlcp="http://
www.adlnet.org/xsd/adlcp_rootv1p2" xmlns:xsi="http://www.
w3.org/2001/XMLSchema-instance" xsi:schemaLocation="http://
www.imsproject.org/xsd/imscp_rootv1p1p2 imscp_rootv1p1p2.xsd
http://www.imsglobal.org/xsd/imsmd_rootv1p2p1 imsmd_
rootv1p2p1.xsd
http://www.adlnet.org/xsd/adlcp_rootv1p2 adlcp_rootv1p2.xsd">
<metadata>
<schema>ADL SCORM</schema>
<schemaversion>1.2</schemaversion>
<lom xmlns="http://www.imsglobal.org/xsd/imsmd_rootv1p2p1">
<general>
<title>
<langstring>Chemistry Assessment</langstring>
</title>
```

Figure 10.2 ADL SCORM 1.2 example of XML code for an assessment object (http://www2. warwick.ac.uk/elearning/aboutus/steve/flash/questionwriter)

10.2.1 Assessment content metadata

Although there are numerous standards and specifications written for learning objects, there are fewer written specifically for assessments. The IMS QTI specifications (http://www.imsglobal. org/question) are discussed in more detail in Chapter 10.4, however it is noted here that they are quite complex and the specific details are usually beyond the scope of the assessment activities of classroom teachers. They have been written with commercial vendors and dedicated assessment creators in mind. The specifications cover attributes for most of the question types currently used in e-assessments, and the latest IMS QTI specifications contain new qtiMetadata tags and a new vocabulary for the exchange of item and distracter statistics. Metadata is data about data; it is information that allows a person or a program to find content based on a search using the metadata tags. IMS QTI incorporates the passing score, the minimum score and the mastery score. The MINE SCORM Authoring Tool allows metadata generation using an inbuilt wizard so that metadata tags related to cognition level, discrimination, instructional sensitivity and difficulty can be incorporated into assessment sequences (http://www.mine.tku.edu.tw).

The Dublin Core Metadata Initiative (DCMI, http://dublincore.org) and the IEEE LOM standard (LOM, 2002) do not themselves address the requirements of those who wish to develop or use e-assessment content. The latest version of the TOIA/COLA assessment metadata schema does include metadata elements for e-assessment objects and processes (Sclater *et al.*, 2005).

10.3 Process standards, specifications and guidelines

The BSI 7988 publication introduces guidelines and minimum requirements for institutions that use computers to deliver assessments and mandates the establishment of good practices for all aspects of the assessment process (http://www.bsi-global.com). The BSI standards are particularly useful for educational institutions since they serve as a benchmarked framework for designing an overall assessment plan; teachers and students can then have confidence in a system that achieves consistency by following a well-articulated plan. BSI 7988 covers 17 sections of e-assessment activity, the first four relating to generic issues and the remaining one to specific components of the e-assessment framework:

An interesting paper by Kleeman *et al.* (2002) describes how e-assessments delivered through the commercial application Questionmark Perception™ can comply with BSI 7988. The software itself does not ensure compliance; rather it is the processes that are established around the use of the software that aid with compliance. These processes include procedural and technical issues and staff development activities to ensure an understanding of how standards can be translated into consistent actions. There are practical issues that must be considered at the local context and

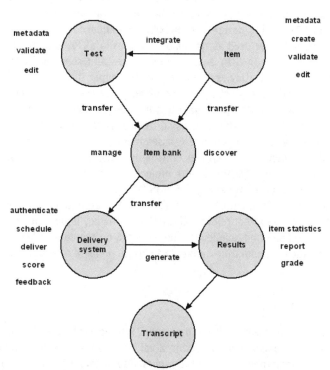

Figure 10.3 ELF description of e-assessment components (adapted from http://www.frema.ecs.soton.ac.uk/overview)

various institutions will likely deal with these differently, but with the overall aim of ensuring compliance at the local level.

FREMA is the Framework Reference Model for Assessment project and attempts to define how the components of assessment, namely the services associated with the construction, delivery and recording of e-assessments, interact in a webservice environment (http://www.frema.ecs. soton.ac.uk). These components have been described by ELF (e-Learning Framework), as illustrated in Figure 10.3. The purpose of ELF is to describe a framework where the various services reference an open specification or standard so that the integration of commercial, institutional and open source components is possible.

It is useful to view the Noun Map and the Verb Map developed in consultation with the e-assessment community as part of the FREMA project (Millard et al.; 2005). The Noun Map describes the resources, along with the stakeholders and roles that might be associated with the use of those resources. The Verb Map covers the activities associated with e-assessment; it attempts to describe what people do in e-assessment, independent of the particular resources that are being used. FREMA is not a standard, but rather an attempt to view how all the components of e-assessment fit together in the real world. It is very beneficial for teachers to be able to view a framework that attempts to describe in relatively simple ways how all the complex issues, standards, specifications, roles and resources fit together. One of the practical issues faced with developing and deploying an e-assessment is that it is relatively straightforward, although very time-consuming, to develop technical specifications. However it is implementation and process issues that are hindering a more widespread adoption of e-assessment in higher and further education. FREMA is working towards a common understanding of how to overcome some of these process problems by concentrating on a Service Oriented Architecture (SOA).

SOA attempts to provide a framework whereby different software systems will work together to produce a result that is efficient and beneficial for the user. SOA is quite different from the dominant paradigm in programming languages today, namely that of object oriented programming, where data and processing are bound together very tightly. Teachers need not be too concerned with these details, except to be aware that some software systems, and the processes they enact, are being designed to maximize modularization and interoperability, and some are being designed to be used as standalone entities in a closed system.

A useful summary paper on SOA e-assessment issues and some practical demonstrations of its application is available (Davies et al., 2005). The paper discusses the Remote Question Protocol (RQP) framework as a practical means of remotely assessing mathematical questions delivered as part of an assessment (http://mantis.york.ac.uk/moodle). A number of projects in the UK have demonstrated the applicability of using item banks to remotely deliver e-assessments through both commercial and open-source e-assessment systems, including ASSIS (Sherratt et al., 2005), APIS (http://www.jisc.ac.uk/index.cfm?name=apis) and SPAID (http://www.jisc.ac.uk/index.cfm?name=toolkit_strath1). The SPAID project showed how items could be packaged, stored and retrieved from an item bank, using IMS QTI specifications. An important component of the project was the development of a customizable metadata tagger that could use the items XML code to automatically extract relevant data. One of the key issues with the use of any item bank is the ability to readily find objects of interest based on searches of key metadata, so tools that assist in automatically populating metadata fields is crucial to a sustainable and usable item bank.

10.4 Interoperability

What is interoperability and why is it so important? Interoperability is the ability of a system, content or activity to be exchanged or used in a variety of situations with the confidence that it will function in a predictable manner. Interoperability allows efficient use of resources and avoids the necessity to design a system, content or activity de novo for every context. How interoperability is achieved is not the primary concern of teachers, but it is essential for teachers to be aware of whether their current e-assessment system, content or activities can be used in a variety of contexts.

Teachers should be generally aware of the issues surrounding interoperability and the considerable efforts that are being made around the world to define the standards and specifications that will allow systems, content or activities to be exchanged seamlessly. This situation of complete exchangeability has not been achieved to date.

The BSI has issued a code of practice for maximizing interoperability between systems in learning, education and training, namely BS 8419-1 and BS 8419-2 (http://www.bsi-global.com). The interoperability recommendations acknowledge that the application profiles for implementing the codes will vary with local context, but provides a framework for defining acceptable standards for these application profiles. BS 8419-1 provides a framework for the use of Dublin Core Metadata and the IEEE LOM (discussed above); it covers issues that are relevant to software designers and content creators on the use of XML DTD, XML schemas, and RDF. As for BS 7988, BS 8419-1 does not ensure quality of the content within the system, and a poor system, content or activity may still meet the interoperability requirements. BS 8419-2 provides recommendations on the mapping between different vocabularies (nomenclatures) used in educational software, content or activities. An example of an application profile would be the TOIA/COLA Assessment Metadata Application Profile as part of the development of assessment item banks in the UK (COLA, 2003). It was produced as part of the COLA project, an initiative to develop item and assessment banks for further education. The latest version of the IMS QTI specification includes a new usage data class that will be beneficial for the incorporation of items into interoperable item banks.

An important website for maintaining a current understanding of interoperability issues is CETIS, the Centre for Educational Technology Interoperability Standards (http://www.cetis.ac.uk). Sclater *et al.* (2002) have written an excellent summary for teachers on IMS QTI v1 specifications. It covers the basic concepts of the complex documentation and explains what teachers should be aware of, without becoming too technical. The XML elements of the specifications are placed in context; so is the need for appropriate XML editors so that content creators are not writing the required XML code themselves, but rather they are building the e-assessment items in an appropriate application and then packaging the content in a format that generates the required XML code automatically. It is a consequence of application and content development that assessment items will be constructed in a variety of formats, so the IMS QTI specifications are about seamless importing from and exporting to other systems.

The recent release of the open-source IMS Learning Design application CopperCore v3.0 allows the integration of a number of services relevant to an e-assessment environment (http://coppercore.sourceforge.net). CopperCore includes a runtime application for the APIS QTI player, which means that e-assessment content conforming to the latest IMS QTI v2 specifications can be delivered within the same content package as those created with IMS Learning Designs. APIS has been developed as an open-source engine to provide a player for assessment items that are constructed to IMS QTI v2 specifications (http://sourceforge.net/projects/apis). Why should this be of interest to teachers? Potentially, it allows a much tighter integration of learning and assessment content and activities. The ability to have an integrated environment for learning and assessment will benefit students and allow teachers to incorporate more sophisticated implementations of diagnostic and formative assessments that will link seamlessly with learning content and outcomes-based design principles. The CopperCore webplayer is also available as a separate package, which means that alternative players that integrate other services may be used.

RELOAD (Reusable eLearning Object Author and Delivery) provides tools for software and content developers such as an open-source Content Package and Metadata Editor, a SCORM Player and a Learning Design Editor and Player based on ADL SCORM and IMS specifications (http://www.reload.ac.uk). The RELOAD tools are used to package content that may be used in a variety of learning management or assessment systems, so is a practical tool to demonstrate the

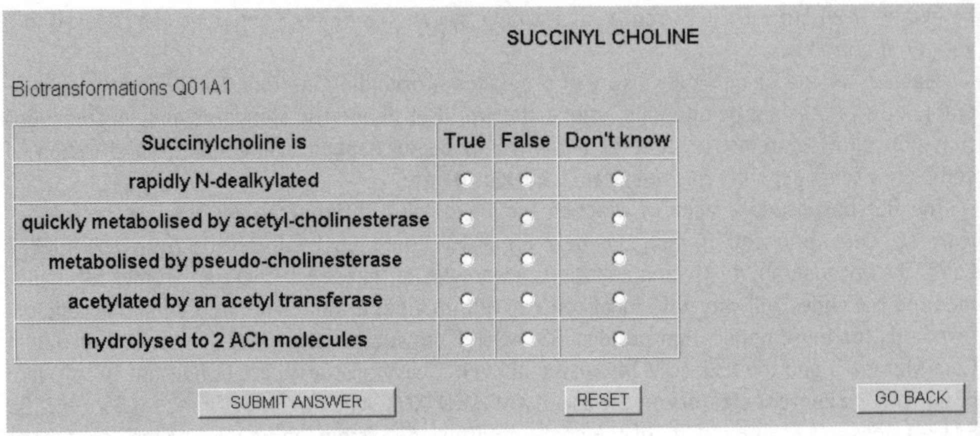

SUCCINYL CHOLINE

Biotransformations Q01A1

Succinylcholine is	True	False	Don't know
rapidly N-dealkylated	○	○	○
quickly metabolised by acetyl-cholinesterase	○	○	○
metabolised by pseudo-cholinesterase	○	○	○
acetylated by an acetyl transferase	○	○	○
hydrolysed to 2 ACh molecules	○	○	○

SUBMIT ANSWER		RESET		GO BACK

Figure 10.4 Example of an IMS QTI item (http://qtitools.caret.cam.ac.uk/qtiv2/examples/V2V1examples.html)

benefits of interoperability and the ability to package content that will be delivered successfully in a number of alternate systems. WELOAD is a web-based version of the RELOAD Editor and is available from http://weload.lernnetz.de.

The IMS QTI v2 specifications have enabled content creators to build e-assessment items that are interoperable, reusable and suitable for incorporation into test banks (http://www.imsglobal.org/question/index.html). The metadata tags have been developed so that the quality of individual items can be monitored and items can now be incorporated into learning designs and simple sequencing events. An example of a QTI item is shown in Figure 10.4, and a portion of the XML file describing the item is shown in Figure 10.5.

The IMS QTI v2 specification has described 15 types of interactions that may occur in an e-assessment, similar to those outlined in Chapter 3 (http://www.imsglobal.org/question/qti_v2p0/imsqti_mdudv2p0.html). It is useful for teachers to review the different question types,

```
- <assessmentItem xmlns="http://www.imsglobal.org/xsd/imsqti_item_v2p0"
    xmlns:xsi="http://www.w3.org/2001/XMLSchema-instance"
    xsi:schemaLocation="http://www.imsglobal.org/xsd/imsqti_item_v2p0 imsqti_item_v2p0.xsd"
    identifier="Succgrp" title="Succinyl Choline" adaptive="false" timeDependent="false">
  - <responseDeclaration identifier="RESPONSE" cardinality="multiple" baseType="pair">
    - <mapping defaultValue="0">
        <mapEntry mapKey="B T" mappedValue="1" />
        <mapEntry mapKey="B F" mappedValue="-0.5" />
        <mapEntry mapKey="A T" mappedValue="-0.5" />
        <mapEntry mapKey="A F" mappedValue="1" />
        <mapEntry mapKey="C T" mappedValue="-0.5" />
        <mapEntry mapKey="C F" mappedValue="1" />
        <mapEntry mapKey="D T" mappedValue="-0.5" />
        <mapEntry mapKey="D F" mappedValue="1" />
        <mapEntry mapKey="E T" mappedValue="-0.5" />
        <mapEntry mapKey="E F" mappedValue="1" />
      </mapping>
    </responseDeclaration>
    <outcomeDeclaration identifier="FEEDBACK" cardinality="multiple" baseType="identifier" />
  - <outcomeDeclaration identifier="SCORE" cardinality="single" baseType="float">
    - <defaultValue>
        <value>0</value>
      </defaultValue>
    </outcomeDeclaration>
  - <itemBody label="Succgrp">
```

Figure 10.5 Example of portion of XML code for IMS QTI item (http://qtitools.caret.cam.ac.uk/qtiv2/examples/v2v1examples.html)

because it encourages a more diverse approach to setting e-assessment items. When teachers use only the traditional e-assessment formats such as MCQs, true/false and short text entry items they often restrict the type of concepts that need to be assessed in a course. An awareness of the full range of question types may assist teachers in designing items suitable for testing multistructural or relational concepts.

11 Security issues

11.1 Security

11.1.1 Authentication of appropriate access

The Joint Information Systems Committee (JISC, http://www.jisc.ac.uk) has recommended Shibboleth (http://shibboleth.internet2.edu) for use in higher and further educational institutions for controlling authentication and access to online resources and e-assessments. Shibboleth is an example of *middleware*, a term used to describe either software or a process that connects users with particular resources they require. Middleware is most often a computer application that allows other pieces of software to communicate with each other, and so pass information from one application for use in another. The ability to pass on appropriate authentication access is critical for high stakes summative e-assessments, and robust systems and procedures are required.

Most educational institutions will have an enterprise authentication system that uses services such as LDAP (Lightweight Directory Access Protocol) or Kerberos to control access to the computer network and various associated applications. Teachers and students do not usually have to be unduly concerned about these issues except to ensure that students have been allocated a user name and password so that they may participate in e-learning and undertake e-assessments.

11.1.2 Secure assessment environments and software

A number of the e-assessment systems presented earlier in Table 5.4 facilitate the construction of a secure environment for high stakes summative assessments. Questionmark Perception™ allows assessments to be accessed via the Internet, but Questionmark Secure will enable computers running Windows operating systems to deliver a secure version of a Questionmark assessment (http://www.questionmark.com). Questionmark Secure prevents students from printing the assessment or using the right-click feature on the computer mouse; opening new applications during the assessment is also prevented, as is saving or viewing the source code for web pages written in HTML. Respondus LockDown Browser® is another such application that allows a custom browser to be presented to students that locks the assessment environment within a WebCT™ or Blackboard™ presented quiz. Once again, students are prevented from printing, copying content or searching the web or the computer hard drive during an assessment (http://www.respondus. com). Figure 11.1 illustrates an example of an assessment delivered via the Respondus LockDown Browser®.

For medium and high stakes summative assessments that are invigilated, students can be required to furnish proof of their identity through photo identification, to access a computer terminal. The physical environment for the assessment can be made as secure as for the more familiar paper-based examinations. However, invigilators need to be aware of the array of portable network and telephony devices that students now have available to them that allow external access to non-authorized content and assistance.

The stake of the e-assessment will determine the extent of the security required and the appropriate delivery environment (Shepherd *et al.*, 2003). The higher the stake for the assessment, the more awareness teachers and invigilators will need of security issues and the more detailed the plans for emergency actions in cases of technical breakdowns within the assessment environment. Purpose built assessment centres provide controlled environments where consistency can be

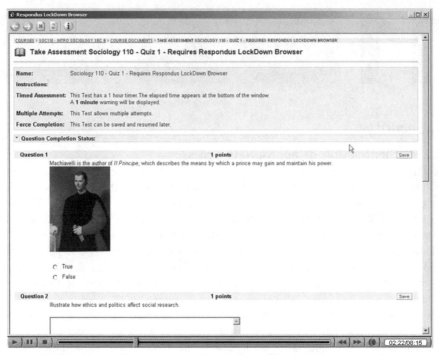

Figure 11.1 Respondus LockDown Browser® quiz (http://www.respondus.com)

maintained and adherence to protocols is relatively straightforward. Students can usually be confident that such an environment will be stable and provide a consistent experience over time. The assessment process in such environments is usually considered fair and valid. For high-stake assessments the environment can be monitored through the presence of a trained invigilator or proctor. Purpose built assessment centres will usually be designed so that they are quiet, free from external disturbances and have controlled temperature atmospheres. The computer terminals will be arranged so that students cannot see other screens, and will have secure environments where access to digital resources is restricted. Each terminal will be similar and items such as screen resolution, sound, keyboards, mouse, etc. will be consistent. Photo identification will normally be required and video surveillance may be present, as well as technical assistance.

Tertiary institutions often have computer suites that have some of these features, but can cause problems for both teachers and students. Some of the disadvantages of computer suites for high stakes e-assessments include:

■ terminals tend to be visible to a number of students
■ non-secure desktop environments mean students may access numerous resources during an assessment
■ mobile telephony devices can be used for non-authorized assistance.

Low and medium stakes assessments usually do not require elaborate, purpose-built environments. Diagnostic and formative assessments are designed to improve student learning, so only the students' learning suffers if they are dishonest.

Security for e-assessments can be increased by the use of encrypted communications through the use of Secure Sockets Layer (SSL), a protocol that allows the browser and web server to encrypt their communications. This means that anyone intercepting the communication will not be able to read it without the appropriate decryption code. Recent versions of the common web browsers support SSL, and by convention, URLs that require an SSL connection start with 'https' instead of 'http'. Another protocol for transmitting data securely over the web is Secure HTTP

(S-HTTP) which is designed to transmit individual messages securely, in contrast to SSL which transmits all information securely.

11.1.3 Security standards and guidelines

The International Organization for Standardization (http://www.iso.org) published ISO 9126 on 'Information Technology – Software Quality Characteristics and Sub-characteristics' in 1991. ISO 9126 covers expectations for the evaluation of computer software and covers six characteristics that are to be included in the evaluation: functionality, reliability, usability, efficiency, maintainability and portability. A new set of documents, ISO/IEC 25000:2005 'Software Engineering – Software product Quality Requirements and Evaluation (SQuaRE)' provides an update to ISO 9126 and also presents information on how to use the ISO/IEC 9126 and 14598 series in their previous form. Valenti *et al*. (2002) have examined e-assessment systems, as typically used in educational settings, in relation to the ISO 9126 requirements and highlighted some of the quality issues that should be addressed to ensure a valid and reliable assessment experience by students.

Kleeman *et al*. (2002) have described how e-assessments may be delivered to comply with BS 7988 standard using Questionmark Perception. The standard includes items on security and authentication; verification of students who may be at remote locations and guidelines on the provision of practice tests to familiarize students with the computer interface; mandatory breaks from the computer screen for e-assessments exceeding 1.5 hours, and the prevention of students viewing other screens, sending emails or accessing unauthorized websites. For assessments that exceed 1.5 hours, it may be inappropriate to allow students to leave the room, so assessments might have to be divided in sections, with different start times. BS 7988 recommends that the computer interface be restricted to only allow certain digital resources to be used. Some of the lock down features present in software security packages may cause problems with interactive e-assessments that require the use of third party applications during the assessment. Most secure software systems possess features that allow administrators to specify applications that may be used in a secure environment. The BS 7988 standard requires procedures to be in place in cases of network congestion or breakdown.

One of the key guiding principles contained in BS 7988 is that 'back-up facilities and fall-back procedures should be in place to minimize disruptions so that the candidate is not disadvantaged, especially in high stakes assessment.' BS 17799:2005 sections 10.4 and 10.5 also cover relevant guidelines on the integrity of the e-assessment software (http://www.bsi-global.com/ICT/Security/bs7799-1.xalter).

11.2 What to do when things go wrong?

Harwood (2005) has published an interesting paper on what happens when a high stakes e-assessment goes wrong. The particular hardware and software used for the assessment were not responsible for the problems, rather a combination of factors related to the configuration of the hardware and the processes used to organize the e-assessment. Many educational institutions would be in a similar situation, and as e-assessments become more prevalent it is a timely reminder for teachers and institutions to reflect on their risk management strategies for assessments. Server environments are often working at peak capacity in educational institutions, and e-assessments place an additional burden on these systems, especially if the number of concurrent users peaks at particular times of the year, and the load is much lower at other times. Student behaviour in an e-assessment is also an important factor, as students tend to expect an immediate response from the computer screen when a keystroke or mouse button is activated. The students' natural tendency when they receive no immediate response is to keep trying the keystroke or mouse button until something happens. This can further aggravate an overloaded server. Student results may not be recorded by a server if there is an overload, or the system crashes immediately after students have submitted their responses. The student response factor may be alleviated if formative e-assessment opportunities have been provided before summative e-assessments are delivered, and students can be informed that in the case of significant disruptions to summative assessments, their formative results may be used. This also has the advantage that formative assessments will be taken more seriously. However, formative assessments are used to improve learning, not to judge performance, so multiple formative opportunities should be provided, and a student's best performance used for any summative purposes. Alternative paper tests can also be made available in case hardware or network problems arise. This would only be suitable for some forms of assessment, but the teacher should reflect on the core objectives being tested, and anticipate how they could be assessed in alternative formats, since this may be required for students with disabilities in any case.

12 Accessibility Issues

12.1 Accessibility

12.1.1 Statutory requirements for accessibility

Many countries have laws covering the responsibilities of educational institutions when providing services to students with some form of disability. In the UK the Disability Discrimination Act 1995 covers general requirements related to appropriate accessibility and the reporting of how students with disabilities have been accommodated (http://www.opsi.gov.uk/acts/acts1995/1995050. htm). The Special Educational Needs and Disability Act (SENDA, 2001) introduces the legal right for disabled students not to be discriminated against in education and training. This includes all forms of assessment where students with a disability cannot be treated 'less favourably' than other students in relation to the disability. Educational institutions are required to take reasonable steps to prevent any disadvantage to the disabled student, which for assessment might include the provision of materials in an alternative format, provision of assistive technologies or the provision of an appropriate physical location. Educational institutions usually employ specialists to provide advice on what constitutes reasonable accommodation, and it is often a matter of the provision of an assessment in alternative format, or a longer time for the completion of the prescribed task, or the use of assistive technologies that allow students with a disability to successfully complete the assessment. Costs are often a factor in some forms of accommodation, and more expensive physical accommodation may have to be introduced over time, although a number of educational institutions could collaborate on the provision of expensive assistive technologies.

In the USA, state-wide mandatory testing of core skills is quite common, and various laws, such as 'The Improving America's Schools Act' (http://www.ed.gov/legislation/ESEA/index.html) and the 'Individuals with Disabilities Education Act Amendments' (http://www.ed.gov/policy/speced/guid/idea/idea2004.html) of 1997 reinforce the requirements that all students must be included in such tests, especially those with disabilities. These requirements were reinforced in the 'No Child Left Behind Act' of 2001, which requires that all students with disabilities participate in general assessments at the state and local level so as to maximize their access to the same general academic content standards as other students (http://www.ed.gov/policy/elsec/leg/esea02/index.html). Participation of students with a disability can be through the general assessment that is taken with or without accommodations, or through an alternate assessment. These laws set two competing priorities for states: assess students with disabilities on grade-level standards and make sure that all students with disabilities participate in state assessment programmes. Special accommodation for students with a disability is designed to remove unfair disadvantages from assessments, and teachers could reflect on whether the assessment process itself is restrictive, and whether the ability of students to respond to questions in an assessment is being primarily determined by the process or their cognitive abilities.

Table 12.1 summaries the various legal requirements for accessibility that impact on e-assessments from a range of nations.

12.1.2 Good practice guidelines

The IMS Guidelines for Developing Accessible Learning Applications (Barstow *et al.*, 2002) is an important document covering accessibility in the broader context, not just students with particular physical disabilities. It covers how e-learning and e-assessment may be made

Table 12.1 Summary of various legal requirements for accessibility related to e-assessments

United Kingdom	Disability Discrimination Act 1995	http://www.opsi.gov.uk/acts/acts1995/1995050.htm
	Special Educational Needs and Disability Act 1 September 2002	http://www.opsi.gov.uk/acts/acts2001/20010010.htm
United States	Improving America's Schools Act	http://www.ed.gov/legislation/ESEA/index.html
	Individuals with Disabilities Education Act Amendments 1997	http://www.ed.gov/policy/speced/guid/idea/idea2004.html
	No Child Left Behind Act 2001	http://www.ed.gov/policy/elsec/leg/esea02/index.html
Australia	Disability Discrimination Act (1992)	http://www.hreoc.gov.au/disability_rights/standards/www_3/www_3.html
	World Wide Web Access: Disability Discrimination Act Advisory Notes 2002	http://www.hreoc.gov.au/disability_rights/standards/www_3/www_3.html
Canada	Canadian Human Rights Act (1977)	http://laws.justice.gc.ca/en/H-6/141385.html
	Provincial and Territorial Human Rights Statutes (2005)	http://www.ldac-taac.ca/LDandtheLaw/ch03-1_Law-e.asp
	Right to Reasonable Accommodation for a Disability (2005)	http://www.ldac-taac.ca/LdandtheLaw/ch04_Law-e.asp
	Disability Standards for Education 2005	http://www.comlaw.gov.au/ComLaw/Legislation/LegislativeInstrument1.nsf/all/search/4B28EE956766891FCA256FCC0004EF81
South Africa	Electronic Communications and Transactions (ECT) Act 2002	http://www.acts.co.za/ect_act
United Nations	The Standard Rules on the Equalization of Opportunities for Persons with Disabilities (1993)	http://www.un.org/esa/socdev/enable/dissre00.htm
European Union	European Institute for Design and Disability (EIDD)	http://www.design-for-all.org
International	Introduction to Web Content Accessibility Guidelines (WCAG) 2.0 Working Draft Documents (2006)	http://www.w3.org/WAI/intro/wcag20.php
	IMS Guidelines for Developing Accessible Learning Applications (2002)	http://www.imsglobal.org/accessibility

accessible for everyone, anytime and in any location. The extensive documentation highlights the roles and responsibilities of the various stakeholders in e-education and the accessibility issues associated with synchronous and asynchronous communication and collaboration tools; interactive environments, such as simulations, role-plays and games; multimedia environments and e-assessments.

These IMS guidelines propose six principles that can be applied to all online participants who have some form of sensory or mobility disability:

- allow for a degree of customization that can be controlled by the user
- allow both auditory and visual access to content
- allow the use of assistive technologies and provide keyboard access for all functions
- provide appropriate context information
- use IMS and other relevant specifications and standards
- use XML where possible.

These principles can be enacted by allowing users to have some control over the presentation variables, including font style, colour and size; the cursor size and style; the size of images and video; the screen layout and colours; as well as the timing of events and keyboard settings. By including accessibility in the initial stages of the design of an e-assessment, teachers can minimize later costs and work that might be required to alter materials to meet specific guidelines.

The IMS guidelines emphasize that a valid assessment, from the perspective of a student with disabilities, is one where the score obtained reflects how well the stated learning objectives have been met and not one that reflects how well a student can cope with the processes used for the assessment. Appropriate accommodation of disabilities should reduce this threat to validity. Text to speech and read-aloud assistive technologies may be used for some students, when the purpose of the assessment allows multiple forms of representation of the questions.

Constructing assessments using an evidence-centred design focus will assist all students, and improve the validity and reliability of the assessment (Almond et al., 2002). This process should assist teachers determine the knowledge, skills, and capabilities that are to be tested during the assessment, and determine the extent to which multiple representations are possible with the maintenance of appropriate reliability and validity. Evidence-centred design encourages teachers to reflect on the relationship between student scores and what they actually mean in terms of the skills acquired and knowledge assimilated.

Students with some form of unrecognized disability may underachieve in an assessment, not because they lack the required skills or capabilities, but because their disability has not been recognized or accommodated. It is recognized, however, that students also have a responsibility to bring to the teacher's attention any specific disability that they know will adversely affect their performance, and which can be readily accommodated. Teachers and test designers can also assist by informing students that multiple representations of assessment items and responses can be made available. Assessments should be designed to provide opportunities for students to demonstrate what they can do, rather than what they cannot do. When a particularly appropriate test design has been constructed and found to be effective, it is often useful to use it as a template. This also applies to particular digital objects that may be reused in different presentation formats, for example as a visual display, or as synthesized speech or Braille. Preparing digital content in alternative formats allows a more efficient reuse of content, thus reducing the overall costs of accessibility compliance.

The concept of a Universal Design for Learning (UDL) proposes that accessibility is a broad issue of accommodating all learning styles, including a variety of abilities in addition to disabilities. The UDL principles of providing multiple, flexible methods of presentation, engagement and expression are all compatible with improving accessibility (Rose et al., 2002). The UDL principles attempt to move the focus away from accommodating a disability, where the disability is perceived as a negative attribute, to acknowledging that all students learn and express themselves in different, but equally valid ways.

The UDL framework proposes that good learning and assessment designs minimize the barriers for students with differing styles and assistive technologies may be used to provide multiple representations of content in the context of ongoing assessment. For example, e-assessment tasks may be in text or audio format, and student responses may also be in text, audio or multimedia format. Multiple representations separate the medium of transmission from the actual learning objective. However, teachers will need to be clear when the ability to respond in a

Table 12.2 TechDis – Web accessibility evaluation form (http://www.techdis.ac.uk)

Criterion	Why it matters	How to check it
Is the text re-sizeable?	Students with poor sight may need larger text sizes. Students with tunnel vision may need smaller text sizes	Using Internet Explorer, select View > Text size and select either larger or smaller text size
Can responses to the items be selected using the keyboard only?	Some students have difficulty using a mouse	Use the Tab key to see if successive clicks highlight the different options on the page. Use the Return key to see if the option can be selected.
Do the various options come up in a logical sequence when selected using the keyboard only?	Students using a screen reader will use the Tab key to move through options. If the options are highlighted in a confusing order it can be difficult to make sense of the assessment.	Use the Tab key to see if successive clicks highlight the different options of the page in turn. See if these come up in logical order from top to bottom and left to right.
Do selectable options (e.g. radio buttons or check boxes) appear after the descriptive text?	Students relying on screen readers want to select an option *after* they have had it read to them, not before	Inspect the page layout to see if the selection buttons are before or after the text.
Where images are used, do they have appropriate descriptions (<ALT = "">) that inform students without disclosing the answers? An example is shown below: `<IMG SRC="http:// server/graphics/ ch7_03.jpg" WIDTH="378" HEIGHT="332" BORDER=0 ALT="This is an image of a Z-hex- 3enemolecule"> `	Students relying on screen readers may not be able to see the image so a text description is required. However, the description should not reveal the correct response	Move the mouse cursor over the image and see if a description appears

particular way is the core component of the assessment, and decide if this is a key competency, or an artefact of the context.

The principles for UDL have been extended to assessment through the proposed Universally Designed Assessment (UDA) system which determines students' needs and proposes methods to match those needs with appropriate assessments (Ketterlin-Geller, 2005). UDA systems provide flexibility in the assessment platform so as to test the stated learning objectives and not the method of assessment. The key feature of UDA is that accommodation for students with disabilities is built into the assessment; it is not an external accommodation. UDA uses a series of diagnostic and formative tests to determine student performance, and whether the test environment itself is causing lower scores. Accommodation is then built into subsequent assessments, and an iterative process ensues. This also facilitates the reuse of content with different cohorts of students. Multiple presentation formats can be tested to find an optimum format, and the diagnostic and formative tests can be reused.

Assessment providers also have a legitimate need to control, in a flexible manner, which alternative formats are presented to students in order to protect the validity of the inferences made from the resulting scores. It could be the case that allowing some items in an e-assessment to be presented in alternative formats has no adverse consequences on the validity of the inferences drawn from the scores, but some alternative formats for specific items will not result in equally valid inferences. It would be useful if the software itself allowed some control over which items could be presented in alternative formats, and which could not.

Teachers and e-assessment administrators could make effective use of alternative formats when designing an e-assessment. TechDis is a UK Joint Information Systems Committee (JISC) funded service to assist those involved in the design and delivery of e-assessments (http://www.techdis.ac.uk). A summary of the TechDis web accessibility evaluation form is shown in Table 12.2 and provides a useful set of questions for teachers and assessment administrators to reflect upon while designing.

Web pages may be conveniently designed using Cascading Style Sheets (CSS) that deliver formatting which is compatible with screen readers. Students can also design their own CSS (or have one designed for them) to suit their own specific requirements. CSSs can improve accessibility by separating the content from the presentation format and allowing students to control preferences such as font type, size and colours. The World Wide Web Consortium has a number of validation tools available for general use, including a CSS validator (http://www.w3c.org).

When using various question types in e-assessments, teachers should enable both mouse and keyboard navigation. Navigation tools such as the total number of questions in an assessment, which question the student is currently doing and overall time limits are critical pieces of information for all students. The ability to return to previous questions and change responses, or to move ahead to answer questions, may also be important for students. Screen readers should be able to let students know how many questions there are and how many options there are to each question.

Text can be converted into speech using recordings or via digitally synthesized sound. Text and music can also be printed using a Braille embosser (http://www.utoronto.ca/atrc). One of the common problems encountered by students with impaired vision is text that uses hard-coded fonts or where an image is used to display text. This prevents many of the commonly used assistive technologies from translating the text and making it available to the student.

12.1.3 Testing accessibility

Teachers and test administrators can check e-assessment files for compatibility with various aspects of accessibility by using free services such as WebXACT, which uses the W3C web content accessibility guidelines as a template and generates a report as shown in Figure 12.1 (http://www.watchfire.com). The report highlights the areas of incompatibility, and teachers can decide what action needs to be taken for the particular group of students taking the assessment.

Check another page:

http://quiz1.science.adelaide.edu.au/servlet/TestPilot3/tp3   Go!

Show Advanced / Accessibility Options Terms of use

Results for http://quiz1.science.adelaide.edu.au/servlet/TestPilot3/tp3/chem/gcrisp01/chemistry1/ch1tute01/ ⇨

Page last checked on Mon 30/01/2006 at 9:37pm.

| General | Quality | Accessibility | Privacy | | Expand All | Collapse All |

⊗ This page **does not comply** with all of the automatic and manual checkpoints of the W3C Web Content Accessibility Guidelines, and **requires repairs and manual verification**.

	Automatic Checkpoints			Manual Checkpoints		
	Status	Errors	Instances	Status	Warnings	Instances
Priority 1	✓	0	0	⚠	4	4
Priority 2	⊗	3	6	⚠	15	20
Priority 3	⊗	3	3	⚠	11	11

Figure 12.1 Report from WebXACT for compatibility of an e-assessment with W3C guidelines (http://www.watchfire.com)

Table 12.3 Tools for testing accessibility

WebXACT is a free online service for testing web pages for accessibility compatibility	http://webxact.watchfire.com
Watchfire® Bobby™ 5.0 is a commercial tool for testing web accessibility. Bobby checks HTML pages against select accessibility guidelines and then reports on the accessibility of each web page	http://www.watchfire.com
WAVE Accessibility Tool is a free service; online service tests web pages for accessibility	http://www.wave.webaim.org
Vischeck is a free application providing an online method of checking how a web page would appear to someone who is colour-blind	http://www.vischeck.com
TechDis User Preferences Toolbar is a free application that allows users to change the appearance of an observed web page conveniently. The toolbar enables changes to zoom, colour contrast and font	http://www.techdis.ac.uk
Lynx Viewer, open source software for loading a text-based web browser	http://www.delorie.com/web/lynxview.html

Some of the available software and services for testing digital files for accessibility are shown in Table 12.3. Many of these services and applications are free and do not require a significant amount of time to use, so teachers are encouraged to check their web-based e-assessments for compatibility with the major requirements for disability access.

12.2 Improving accessibility

TechDis is funded by JISC and provides a variety of services for educational institutions, including the 'TechDis User Preferences Toolbar' (http://www.techdis.ac.uk). This useful tool allows students to have some control over the colour, font and size of objects on a web page (Figure 12.2).

The toolbar uses style sheets as presented by the TechDis User Style Sheet Wizard. TechDis has produced staff development materials (http://www.techdis.ac.uk/staffpacks) of which one element focuses on e-assessment in depth and includes a table of important points to consider. TechDis is also working to make the e-assessment experience more accessible by identifying areas in the e-assessment process where further guidance is required to enable accessibility to be enhanced (http://www.techdis.ac.uk/index.php?p=9/11).

Figure 12.2 TechDis User Preferences Toolbar (http://www.techdis.ac.uk/gettoolbar)

An authoring tool to add captions, subtitles and audio descriptions to digital media is available free of charge for content creators and educators. This tool, MAGpie (Media Access Generator), is available from the National Center for Accessible Media (NCAM; http://ncam.wgbh.org/webaccess/magpie). Proprietary software exists that allows web authors to add sign language to a web page using animated characters, such as the SigningAvatar® character from Vcom3D shown in Figure 12.3, and renders web content in 'Signed English' and 'Pidgin Signed English' (http://www.vcom3d.com).

For multimedia content, such as video or animation, an audio commentary of what is happening, along with text captioning for any sound should be provided for students who are unable to see or hear such content. If this is too difficult to do, then it would be more appropriate to present the information in a different way.

If colour is used to define specific text or parts of an image, then alternative representations of the object should be made available so that students with various levels of colour perception can still respond to the purpose of the question and not be discriminated against by its format. Coloured buttons should be accompanied by text that allows screen readers of plain text reading to distinguish non-contrasting objects.

Figure 12.3 SigningAvatar® from Vcom3D (http://www.vcom3d.com)

When using web pages for the delivery of e-assessments, it is useful for teachers to be aware of specific HTML tags such as 'LANG', which is used when a change in the language occurs on the page; the 'ACRONYM' tag and the 'ABBR' tag for abbreviations. Acronyms should be written as individual letters with spaces, such as S V G for Scalable Vector Graphics, otherwise screen readers will try to pronounce 'SVG' as a single word and it will make no sense to a student taking an assessment. In e-assessments which use various languages, the 'LANG' tag should be used to alert screen readers that a change in language has occurred, e.g. < lang="fr">.

Table 12.4 Accessibility issues to consider when designing an e-assessment (Ball, 2005)

Forewarning	Is appropriate information provided for all students on assessment format and expectations?
Equivalence	Do students have an opportunity to seek clarification on assessment format and expectations?
Alternatives	Are alternative assessment formats available for students who have particular needs?
Clarity	Are all instructions clear and accessible to students who have vision or speech impairment, or for whom complex language may be a difficulty? Is the content of the assessment worded using plain language terms?
Guidelines	Is the teaching staff aware of accessibility guidelines, the TechDis Website Accessibility Evaluation Tool, WAI Web Content Accessibility Guidelines?
Navigation	Can students use the mouse, keyboard or joystick to access and respond to questions? Are simultaneous keystrokes required?
Error Tolerance	Can a student return to questions and change responses readily?
Audio	Can text and speech be used for each question? Have acronyms, abbreviations and changes in language been accommodated with appropriate tags?
Pixelation	Can essential images be enlarged without distortion?
Images	Do images have full text descriptions for those that cannot see the image?
Colour	Is colour used to distinguish options, provide essential information or elicit responses? Will students with colour-impairment be able to respond appropriately? Is there appropriate contrast between different colours, especially essential text or images?
Text	Can students change text attributes, such as font type, colour and size? Can students apply their own style sheets to the assessment?
Tolerance	Are dyslexic students disadvantaged by fill-in-the-gap questions? Is exact spelling essential?
User-Testing	Have students with a range of learning styles and some with disabilities tested the assessments?
Policy	Does your assessment have to comply with internal policies of the institution?
Advice	Does your institution have readily available advice on accessibility issues in assessment?
Screen Reader	Has text been checked with a screen reader? Do navigation and links make sense when read by a screen reader? Do the assessment questions and response types make sense when read with a screen reader? Can tables be read and do they make sense?

Writing mathematical expressions on the web often requires specialist applications and this can make the text incomprehensible to standard assistive technologies used by some students. It is possible to use MathML with an appropriate web browser plugin such as MathPlayer to assist in the interpretation of mathematical expressions by students with disabilities (http://www.dessci.com/en/products/mathplayer). MathPlayer 2.0 will allow text-to-speech, so that screen readers such as Window-Eyes (http://www.gwmicro.com), HAL (http://www.zabaware.com/reader) and JAWS (http://www.freedomscientific.com) can all be used by students.

The IMS Guidelines for Developing Accessible Learning Applications contains detailed information and links for teachers and developers of e-assessments on the principles and guidelines for enabling a higher level of accessibility for individual students with varying levels of disability (http://www.imsglobal.org/accessibility). This is a particularly informative website with respect to discipline specific issues.

Ball (2005) has provided a practical summary for teaching staff involved in e-assessment to make their assessments more accessible, within reasonable workload limits. The time to prepare appropriate e-assessments will be an issue with most teaching staff, as the accessibility documents are quite detailed, and the effort required to translate them into the discipline context of the assessment can be quite onerous. Ball has concentrated on the more common issues, and how teachers and assessment designers might reflect on accessibility issues using the 'Universal Design of Assessment' principles (Ketterlin-Geller, 2005). A summary of main accessibility issues to consider when designing an e-assessment are shown in Table 12.4.

12.3 Assistive technologies

Assistive technology (AT) for e-learning and e-assessment describes any hardware or software that helps students with some form of disability to access and respond to digital resources. This can include screen readers that use text-to-speech audio so that web content can be read aloud for students with vision impairment. Modified keyboards with extra large fonts and contrasting colours, such as that illustrated in Figure 12.4 are also available for students with vision impairment. Tactile devices generate Braille code for text and graphics so that severely vision-impaired students who cannot use screen enlargers, or modified keyboards, can feel the content. Screen magnifiers allow the user to enlarge the size of images and text displayed on screen. However, teachers should be aware that not all content on the screen might be enlarged in static proportions.

Adaptive keyboards can also be designed for students with varying degrees of physical disability and may contain fewer choices with larger keys, or touch screens may be used so that

Figure 12.4 Example of modified keyboard for students with vision impairment (http://www.keys-u-see.com/)

Figure 12.5 Example of joystick for students who cannot use a standard keyboard to move around the screen (http://www.donjohnston.com/catalog/pengild.htm)

a keyboard is not required. Voice recognition software may also be used instead of a keyboard or mouse. For students with limited mobility, a joystick may be appropriate, and allows full control over mouse movements and the selection of options on the screen (Figure 12.5).

Section 5 **How do I make e-assessments interactive?**

13 Assessing discussion groups and collaborative tasks

13.1 Communicating and collaborating online

13.1.1 Overview

Computer-mediated communication (CMC) may be classified as synchronous or asynchronous, and it may be either public or private (Naidu *et al.*, 2006). Synchronous communication requires participants to be online at the same time and includes activities such as chat, videoconferencing, interactive whiteboards and moo (*mud* object oriented, where mud is a *m*ultiple *u*ser *d*omain, and is based on role-playing games). Asynchronous communication allows participants to read and respond to messages in their own time and includes activities such as email or listservs, bulletin boards, discussion boards, interactive web pages and newsgroups, wikis, blogs and podcasting. For CMC that is public, anyone with an Internet connection may read and respond to the messages. Private CMC includes a number of variations, ranging from anyone with an internet connection being able to read but not respond to messages, through to websites requiring a password or registration key in order to read or respond to messages.

Computer supported collaborative learning (CSCL) is a recent variation of a wider set of activities dependent on computer-based network systems that facilitate group work for members in disparate physical locations and commercial groups undertaking a common project task (Weinberger *et al.*, 2006). CSCL attempts to scaffold learner support so that the group is able to achieve an outcome that is more complex, and frequently of a higher quality, than that expected from individual students. CSCL systems use computer networks to help students to communicate their ideas and obtain feedback from other group members, as well as from the teacher.

Email and email listservs are the simplest type of CMC, and usually function through the use of a central email address, belonging to an administrator, to which participants post text messages or attached documents. Participants then read and respond to what other participants have posted. Listservs usually require some form of registration or subscription, a process whereby the administrator approves the access rights of each participant. The administrator may also monitor the posted messages, and may also be required to approve postings before they are made available to other participants. This is an inexpensive form of CMC and usually requires minimum training and technical knowledge on the part of the participants. However, there is little structure to the sequence of messages, and the number of entries may grow so rapidly that it is difficult to find particular messages of interest. Newsgroups are generally specific to a particular topic or issue, and require participants to subscribe in order to read and respond to messages or notices. Unlike email, which is an active form of CMC since messages are sent to individuals, newsgroups are passive and participants must access the newsgroup website to read messages. Newsgroup entries are structured similarly to emails, where the participants can read the titles of messages and decide which ones to read. Posting to a newsgroup requires only a limited amount of technical knowledge and is similar to email.

Websites that host synchronous chat sessions allow participants to engage in an online text-based conversation. Examples include Instant Messaging applications such as AIM (http://www.aol.com.au), Skype (http://www.skype.com), Windows Live Messenger (http://join.msn.com) and Yahoo! Messenger (http://messenger.yahoo.com). These sessions may involve two or more participants, and are useful when participants are separated by geographical distance, although differences in time zones around the world may mean that some participants must be online in the early hours of the morning. Chat sessions are a form of linear CMC, but they capture the flow of the text-based conversation for later review, and so are useful for group work. Like email and listservs, the volume of information for chat sessions can be large, and the conversation can become disjointed since each entry is recorded as it occurs in real time. Discussion boards or bulletin boards are more structured versions of chat sessions, and may be either linear or threaded. The linear format is similar to a newsgroup, but the volume of data usually makes it difficult to find individual entries. Threaded discussion groups allow ordering, and recent applications allow some tracking and searching for specific key works or participants within the data recorded.

Salmon (2000) has discussed the importance of the role of the e-moderator in CMC, and the need for participants to feel that they belong to a community. The e-moderator allows all participants to have a voice and contribute to the community, and must anticipate and accommodate different styles of participation ranging from those who are reluctant through to those who are dominant. When CMC is used as a learning and teaching tool, students must be provided with clear guidelines about expectations, behaviour, outcomes and assessment procedures. It is useful to commence CMC sessions with some form of social activity, much as one would include in a face-to-face workshop (Benfield, 2002). For CMC to be an effective educational tool an appropriately trained e-moderator or facilitator is required. Effective CMC requires that students perceive the purpose of the activity is important to their studies and that they can relate to the expected outcomes. Teachers thinking of using CMC need to be able to articulate the educational benefits of the exercise in terms of the amount of time students are expected to put into constructing, reading and responding to entries.

Why require students to communicate online, rather than face-to-face? Apart from the obvious reasons of geographic dispersion associated with fully online programs, students might be studying part-time and unable to attend face-to-face sessions because of work related or family reasons. Many mature students with families would find it difficult to attend all face-to-face sessions at fixed times. In addition to these issues related to flexibility in timetabling prescribed learning or assessment activities, there are pedagogical reasons for offering students the opportunity to communicate online. Students may access a variety of resources during an asynchronous discussion, informing themselves of relevant information and reflecting on this before responding. Students who are less active in verbal discussions have an opportunity to make an entry without feeling dominated by others, thus allowing the teacher to cater for a variety of learning, communication and assessment styles.

Students require an authentic task with outcomes that are meaningful in order to be engaged in an online discussion (Laurillard, 2002). Examples could include tasks such as undertaking a public inquiry, preparing a government report or debating a current issue appearing in the press. Authentic tasks have meaningful outcomes; they allow students to make informed decisions where choices are made and consequences explained. Current affairs often offers appropriate topics for an online discussion and an added feature of using such topical issues is that students can also analyse and comment on the public responses to the issues.

How many students should be involved in an online discussion group? This will depend on the purpose of the discussion, and for the examples given above groups of 5–8 students would be suitable. Some discussion boards may have more, but classes of several hundred should be divided into groups, and where different groups of students have been allocated the same topic, additional sessions may be used to compare how different groups approached the topic. Alternatively, the different groups may be allocated different topics, and the additional workload for the teacher will be to find a sufficient number of suitable topics. It will assist teachers who assess the discussions if the number of entries is limited, and specific criteria are used to assess entries.

Salmon (2000) has emphasized the need to specify clearly the time commitment expected of students and any tutors in online discussions, and to ensure that there is a purpose for discussing the task. Students are quick to ascertain when an assessment task has been allocated simply to 'fill in the space'. The topic should be engaging, but also relevant to the course and to the development of the student as a professional. The e-moderator can assist by summarizing key issues arising during the online discussion, and aspects that may require more attention by the students. The discussion should have a definite conclusion, students should feel that the key issues have been drawn together, and a final recommendation, decision or consensus has been arrived at from the discussion. This is a critical part of the discussion, and one that is sometimes overlooked by teachers. For on-campus students it is often useful to schedule a face-to-face session to draw the activity to a close and allow students the opportunity to clarify any remaining issues.

Online discussions make use of Vygotsky's (1978) concept of the social construction of knowledge to engage learners by providing a framework that allows collaboration. e-Moderators can assist in the construction of a social context for student engagement, either by providing an initial face-to-face meeting of students before the online discussion commences, or an equivalent, synchronous, virtual meeting. This initial engagement is crucial in order to establish shared values, a sense of purpose for the activity and the ground rules for interaction.

It is important to appreciate the difference between technologies that allow collaboration and technologies that facilitate collaboration (Gao *et al.*, 2005). Many of the current learning management systems tend to allow collaboration to take place; they are designed to provide a conduit through which students may communicate with each other. More recent examples of purpose-built systems that facilitate the online collaboration are discussed in the next section of this chapter.

13.1.2 Examples of software for e-collaboration

Some online discussion software uses a framework that resembles a meeting room, with virtual chairs and tables, and doors by which students may enter and leave the room. The navigation tools mimic those that are encountered in the real world. For example, a library icon might be a path for students to access online resources, a coffee machine might signal a break in the discussion (Figure 13.1). Interactive whiteboards provide tools for students to share information and so encourage active participation.

Figure 13.1 Tools that facilitate collaborative problem-solving and group work (ACollab, http://www.atutor.ca/acollab/demo.php)

For group-based discussions it is helpful if students are aware of each other's attributes and strengths as the tasks that must be accomplished online may be divided between group members. Whether the discussion is designed for groups or individuals, students should be reminded at regular intervals to refer to the task that must be completed and the actions that are required to complete that task (Gao *et al.*, 2005). Completing a group task online is often complicated, and involves planning specific actions for each group member. It is often helpful for each member of the group to compile of a list of the required resources and timelines for completing specific tasks, and for there to be a general consensus about when a task has been completed to the necessary standard. Online collaboration is facilitated when the system presents tools that allow each of these essential functions to be organized by the students and where the e-moderator has a plan that involves scaffolded support for the group (Lipponen *et al.*, 2004).

Lipponen *et al.* (2004) have proposed four necessary criteria for technology to support collaboration:

- the design model should be based on an explicit pedagogical theory
- the technology should be based on groupware (multi-user and multi-location facilitation)
- there should be explicit facilitation of essential procedures and appropriate scaffolding through the active use of prompts and suggestions
- the technology should facilitate community-building and equity.

Examples of software products that are specifically designed to scaffold collaborative online activities include Knowledge Forum™ (http://www.knowledgeforum.com); the open source server software Fle3 (http://fle3.uiah.fi) and Swiki (http://minnow.cc.gatech.edu/swiki). Swiki is based on the popular wiki concept (http://jot.com), software that facilitates the creation of a website that can be developed by many concurrent users. Figure 13.2 illustrates an example of an electronic group workspace by Knowledge Forum™; this application allows a form of scaffolding where group members can identify the purpose of their contribution, such as describing whether

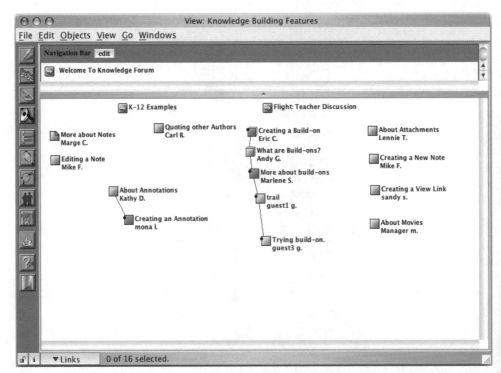

Figure 13.2 Example of learner interface for collaborative online group discussions and knowledge construction (Knowledge Forum™, http://www.knowledgeforum.com)

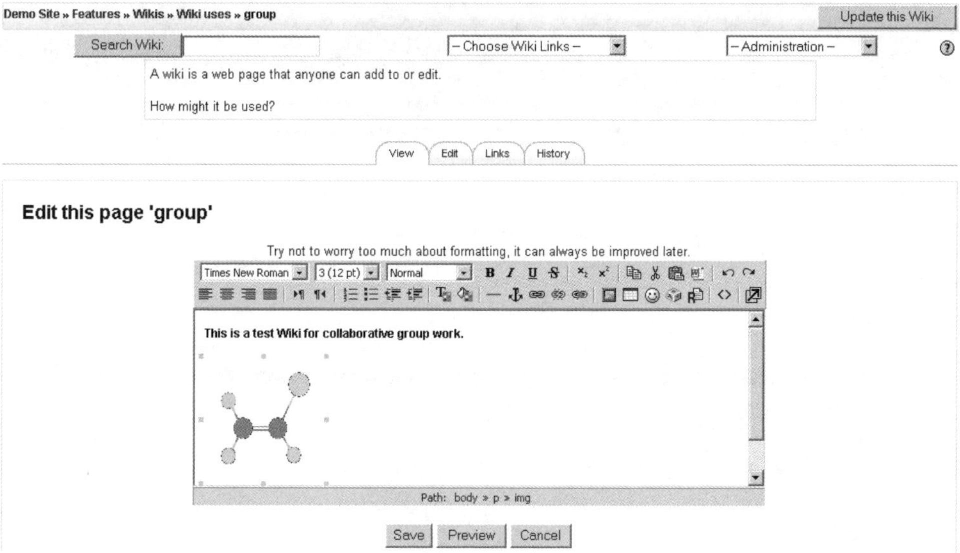

Figure 13.3 Example of learner interface for a wiki (Moodle, http://moodle.org)

it is based on theory, opinion or reflection; or building on someone else's idea; or a question or a critique. Group members may apply titles, annotations or references to their entries, as well as view the same content from different perspectives or contexts. Once the group, or a group leader, is satisfied with the document or contents, permission to publish to a larger or public group may be given.

Collaborative group work often involves the creation of a shared document, and a number of technical issues arise when group members are required to work on a common document. The document needs to be available for all group members to annotate, but versioning control must be available so that group members and the teacher can readily track contributions by individuals. Wikis (wiki means quick in Hawaiian) facilitate group activities online by enabling anyone with a web browser and an Internet connection to work on a shared document or web page. An example of a wiki interface in the learning management system Moodle is shown in Figure 13.3. Features commonly found in wikis include the ability to construct documents online with embedded web links, the archiving of recent changes and their authorship, the ability to revert to previous versions of a shared document and numerous security features such as password access or protection for specific documents. The assessment of group work undertaken on wikis may be an issue if individual contributions need to be identified and verified, so if this is a requirement for the assessment scheme, the particular software used for the wiki should be capable of authenticating and tracking individual activities.

Fle3 consists of server-based, open-source software freely available under the GNU General Public Licence (GPL) for computer-supported collaborative learning. Fle3 contains three components, as seen in the screenshot depicted in Figure 13.4. The section 'WebTops' is used to store documents, files and web links that may be shared with others; the section 'Knowledge Building' is used by group members to construct knowledge, build theories and engage in debates; the section 'Jamming' is used for the collaborative construction of digital content and can track changes, revisions and authorship.

13.1.3 Design principles for e-collaboration
How do teachers know whether online communication and collaboration is appropriate? What are the design principles that can be applied to e-collaboration? Will students be required to interact with each other, as well as the content for the course or task? Teachers would like to

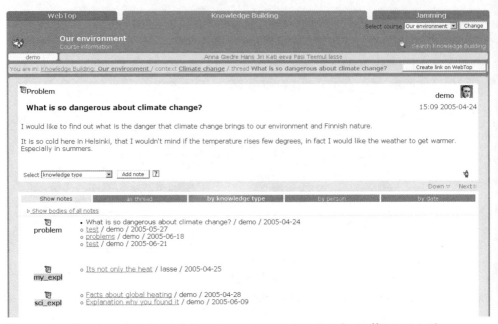

Figure 13.4 Fle3 interface for collaborative group work online (http://fle3.uiah.fi)

predict the relationship between the outcomes expected for the task and the framework for the interactivity designed for online collaboration. Strijbos *et al.* (2004) have proposed six principles, based on process-oriented design methodology, for e-collaborative activities and tasks. These six design principles, presented below, have been modified from the original:

1. Specify the learning objectives for the activity or task:
   - What are the skills and capabilities that students will develop by interacting with each other?
   - Are all students expected to master the same skills to the same level?
2. Specify the expected level of interaction between the students:
   - Is the purpose of student interactivity to obtain feedback, to exchange or create knowledge, to engage in discourse or to develop a logical argument?
   - Are students expected to reach a consensus in order to present a single report?
3. Select the task based on the learning objectives and the expected level of interaction:
   - Will the task enable closure of the discussion and a consensus report?
   - Will the report enable students to show the skills and capabilities they have developed?
4. Specify the level of scaffolding the teacher or e-moderator will provide to the groups:
   - Will the teacher or e-moderator prescribe the limits of the task and provide feedback during the interactivity?
   - Will students each have a specific sub-task to complete on behalf of the group?
   - What will be the level of dependency on individual students within the group; if one member fails will the group fail?
   - What is the marking scheme for the task and does it involve peer assessment?
5. Specify the expected group size and student responsibilities based on the learning objectives and the expected level of interaction:
   - Will each group contain a fixed number of members with specified responsibilities?
   - Will there be a set number of entries and will the format of entries be prescribed?
   - Will all students make the same type of contribution, are they expected to negotiate tasks and outcomes, what happens if there is disagreement within the group?

6. Specify how the online environment supports collaboration and achieving the learning objectives:
   - Will students be provided with examples of what is expected of them?
   - Will face-to-face sessions be used as well as online sessions?
   - Will students use synchronous or asynchronous interactivity?
   - Will training sessions be held to show how to use the system, how to upload or share files, how to work with a shared document for the report?

Online discussions and collaboration afford an opportunity for students to engage in knowledge construction and new meanings according to the principles of social constructivist theory (Pena-Shaffa et al., 2004). Effective learning is enhanced by students interacting with peers and teachers in a community of practice that shares common perceptions of tasks and outcomes. An active environment is required for the application of social constructivist theory and multiple skills can be developed as a result. Participants search for, and assimilate, knowledge into new forms and construct meaning for themselves and the group. Members learn to recognize strengths and weaknesses in themselves and others; they learn to negotiate and prioritize, and work towards a common goal.

E-moderators and course designers need to take into account the relationship between a student's intrinsic competence and capabilities and affective factors such as their confidence in the online environment and in dealing with group dynamics (Macdonald, 2003). Effective communication also requires students to gain an understanding of the discipline-specific discourse and ways of thinking. In order to complete a task through collaboration, students may need to acquire additional skills, including how to work in a team and how to negotiate with other team members. Students will require some guidance with affective issues such as group cohesion and mutual trust. They will need to be provided with opportunities to practise achieving a formative task before being expected to complete a summative task, so adequate time must be allowed for the recognition and development of these essential skills. The summative assessment of both the process and product of collaborative work can be complicated, and teachers will need to allocate sufficient time to design tasks that allow students to develop the appropriate group skills before summative assessments are undertaken.

Tuckman's (Tuckman et al., 1977) model of leadership and group dynamics is useful for reflecting on the role of e-moderators and group members. The model uses the stages of *forming, storming, norming* and *performing*; it describes a shift from a dependence on the group leader (or e-moderator) for guidance and direction through to a situation where the group is self-aware and productive (Figure 13.5). The model is useful for designers of online group activities

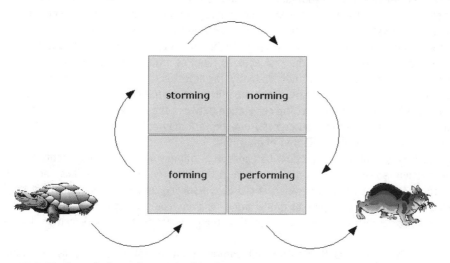

Figure 13.5 Tuckman's (1977) model of leadership and group dynamics

because it highlights the fact that groups require time to move through the different stages of development and that attention to process avoids unnecessary conflict within the group that may delay productive activity. A fifth stage can be added to the model, that of adjourning or the discontinuance of the group once the task has been completed. For online group work this debriefing is also important, and teachers should consider how to conclude the activity with either a face-to-face or virtual synchronous wrap-up session. This gives a sense of completion for the group members.

13.2 Assessing collaborative problem-solving and group work

What are the definable characteristics of a good problem-solver and can they be ascribed to a group as a whole, as well as to the individual members? According to O'Neil Jr *et al.* (2003) a good problem-solver has an appropriate understanding of the required content, possesses skills that allow for a strategic approach to tackling a task and is capable of self-awareness and self-regulation. The tools used for the *evaluation* of problem-solving skills include items such as surveys, reflective journals and ethnographic investigations, but the summative *assessment* of problem-solving skills often requires processes that are quantitative and reproducible. Herein lies a dilemma for the teacher since collaborative learning occurs within a community of practice, and the group is expected to achieve a common goal or solve a common problem, but the individual members of the group usually require a mark or grade that reflects the development of individual capabilities.

One approach to solving this dilemma is the CRESST teamwork process model for collaborative problem-solving which describes six skills that might be assessed for problem-solving, including adaptability, coordination, decision-making, interpersonal skills, leadership and communication (O'Neil Jr *et al.*, 1997). Adaptability is usually associated with a reasonable level of prior knowledge by the group members, and would not be expected to be a significant component of the assessment for novices (O'Neil Jr *et al.*, 2003). Coordination is determined by the way in which tasks are integrated, synchronized and completed, and the awareness shown by the group of the timelines within which this must happen. Decision-making is dependent on discussions within the group, and the effective use of information to expedite the completion of the task. Interpersonal skills assist in reducing the chances of conflict within the group and good leadership would also be expected to positively influence group outcomes. The levels of productive communication are expected to show a positive correlation with group performance.

In the CRESST model group members collaborate on the construction of a knowledge map and the performance of the group and its members is measured by scoring the knowledge map against expert maps. The use of the knowledge map approach to measure group performance is dependent on whether an individual group member could successfully complete the task without the input from other members. This will always be an issue with group work, and the teacher will need to reflect on whether the task actually requires group collaboration, or whether each member could complete the task independently. The assessment criteria for group work will need to take this into account and there should be a genuine match between the real objectives for the task and the marking scheme. The correlation between the CRESST teamwork process model parameters and the measured outcomes from the task may not always be positive for each of the six skills in the taxonomy (Chung *et al.*, 1999).

O'Neil Jr *et al.* (2003) have proposed a conceptual framework for the components of collaborative problem-solving, as outlined in Figure 13.6. This framework describes the attributes that are associated with collaboration and problem-solving as well as the skills that could be developed and assessed as part of group work. Teachers could use this framework to propose the assessment criteria for group work based on the priorities that will be placed on the various attributes.

Are the characteristics that foster collaborative problem-solving amenable to summative assessments that are valid and reliable? The content specific knowledge and level of self-

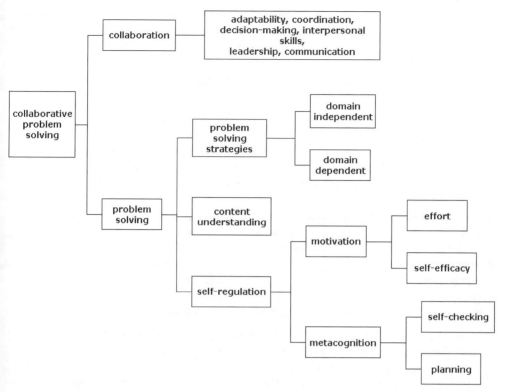

Figure 13.6 Conceptual framework for collaborative problem-solving (O'Neil Jr *et al.*, 2003)

awareness of individual group members will vary, but the quality of the group output will be dependent on the leadership and interactions within the group. The teacher will need to decide whether the objectives and the assessment criteria will treat the group as a single entity, or as a group of individuals, and whether the assessment will attempt to also measure interpersonal skills and leadership qualities.

Assessing problem-solving skills is challenging because it involves complex judgements about multiple actions from numerous learners in a specific context (Bennett *et al.*, 2003). Computers are able to archive every keystroke and action during an online session, and in principle this information could be used to assess many aspects of collaborative problem-solving. However, the volume of information collected during an online group activity, even with a relatively small class of students, is enormous and teachers require assistance in interpreting the data and matching it appropriately to the learning objectives for the task. A general framework, described as evidence-centred design, helps teachers to conceptually design assessments that will generate evidence that can be correlated with student activities and then translated into inferences about performance (Mislevy *et al.*, 2004). This is an important principle that can be applied to most assessments: the necessity to design an assessment task that will actually measure what one is intending to measure, and reflecting beforehand on the evidence that will be required to draw inferences between activity and performance.

Assessment of group activities needs to measure the complex relationship between the students' intrinsic ability, what they have learnt during the course or programme, as well as affective influences such as student confidence in working within an online environment, student motivation and group interactions (Macdonald, 2003). Assuming that the collaborative effort is to be assessed by means of a collaborative product, the components for the assessment are likely to be the collaborative output matched against the stated objectives and some form of evaluation of the individual's contribution. If both the group and individual components are to be marked, a weighting should be used to match the marking scheme to the objectives for the task. Items that might be assessed in collaborative problem-solving include activity levels, the final product of group work, individual self and peer reviews, as well as leadership and negotiation skills.

Macdonald (2003) has proposed the following guidelines for the assessment of collaborative problem-solving:

- if participation in an online collaborative project is mandatory, then it should be summatively assessed
- if the level of computing skills varies in a class, then appropriate scaffolding should be provided in the formative stages of the activity and the teacher will need to make clear to students which activities are to be assessed, and which are designed to develop capabilities
- the development of skills specifically associated with collaborative activities, in addition to learning the discipline content, should be part of the objectives for the course, and weighted appropriately in the assessment
- feedback during the initial stages of the collaboration is important for defining expectations and the level of activity required to complete the task
- the final group outcome should be subject to peer-review, and so the development of peer-review skills should be incorporated into the learning activities.

Collaborative group work is suitable for an authentic learning and assessment activity, and it allows more sophisticated, real world problems to be set for students (those at the relational and extended abstract levels of the SOLO taxonomy). Peer assessment is often an important component of the assessment of collaborative problem-solving and a number of models may be used. One involves the teacher grading the group output, multiplying the mark by the number of group members and allowing the members of the group to divide the resulting group mark amongst the individual members. A consequence of this approach is that peer pressure may occur and an inappropriate distribution of the marks may result. An alternative model involves each group member assessing themselves and other group members against a set of predetermined criteria, and the teacher then aggregating those marks and assigning an individual final mark. This method allows each student to evaluate their own contribution in relation to the other group members, but a consequence could be collusion or peer pressure within the group to assign inappropriate marks that maximize each individual's final mark. An example of a group assessment peer review form is illustrated in Figure 13.7.

An example of software that is designed to measure the contributions of individual group members to group work in the design of Java computer code is VorteX (http://www.studentcentredlearning.com). VorteX does not record activity by simply logging keystrokes but attempts to capture the actual construction process of a collaborative effort to complete a task. The teacher is able to provide feedback for the group on their approach to solving the problem. VorteX is similar to project management software, and allows detailed tracking of the design process.

Individual group members must be convinced that the teacher is able to reliably assess their contribution, and that the marking scheme appropriately rewards the stated outcomes expected for the group. Teachers should decide whether a norm-referenced or criterion-referenced assessment scheme is more appropriate for the particular outcomes and whether the *process* of group learning and the *product* of group activity are both assessed, and what is the relative weighting for the two components. The relative contribution of each group member to both the process and product may be an important aspect to measure, depending on the stated objectives for the task. The importance of individual activity during the group work needs to be clear from the beginning so that each member can make an informed decision about how they will contribute. Table 13.1 summarizes the tasks and corresponding teacher and student activities associated with assessing group work.

1. How many of the group members actively contributed to the final group product?

○ 1   ○ 2   ○ 3   ○ 3   ○ 4   ○ 5   ○ 6

2. How many of the group members consistently contributed to group activities?

○ 1   ○ 2   ○ 3   ○ 3   ○ 4   ○ 5   ○ 6

3. Overall, our group worked effectively to produce the final product.

○ Strongly agree   ○ Agree   ○ Not sure   ○ Disagree   ○ Strongly disagree

4. I have learnt new skills by working with others in a group.

○ Strongly agree   ○ Agree   ○ Not sure   ○ Disagree   ○ Strongly disagree

5. Other members of the group benefited from my contribution to the final product.

○ Strongly agree   ○ Agree   ○ Not sure   ○ Disagree   ○ Strongly disagree

6. One thing I would like to change about this particular group activity is:

Figure 13.7 Example of a group assessment, peer review form

Teachers should reflect on the consequences of how groups are selected, and how this may influence the assessment outcomes. Will groups self select members on existing social contacts, or will teachers assign group membership randomly, alphabetically, by ability level or by skills? These decisions will have an influence on group dynamics and the eventual assessment outcome for the group and for individuals. Is the culture of the discipline to work in groups, or as individuals? Often working in groups (or indeed teaching in groups!) is seen as an artificial construct, because for some disciplines it may be claimed that groups do not naturally form to accomplish tasks in a particular profession. Teachers will need to reflect on the practices that are common for their discipline in the workforce, and will need to align their assessment activities with the culture of professional practice. If the process of working in groups is an important part of the learning of professional skills, then it should be reflected in the assessment scheme.

What can be done to ensure that each group member contributes to the process and product? It is difficult to ensure, but teachers can establish a framework that explicitly states the expectations and the consequences of failing to meet the standards expected, and how individual contributions will be assessed and verified. The teacher and the group can form group rules, including frequency of meetings, meeting deadlines, allocation of specific duties or responsibilities within the group and how progress will be recorded. It is good practice to keep a record of meetings; this may be in the form of a blog, wiki or discussion group. Group members should have a record of their expectations and activities, so that should a member not comply, then documentation exists to present to the teacher. The teacher can then reinforce the expectations and set timelines for the member, and also note the impact this may have on the rest of the group.

Sung *et al.* (2005) have developed a web-based self- and peer-assessment system for group work, Web-SPA, that uses a database server and web application program module. The system allows individual or group assignments to be submitted and the teacher can determine a marking scheme, and set parameters such as self- and/or peer-assessment, group discussions for each assessment and a second stage modification of marks after group analysis. The system keeps track of the marks, and can provide examples of high-scoring and low-scoring work for group analysis. Expert marking may also be used, and the results from self- and peer-assessment can

Table 13.1 Summary of tasks and the corresponding teacher and student activities associated with assessing group work

Decisions to be made by teacher	Consequences for marking scheme	Teacher actions	Student actions
Will the process of group work be assessed?	Marks must reflect the priority of the development of process skills	Assign relative weighting to favour process versus product. Assign authentic task that is appropriate for group work, to develop capabilities in group dynamics	Develop skills that enhance the process side of group work.
Will the product of group work be assessed?	Marks must reflect the priority of the product produced by the group	Assign relative weighting to favour product versus process. Assign authentic task that requires group activity to produce a product	Develop skills that enhance the product side of group work
Will a group mark or individual marks be assigned to the group product?	Individual contributions may need to be measured. The group mark may be the same for all members, independent of their contribution	Develop criteria for assigning marks and an appropriate rubric. Develop procedures that are valid and reliable	Evidence of individual contribution may be required: personal log, time sheets, peer reviews
Will learners assess their own contribution?	Marks may not reflect actual standard of work	Formative exercise in self-assessment with feedback. Develop procedures that are valid and reliable	Develop self-assessment skills
Will learners assess the contribution of other group members?	Peer pressure may influence marks	Formative exercise in peer-assessment with feedback. Develop procedures that are valid and reliable	Develop peer-assessment skills
Will the assessment be norm-referenced or criterion-referenced?	Individual learners may be disadvantaged in norm-referenced assessment depending upon which group they are in	Criteria must be developed	Norm-referenced assessment means learners compete against each other for marks

- Subjects
- Students
- Teams
- Assessment Criteria
- Assessment Results
- Passwords   Logout

Please fill out all fields in the self and peer assessment form and then click on submit at the bottom of the form.

Criteria	John Smith	Sarah Ng	Jane Fong
Writing report:			
Typing	1	-1	3
Producing diagrams, figures, tables	1	2	-1
Getting extra references & appraising their usefulness	1	3	0
Editing format, style, grammar, spell	2	2	2
Number crunching:	John Smith	Sarah Ng	Jane Fong
Getting new data	1	2	1
Finding out how to solve problem	0	0	-1
Data & formula entry and formatting	3	2	1
Analysis and cross checking	2	0	-1

Figure 13.8 Example from the SPARK interface (http://www.educ.dab.uts.edu.au/darrall/ sparksite)

be compared to expert assessment. Self- and peer-assessments enable students to develop new skills; they facilitate a reduction of student dependence on the teacher for all feedback, and encourage students to reflect on their own work. In Web-SPA each student assesses their own work, peer-assesses another student's work, then the group members discuss the results of the self- and peer-assessment. Web-SPA chooses some of the high- and low-scoring works for group discussion.

Self and Peer Assessment Resource Kit (SPARK, http://www.educ.dab.uts.edu.au/darrall/ sparksite) is an open-source product designed to facilitate the effective assessment of group work (Freeman *et al.*, 2002). The teacher can determine the criteria and assign associated marks using a simple web interface, and students reflect on the performance of group members and rate each other and themselves against each teacher-provided criterion. The teacher or tutor grades the product of the group work, and uses SPARK to provide individual marks as well as summative and formative feedback. An example from the SPARK interface is shown in Figure 13.8.

13.3 Assessing online discussion groups

An online discussion group (also referred to as an online forum discussion board) is one form of CMC that allows students and teachers to interact in an asynchronous manner. For students who are reluctant to contribute in a face-to-face environment the use of the online environment may align more readily with their preferred communication style. There is also a sense of more control for individual group members in this asynchronous environment. However, some students prefer to communicate face-to-face, and some students are intimidated by having to use computers to participate in an assessable discussion. Teachers will need to provide students with a rationale for the purpose of any online discussions that are mandatory and assessable. In order for a student to participate in an online discussion they usually require only an Internet connection and interact with the server-side software through their web browser.

The interface for constructing an entry for an online discussion resembles that for email (illustrated in Figure 13.9), with a subject heading and a text box to write the entry. Files may also be attached to the entry using the familiar 'browse' button as for email attachments. The technical knowledge required by students to participate in an online discussion is usually no more than that required to send and read emails.

191

Your new discussion topic

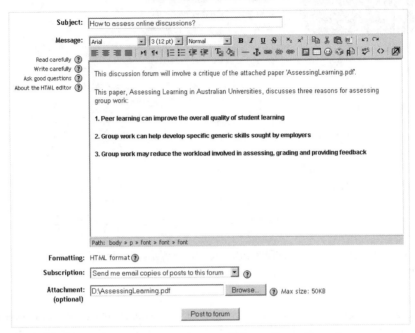

Figure 13.9 Moodle interface for discussion group (http://moodle.org)

The student can read discussion entries by opening the hyperlinked text containing the subject heading for the topic of the discussion. The interface is again very similar to email, usually containing the subject, the author and the date the entry was made (an example from the Blackboard™ discussion board is shown in Figure 13.10). Responses to entries are arranged in nested form, frequently indented to allow students and the teacher or tutor to readily distinguish new entries from replies to existing entries. Different software applications allow a variety of options for both the teacher and the student with respect to the format of the interface, how many entries may be made, whether new threads may be commenced, whether entries may be

Figure 13.10 Blackboard™ interface for discussion group (http://www.blackboard.com)

graded or critiqued, whether entries are anonymous or the author's name visible, whether entries may be modified after posting and whether some learners may be blocked from making further entries. Online discussions require agreed rules for participation, and just as email messages are subject to 'netiquette' or net-based etiquette, so are online discussions (Shea, 1994).

Online discussions allow more students to participate in course discussions than would be possible in a traditional classroom setting. In order for students to see a purpose in allocating time to actively participate in an online discussion it should involve a well-defined task with explicit outcomes. The assessment of discussion group entries may be either formative or summative, but there should always be a readily recognizable benefit to the student for participating in the discussion. The assessment criteria should be related to the objectives and purpose of the defined task and may relate to the level of learner understanding of content or issues, the generation of new content or the critiquing of existing content, as well as to the quantity and quality of participation. Formative feedback may be used in the initial stages of a group discussion in order to clarify expectations and establish standards. This will allow students to gauge the quality of their contributions against other participants and to identify what is valued in online discussions. Various options are available to the teacher in terms of how to summatively assess the discussion, including marking all entries, marking later entries but not earlier ones, averaging marks over a number of entries or using the highest mark from a series of marked entries.

An example of criteria that might be used for grading online discussion entries is shown in Table 13.2. Requiring students to participate in an online discussion will not necessarily lead to

Table 13.2 Grading descriptors for online discussion entries

Grade	Understanding content	Participation rate	Participation quality
Fail	No understanding, significant misunderstanding	No participation	Off the topic, irrelevant entries
Pass	Superficial understanding, opinion without evidence, unistructural approach	Minimum participation, needs prompting to respond	Entries relevant but no critiquing of content or other entries
Credit	Some deep-level understanding, some evidence-based opinion, multistructual approach	Regular participation, needs prompting to respond	Entries relevant to topic with some critiquing of content and other entries
Distinction	Deep-level understanding, evidence-based opinion, multistructual approach using compare, contrast, analyse	Significant number of good entries, no reminders required	Entries relevant to topic with significant critiquing of content and other entries
High Distinction	Deep-level understanding, reflective and relational approach, critiques others using evidence to support opinion, new interpretations	Significant number of high-quality entries, no reminders required	Entries highly relevant to topic with significant evidence-based critiquing of content and other entries

meaningful engagement with the allocated topic or task. If the assessment for participation relies solely on making an entry and no standards or criteria are applied to the quality of the entry, then it is likely that students will minimize the amount of time allocated to constructing their entry (Benfield, 2002). The teacher, or e-moderator, should provide clear guidelines on expectations in terms of the number and size of entries, the type of content and language expected, whether references from the primary literature are required to support arguments, as well as the deadlines for initial and final entries (Salmon, 2000).

Teachers may take an active or passive role in the discussion, and this will depend on the objectives for the activity, the extent of scaffolding that is required and the expected outcomes from the group participation. One of the issues that must be addressed in any online discussion is the ethical treatment of students' contributions (Brem, 2002). Students must be informed whether their entries will be made public, and whether they will be stored or reused in some manner. For discussions that take place within a learning management system subject to password authentication for access, and that are obviously associated with a course or subject site within the system, students would probably be aware that only other enrolled students will have access to their entries. Teachers may have further subdivided the class into groups, and restricted read and write access to only members of the group. However, this may not be the case, and so teachers will need to explain clearly to group members the extent of public access to their entries, and whether the entries will be reused at a later time. In particular, teachers will need to obtain ethics clearance if online discussions will be used for research purposes, so a decision must be made before the discussion starts about the purpose of the discussion; is it only for learning, teaching and assessment purposes, or will it later be used as data for research purposes? Students must be informed about the purpose of the online discussion.

How does a teacher analyse the content of an online discussion? This will depend on the purpose of the discussion, the objectives and assessment criteria articulated to students and the outcomes expected. Research approaches to analysing online discussions include grounded theory and the use of theoretical codes (Glaser, 2005), content analysis (Stemler, 2001) and ethnography. There are various software applications that can assist in the qualitative, large-scale analysis of texts, including NVivo and N6 (formerly NUD*IST, http://www.qsrinternational.com). One of the difficulties for teachers in analysing the content of online discussions is whether there is a direct relationship between the actual discussion content in the form of the words that are recorded, and the latent content that represents what the student intended or the complex interactions that occurred between students in arriving at the recorded text (Murphy *et al.*, 2005). The analysis of the content of online discussions is usually used as a proxy measure for the assessment of knowledge construction and the ability to solve problems, as well as the myriad interactions that took place between the group members.

Content analysis of the text in online discussions may be coded according to Garrison *et al.* (2001), who proposed the categories triggering, exploration, integration, solution and other. *Triggering* constitutes the initial stage of the inquiry and allows the group members to focus on the task; *exploration* involves the interplay between individual group members reflecting on the task and engaging in discourse to explore the possibilities and propose various options; *integration* is the critical phase where meaning begins to develop from the various options presented; *resolution* leads to the proposed solution to the problem presented in the task and involves the articulation or presentation of the outcome. This approach to content analysis allows the teacher to categorize each sentence from the online discussion and assess knowledge construction, critical thinking and how students use other entries to build their own contributions. An alternative method of content analysis is that proposed by Hara *et al.* (2002) and uses five categories for analysing the quality of the cognitive applications inferred in the discussion: elementary clarification, in-depth clarification, inferencing, judgement, application of strategies and other. These tools are suitable for conducting research on discussion groups but would be very time-consuming for use in the routine assessment of discussions for

Table 13.3 Content analysis criteria for online discussions (Hara *et al*, 2002)

Reasoning skills	Indicators
Elementary clarification	Identifying relevant elements Reformulating the problem Asking a relevant question Identifying previously stated hypotheses Simply describing the subject matter
In-depth clarification	Defining the terms Identifying assumptions Establishing referential criteria Seeking out specialized information Summarizing
Inferencing	Drawing conclusions Making generalizations Formulating a proposition which proceeds from previous statements
Judgement	Judging the relevance of solutions Making value judgements Judging inferences 'I agree, disagree'
Application of strategies	Making decisions, statements, appreciations, evaluations and criticisms Sizing up

summative purposes. The transcript analysis tool of Zhu (discussed in Fahy, 2005) involves coding each sentence of a discussion forum as either questions (horizontal or vertical), statements (referential or non-referential), reflections, scaffolding comments or paraphrases and citations. In order to conduct a content analysis of an online discussion output Hara *et al*. (2002) have proposed the use of the reasoning skills and associated indicators as outlined in Table 13.3.

Naidu *et al*. (2006) have proposed that the procedure for CMC content analysis should comprise of the following critical steps:

- determination of the unit of analysis
- development of a segmentation procedure
- determination of the reliability of the segmentation procedure
- development of coding categories and rules
- determination of the reliability of the coding categories.

The marking scheme for an online discussion can be quite simple, and based on a rudimentary 0–3 point scale that covers minimum criteria for responses to a specific question. An example is shown in Table 13.4 below. The entries are awarded a mark of 1 for minimum effort that is

Table 13.4 Simple marking rubric for online discussion

0 Point	1 Point	2 points	3 points
No response to question	Minimal response to question but relevant to topic	Acceptable to good response to question, relevant to topic but no commentary about other learners entries	Good response to question, relevant to topic and commentary about other learners entries

Table 13.5 Detailed grading rubric for online discussion

Criteria	Excellent	Good	Acceptable	Below standard
Analysis and critical thinking	Entry is highly relevant, insightful and shows comprehensive analysis and depth, draws conclusions from information presented	Entry is relevant, insightful and shows thoughtful analysis, summarizes known information	Entry is relevant, but superficial with minimal analysis, recalls known information	Entry is not relevant, no analysis
Integration	Entry contains new content and critiques responses from others	Entry related to topic and comments on responses from others	Entry related marginally to topic and only agrees or disagrees with responses from others	Entry not relate to topic and no mention of responses from others
Resources	Provides appropriate references to literature to support own entry and critiques on responses from others	Provides appropriate references to literature to support own entry and general references for comments on responses from others	Provides general references to literature to support own entry but not to comments on responses from others	No references o citations
Individual contribution	New ideas presented which add significantly to the discussion	New ideas presented which are relevant to the discussion	Common knowledge only presented	Restating cours content already presented or misses the poin
Milestones	Exceeded number of minimum entries, responded without prompting	Completed minimum number of entries, responded without prompting	Completed minimum number of entries, but responded when reminded	Did not contrib unless prompte some entries missing
Language and grammar	Scholarly language with minimal grammatical errors	Appropriate language with minimal grammatical errors	Common use of language with some grammatical errors	Misuse of language, diffic to understand, significant grammatical errors

relevant, 2 marks for an acceptable or good response but no comments about other entries and 3 marks for a good response and comments about other entries. A more detailed grading rubric is shown in Figure 13.5 and sets a number of criteria and the associated standards that are expected from the students.

Gilbert *et al.* (2005) have defined meaningful discourse in online discussions

as the ability of students to demonstrate critical thinking skills by (a) relating course content to prior knowledge and experience, (b) interpreting content through the analysis, synthesis, and evaluation of others' understanding, and (c) making inferences.   (p. 275)

In order for students to benefit from this meaningful discourse the teacher must structure the tasks so that genuine collaboration is encouraged. Students should be provided with the opportunity to explain concepts and information to other participants, and to engage in peer review by critiquing the responses of other students. What are the instructional design principles that facilitate this meaningful discourse? The scaffolds provided by the teacher, the rules of engagement and the assessment criteria all play a crucial role in encouraging meaningful discourse. Guidelines provided by the teacher will encourage student responses, especially if they provide examples of the length and depth of discussion entries. Similarly, an explicit assessment rubric that explains the relative weightings that will be applied to different components of the entry and rewards analysis and critical thinking will elicit more meaningful discourse and inferences. Online discussions can potentially empower students to be less dependent on the teacher for content clarification, and facilitate student awareness of the extent of their own cognitive abilities.

Further examples of marking and grading rubrics can be found in Appendix A.

14 Interactive assessment and Java applets

14.1 Interactivity and learning designs

One of the characteristics of the online environment is its ability to facilitate interactivity; to provide participants with instant feedback to their individual keystrokes or mouse movements. This characteristic can be used to enhance the learning and assessment environment through a judicious use of online features and learning designs.

Interactivity in the online environment can occur between individual students, between students and teachers or between students and content. For e-learning, the student, teacher or computer may initiate the interaction or the subsequent response. In order to develop a framework for interactivity heuristics, Evans *et al.* (2003) have proposed a three-way model of interactivity involving the ordered components of initiation, response and feedback (Figure 14.1). Each initiation action involving the computer and the student involves a one-way flow of information that results in a further response that subsequently generates some form of feedback. These three actions are common to all interactivities involving students and a computer, and give rise to an iterative interactivity cycle.

These three actions are seen when a student is presented with a typical MCQ; responding to an online MCQ involves the computer presenting the question to the student (initiation), the student answering the question (response) and the computer marking and responding to the answer (feedback). Evans *et al.* (2003) used this framework to describe nine heuristics for the evaluation of online interactivity and the common problems encountered by students. These have been adapted below to provide the following guidelines for teachers who are designing interactive e-assessments:

■ navigation should be easy with obvious tools on each screen that allow the student to see where they are and where they will be proceeding to next
■ the student should be engaged in frequent and varied interactions, including the use of multimedia
■ the student should be required to reflect on what they are doing and not only respond using recall
■ the student should be provided with opportunities to apply their recently learnt content in order to reinforce key concepts
■ assessment activities should be relevant and timely to the key course objectives.

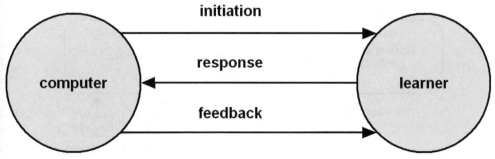

Figure 14.1 Three-way model of interactivity for the flow of information in the online environment (Evans *et al.*, 2003)

When students undertake assessments that are interactive in nature they have the potential to respond not only in a predictable or predetermined manner, but also with the potential to respond in an unexpected, but equally valid, manner. When students are provided with interactive tools, they have the potential to create new knowledge, or to reorganize existing knowledge in new ways. The assessment design can provide opportunities to enhance the learning experience as well as create new forms of knowledge, especially in the social context of group activity.

Two learning models, constructivist learning and situated learning, have arisen from cognitive research into the ways in which students learn (LearningMate, 2004). A social constructivist approach to assessment offers new pathways for students to demonstrate the relational and extended abstract capabilities they have developed during the learning process (Rust *et al.*, 2005). Teachers are now expected to create learning activities that enable students to acquire a range of meta-cognitive skills and capabilities, in addition to the acquisition of declarative knowledge, and an assessment framework is required that matches this learning environment. In the constructivist approach to learning, students are expected to make decisions and reflect on the consequences of those decisions. Access to information and authentic learning tools are common in the constructivist learning environment; these same tools and information sources should be available in the assessment environment in order for students to demonstrate higher order abilities.

Situated learning environments allow students to solve contextualized problems, often within a collaborative framework (LearningMate, 2004). When the learning design is framed around situational activities, the assessment tasks should align with this paradigm; the problems should be real, interesting and require solutions that have consequences. The interrelationships between the resources available to students, their use of formative assessment and feedback through discussions with peers and the teacher are described in Figure 14.2. In this situated learning environment, portfolio assessment methods are deemed appropriate for the summative assessment component since it encourages an iterative building of evidence of capability. e-Portfolios are becoming a common format in e-assessment since they allow for a holistic

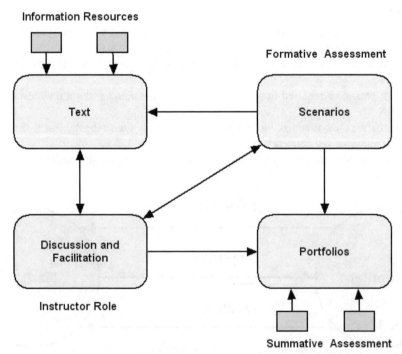

Figure 14.2 Learning and assessment model based on situated learning (LearningMate, 2004)

approach that integrates the pedagogy underpinning the course, the learning designs used to construct the course and the assessment tasks provided to the students (Mason *et al.*, 2004). e-Portfolios also allow students to develop some of the meta-cognitive capabilities associated with life-long learning.

Baldwin *et al.* (2003) have described five essential knowledge components or elements to interactive learning:

- content, which includes the actual discipline knowledge, learning objects and objectives
- learners, including their characteristics and learning styles
- technology, which includes an understanding of the appropriate tools that match learner characteristics and styles
- pedagogy, which includes an understanding of discipline methods and styles of teaching
- interaction, which coordinates and balances the previous components.

In order for an e-learning and e-assessment framework to be effective in engaging students and encouraging productive outcomes, each of these five elements should be present and integrated. The role of the teacher is to facilitate this integration, to use the elements in a manner that is appropriate for the discipline, the content, the objectives and the learning styles of the students.

Figure 14.3 illustrates a composite representation of interactive learning and interactive assessment. It draws on the interactive learning description of Baldwin *et al.* (2003) and their Balanced-Learning Design (BLADE) model, but incorporates interactive assessment. The BLADE model considers the actual learning styles of students and the relative proportion of students with each learning style, as well as the learning styles they may need to adopt to develop skills and capabilities required for the course.

The student interacts with the content initially presented by the teacher and then undertakes diagnostic and formative e-assessments that are designed to test not only the declarative and

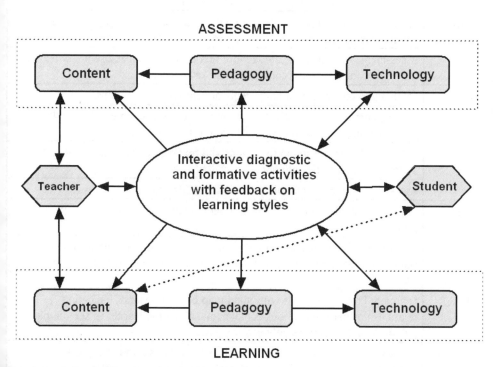

Figure 14.3 Interactive learning and interactive assessment using the BLADE model (adapted from Baldwin *et al.*, 2003)

procedural knowledge aspects of the content, but also the learning styles of the student. The feedback to the student is not only related to the content, but also incorporates the learning styles that might be appropriate for this content and the procedural knowledge in the course. The teacher can use the reports from these assessment exercises to review the pedagogical framework for the course and the manner in which the content is presented so that student outcomes are improved.

Students approach their learning in different ways and they have different learning styles (Koper *et al.*, 2004). The approach that students adopt in learning may be characterized as combinations of the following dimensions:

Table 14.1 Four sets of dichotomous approaches to learning, adapted from Baldwin *et al.* (2003)

Active	Learning: Students provided with frequent opportunities to discuss and apply what they have learnt through group assignments, synchronous discussions and tutorial exercises. Allow students to move ahead by having access to all course resources
	Assessment: Frequent use of diagnostic and formative assessment with detailed feedback. Use of interactive e-assessment will engage students
Reflective	Learning: Allow time between new concepts for students to incorporate material into their own understanding. Use asynchronous online discussions
	Assessment: Frequent use of diagnostic and formative assessment with detailed feedback. Use of simulations that allow students to test understanding
Sensing	Learning: Provide students with case studies and real world examples. Extensive use of multimedia will engage students
	Assessment: Use of simulations and online tools in assessment. Use multimedia for presenting questions and responses in e-assessments
Intuitive	Learning: Provide opportunities for students to use mind maps, presentation of general concepts and abstract ideas. Provide frequent summaries
	Assessment: Assessments can be more text based, minimize use of contextual framework for questions; concentrate on key concept
Visual	Learning: Extensive use of multimedia and visual concept maps
	Assessment: Use of simulations and online tools in assessment. Use multimedia for presenting questions and responses in e-assessments
Verbal	Learning: Use of lecture presentations and text-based resources. Provide appropriate summaries of course concepts
	Assessment: Online group discussions. Text-entry questions and responses
Sequential	Learning: Present content in linear, ordered manner. Complete one topic before proceeding to the next
	Assessment: Questions presented in same order as course content in a logical sequence. Precise responses required to MCQ, true/false, extended matching item
Global	Learning: Provide students with mind map of entire course, indicating relationships between various components. Allow the learner to see the big picture, and connections between the parts
	Assessment: Questions can use content from various areas of the course, allow students opportunity to construct responses using holistic approach and numerous concepts

- active–reflective
- sensing–intuitive
- visual–verbal
- sequential–global.

Table 14.1 summarizes these four sets of dichotomous approaches to learning, with the corresponding matched approaches that could be adopted for assessment. It will be difficult to accommodate all possible combinations, so teachers could consider using a variety of item types in an assessment activity. Students will also need to be aware that their preferred learning and assessment style may not match all activities and question types used in the course, but by being aware of these differences they can make informed decisions about how they will approach the tasks. Teachers should be aware of these issues, and the consequences they may have for the prescribed learning activities and assessment tasks for their courses. Teachers could use diagnostic assessment tools that will assist students to identify their own learning styles and how these might map onto the learning styles that facilitate the development of capabilities that are to be assessed in the course (Cassidy, 2004). An interactive learning and assessment environment helps students to identify their preferred learning and assessment style, since it provides a framework for diagnostic and formative feedback that will allow students to make adjustments to how they approach their learning.

14.2 Interactivity and assessment

14.2.1 Interactivity through simulations

Simulations enable multistructural and relational responses to be assessed in an online environment. They allow authentic learning and assessment tasks to be set for students who can manipulate data, examine consequences and make informed decisions about potential solutions to a problem. Online simulations allow rapid feedback to students, so that they can assimilate this feedback into their learning and so influence their responses to the next assessment task they are required to undertake.

A good example of software that supports the relatively straightforward construction of simulations is the open-source system, JeLSIM (Java eLearning SIMulations; https://jelsim.dev. java.net). The JeLSIM toolkit provides a simple interface for teachers to prepare simulations that are then packaged as Java applets or as IMS Content Packages. The packaged file can be uploaded to an institutional server, and called from within a virtual learning or assessment system using very simple HTML code. JeLSIM uses a set of standard visualization objects such as graphs, tables, digital inputs and outputs (Thomas et al., 2004). More sophisticated objects require the assistance of a Java programmer, but once tools are constructed, they become available for others to use. The JeLSIM software uses Java code to generate a set of standard models and the teacher can add a framework around these models (this framework will be what the student views in the packaged product), so that the model can be reused and adapted for different purposes (Thomas et al., 2004). This is an efficient model since standard code does not have to be written each time, and novice users can construct simple simulations with little knowledge of programming. An example of a simulation prepared with the JeLSIM toolkit is shown in Figure 14.4 and the required HTML code to call the Java applet is shown in Figure 14.5. This simulation allows the student to input the date, time and location of a person on the earth and generate data about the location of the sun. This JeLSIM example could be used within an e-assessment where the teacher has developed either MCQ or text entry items that require the student to generate a numerical response using the simulation, or to use the numerical responses to compare two different scenarios for a relational question. The concepts underlying the simulation are relevant to physics, mathematics and geography and the JeLSIM toolkit allows a modular construction approach so that components may be reused with a different interface for different student levels.

Solar Geometry Calculator

Click on the pale blue fields to input data

Set Date and Time: (Use clock time not apparent solar time)

21	April	2003

Hour	minute
20	30

Set Surface Orientation　　　　**Set Location**

Surface azimuth	Surface tilt	Latitude	Longitude	Standard time meridian
0.00	0.00	55.00	-4.00	0.00

OUTPUT

Declination	Solar altitude	Solar azimuth	Solar incidence
11.93	-11.82	311.85	101.82

Figure 14.4 Example of simulation developed using JeLSIM http://www.jelsim.org/content/applets/solar/index.html

```
<applet code = "org.jelsim.applet.ProgressApplet.class"
  archive = "progress.jar"
  width = "1" height="1">
<param name="loadApplet" value = "solarexpert">
</applet>
<applet code = "org.jelsim.applet.JSApplet"
  archive = "jscore.jar,SolarGeom.jar" name = "solarexpert"
  width = "574" height = "286">
<param name="isPanel" value = "X">
<param name="loadFile" value="solarexpert.jsm">
<param name="modelClass" value="org.jelsim.models.muneer.
solargeom.SolarGeom">
</applet>
```

Figure 14.5 Simple HTLM code used to call JeLSIM Java applet (http://www.jelsim.org/content/applets/solar/solarexpert.html)

e-Assessment should not simply be paper-based assessment delivered via a web interface. The web is interactive, it responds to users and allows users to manipulate information and data. Simulations allow students to explore, to test ideas, to try the unexpected. These types of activities are typically associated with the higher levels of the Bloom and SOLO taxonomies. In order for teachers to construct an interactive e-assessment involving the use of simulations, the tools must be accessible to non-programmers. The authoring tools should allow the ready integration of learning objects that are simulations in their own right, and some means to record and respond to student keystrokes. The first condition is relatively straightforward to meet, and usually requires the teacher to incorporate some very simple HTML directing the e-assessment system to open the simulation at the appropriate time and location. Some simulations are constructed as part of the e-assessment itself, or else combine learning materials and assessments within the one learning object.

In order to increase the reusability of simulations, both as learning and assessment tools, it is usually more convenient to have the simulation exist as a separate object, and call it from within the e-assessment system at runtime. This allows one copy of the learning object to exist on an institutional server and be used many times for different purposes. Complex simulations are usually expensive to produce, and it is unlikely that classroom teachers will be able to allocate sufficient time to produce the variety of simulations required for an interactive learning and assessment environment. It is more efficient to reuse well-produced simulations, and incorporate them into purposely built e-assessments which can be more contextual, and aligned more closely to the objectives for different courses.

Thomas *et al.* (2004) have provided a useful summary of how simulations might be used to assess higher order skills, using the processes associated with a modified Bloom's taxonomy:

1. *Assessing Understanding*
   Exemplify – students could use a simulation to show an understanding of a basic concept, for example by generating some data by running the simulation and using this as a response to the question.
   Predict – students could use the simulation to predict what will happen when given a specific set of conditions, again by generating some output from the simulation that is used as a response to the question.
   Compare – students could be given a particular scenario and be asked to use the simulation to map what would happen in a different context (but using the same principles). Data from the simulation could be used as a response to the question.
   Explain – students could run the simulation and then provide free text entry to the question. This may be suitable for automatic marking, or may require a teacher to read and assign a mark. Extended response questions or EMI (Extended Matching Item) may be suitable here.
2. *Assessing Application*
   Execute – students could use the simulation to process a dataset and generate a result as a response to the question.
   Implement – a student might be required to make a decision or draw a conclusion to an unknown situation. The simulation would allow different scenarios to be run, and the conclusion would require a conceptual understanding of the relationships between the outcomes from the different scenarios.
3. *Assessing Analysis*
   Differentiate – students could be presented with a case study and the simulation could allow them to test a number of potential explanations for the current situation presented in the case study. Both relevant and irrelevant information would be available to the student, and they would need to rationalize which information was useful for the simulation.
   Find coherence – students could be required to find a relationship between information they have, but this relationship would not normally have been presented as declarative knowledge. (Determine how elements fit or function within a structure.)
4. *Assessing Evaluation*
   Check – student could be required to use a dataset, scenario or case study to determine if they are appropriate, or conform to some existing criteria.
   Critique – student could use the simulation to look for inconsistencies in a dataset, scenario or case study.
5. *Assessing Creativity*
   Generating solutions – student is required to generate a hypothesis.
   Evaluating, selecting and planning the appropriate strategy – once the hypothesis has been formulated, how will it be tested? This would consist of designing an experiment, including deciding what equipment was needed and how it will be used to generate a result to test the hypothesis.

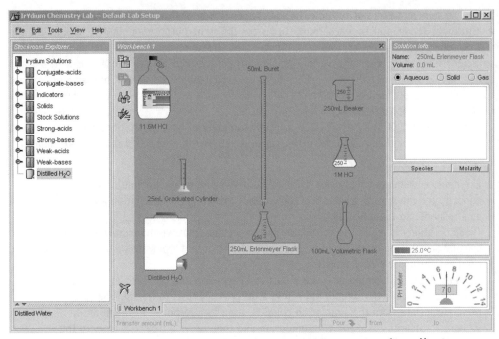

Figure 14.6 Simulated laboratory experiment from the IrYdium project (http://ir.chem.cmu.edu)

Undertaking an activity that solves the problem – carry out the simulation and report the results. Did they support the hypothesis or must a different hypothesis be formulated?

An example of using a simulation to assess creativity would be a simulated laboratory experiment, as illustrated in Figure 14.6. The questions used to assess the various levels of the Bloom or SOLO taxonomies could be in most of the formats summarized previously in Table 3.2 and cover concepts such as the use of appropriate experimental equipment, the ability to take precise and accurate measurements, the ability to perform calculations and the ability to draw valid conclusions from experimental data.

Simulations allow teachers to build authentic learning and assessment environments, since students are actively engaging with tools that enable them to explore possibilities, examine alternatives and use feedback to influence their learning. The means by which simulations are integrated into e-assessments will depend on the format of the simulations. The most versatile simulations are those that are packaged as Java applets or IMS content packages, since these objects may reside on a server and be called from numerous web-based applications using simple HTML. These simulations are separate from the actual assessment, and may be used as a learning object or as an interactive tool in e-assessments. The questions for the assessment may be constructed independently of the simulation and so the difficulty level may be set by the teacher to match the student level. In this case, the question is marked by the assessment engine and not by the packaged simulation. The feedback to the student can be determined by the teacher, and may provide access to extra resources or allow the student to use the simulation to improve their learning before proceeding to new concepts. A total integration of the simulation and the assessment would allow information about the student use of the simulation to be passed to the assessment engine (Thomas *et al.*, 2004). Student keystrokes, simulation variables and student-generated data would be used by the assessment engine to determine a mark and associated feedback for the student responses. This is technically possible but requires more detailed programming and usually involves a project team with a variety of skills.

An example of a medical education simulation is illustrated in Figure 14.7, from the MedicCaseML by MedicMED (http://www.medicmed.de/easa/EASA/AppData/Demo1.htm). This

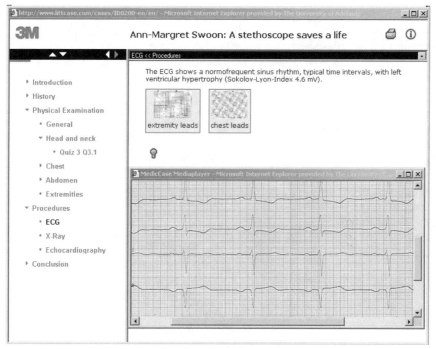

Figure 14.7 Simulation used in medical education from MedicCaseML by MedicMED
(http://www.medicmed.de/easa/EASA/AppData/Demo1.htm)

case illustrates a simulation that might be used in a formative assessment or as a teaching tool, using real case data but fictitious patients. Students may play the scenario as many times as they require, taking alternative paths and reflecting on the consequences of their decision-making in a safe environment. Such simulations could also be used for summative purposes if the number of variations embedded in the simulation was sufficient to ensure that overexposure of specific items or data was avoided.

Commercially available simulation can be quite sophisticated, and used as both learning and assessment tools. The simulations illustrated in Figures 14.8 and 14.9 can be used in both undergraduate and postgraduate business studies programmes, and enable students to practise market analysis and the outcomes of their decision-making. Wall Street Raider (Figure 14.9) allows students to investigate the ethical, legal and moral issues associated with their activities and decisions. Teachers could incorporate such simulations into diagnostic, formative and summative assessments, and provide rich feedback to students. Question types would cover the full range summarized previously in Table 3.2. It is likely that these types of simulations will become more common in further and higher education, and will form core activities for both learning and assessment. The competitive advantage that arises from the ability of institutions to offer sophisticated simulations will undoubtedly encourage additional funding to be inverted into the development of discipline-specific examples.

14.2.2 Interactivity through Java applets

Not all Java applets are automatically suited to assessment tasks, nor are they necessarily suited to all discipline areas. Java applets may complement content or questions presented in other formats by allowing students to interact with the concept being considered. The use of Java applets in assessment may be made more beneficial for students by the use of judicious design elements and the ready availability of teacher-prepared documentation. It is essential that adequate time be allowed for students to become familiar with the use of the Java applets, especially if they are a crucial component of the assessment. There is frequently a steep learning

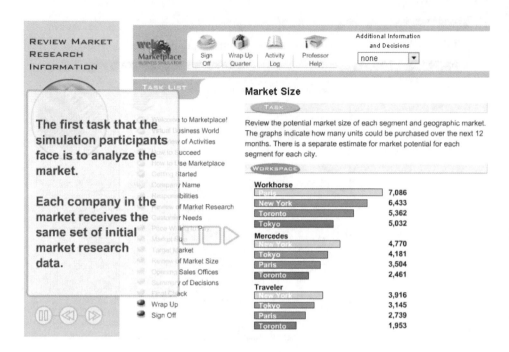

Figure 14.8 Simulation used in business studies (http://www.marketplace–simulation. com)

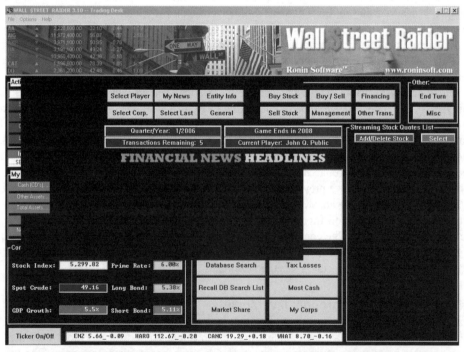

Figure 14.9 Wall Street Raider simulation used in business studies (http://www.roninsoft. com/wsraider.htm)

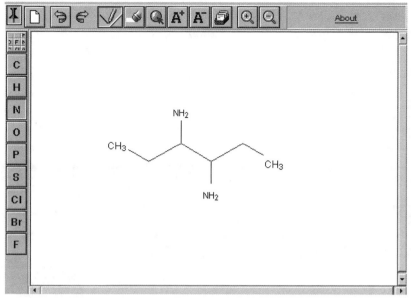

Figure 14.10 Chemical structure drawing Java applet from ACD Labs (http://www.acdlabs. com).

curve for students when they encounter a sophisticated Java applet tool for the first time, particularly for students with minimal web experience.

Teachers who are contemplating using Java applets in their assessments should allow adequate time during the learning stages of the course for students to become familiar with the online tools. A useful activity is to include the Java applets in a number of diagnostic or formative assessments (Crisp, 2002). For example, the chemical structure drawing applet from ACD Labs illustrated in Figure 14.10 allows students to use the standard shorthand representation for depicting a particular chemical. The ability to draw this visual image of the structure is a skill that students in chemistry are required to understand and master. The applet tool allows this familiar skill to be translated to a web interface, and students would be expected to use the template format of the applet tool to assemble the required image. Students would normally be able to draw the structure on paper without difficulty, but it may not be obvious to all students how this could be achieved using this particular applet. The tool bars on the left and top of the applet interface allow students to construct the image and teachers would need to allow time for students to become familiar with this interface before using the tool in a high-stakes, summative assessment, so that students would not be disadvantaged.

Many Java applets are freely available on the web and teachers who wish to use them as standalone tools within the e-assessment task will usually find it unnecessary to write their own applets. For those that are freely available from the web, teachers should download the available *.class or *.jar files and store them on an institutional server where they can be called using the appropriate HTML code. Usually some form of attribution will be required when using such Java applets locally. Alternatively, teachers may wish (or be required to by the applet writer) to use the Java applet from its remote location. From the point of view of the student using the applet, it usually makes little difference whether the applet is served from a local or remote server, although download times may vary. Most sites from which applets are available will contain example HTML code for teachers to use.

What types of Java applets are useful for students? There are simple applets that provide information to students with no, or minimal, interactivity. Such applets can be used as Help menus or to provide course content for use in tutorials, workshops or assessment. An example would be a simple slide show showing information and allowing students to use an index to find

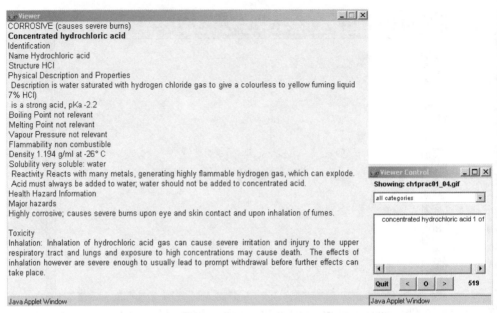

Figure 14.11 Use of a slide show applet in pre–laboratory assessments (Viewer 1.0 by Patrik Lundin, plundin@kagi.com).

relevant material. Since applets can be made to open in a second window, students may toggle between an assessment window and an information window, as appropriate. This is particularly useful in formative assessments since the purpose of the task is to assist student learning. An example of a slide show Java applet used to display indexed information to students during an e-assessment is illustrated in Figure 14.11.

Applets are available that illustrate a basic concept and allow students to explore how the underlying principles can be derived from the examples provided. The discipline areas of chemistry, biology, physics and mathematics are well represented in this class. Examples of such an applet would be titration in chemistry, simple harmonic motion in physics, polynomial equations and their graphical displays in mathematics, statistics displays, geographic information systems for geology or geography, translating a sequence of nucleic acids to generate the corresponding amino-acid sequence in biology. A non-science example can be found in music, where keys on a piano can be related to notes on a staff or played by the speakers on the computer. The interactivity inherent in these applets allows a student to explore, make errors and seek their own solutions. They can all potentially be incorporated into e-assessments and allow students to use authentic tools (Crisp, 2002).

An example of a Java applet that allows students to analyse statistically is shown in Figure 14.12. Such a tool could be used readily in online statistics quizzes, but also in disciplines such as psychology, marketing, biology and geography. The institution would require only one copy of the Java applet on a local server, and many disciplines could incorporate the tool into their courses as both a learning and assessment tool.

Appendix 2 lists some representative examples of Java applets that would be suitable for integration into e-assessments.

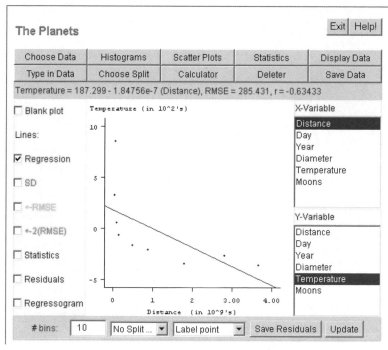

Figure 14.12 Statistics Java applet example by John Marden (http://www.stat.uiuc.edu/courses/stat100/cuwu)

15 Online role-playing and games

15.1 Characteristics of online role-plays

The difference between a simulation as discussed in Chapter 14 and a role-play is that the former uses a set of rules to limit the choices that are available to the participant, usually through the use of computer algorithms, whereas for the latter the responses are normally only limited by what the participant chooses to do (Linser *et al.*, 2004). Role-plays in educational settings involve students taking on a persona as defined by the teacher, and responding to a scenario as a defined character. The outcome from a role-play is not usually predetermined, although the scenario may require a decision or recommendation to be made, and a justification for the outcomes arrived at by the students. By acting out the scenario, students interact with each other, and the material is presented as part of the course.

Simulations, as shown in the Chapter 14, are very well suited to many of the science disciplines since they present models for the concepts that govern physical systems. For simulations, student input will normally be interpreted through an algorithm in order to generate the corresponding output and students will compare this output with that expected from their understanding of the conceptual models related to the discipline topic. The number of choices will necessarily be limited. Role-plays, on the other hand, are often suited to learning and assessment activities that are social or cultural in nature, such as those that involve human interactions and characteristics (Figure 15.1). The role of the technology is quite different in simulations and role-plays. When students interact with a simulation the technology is an active participant, the algorithms are responding to the student input and producing results that the student will use. In an online role-play, the technology is used to facilitate communication and access to information, its role is passive since the student does not use an output generated by the computer before proceeding.

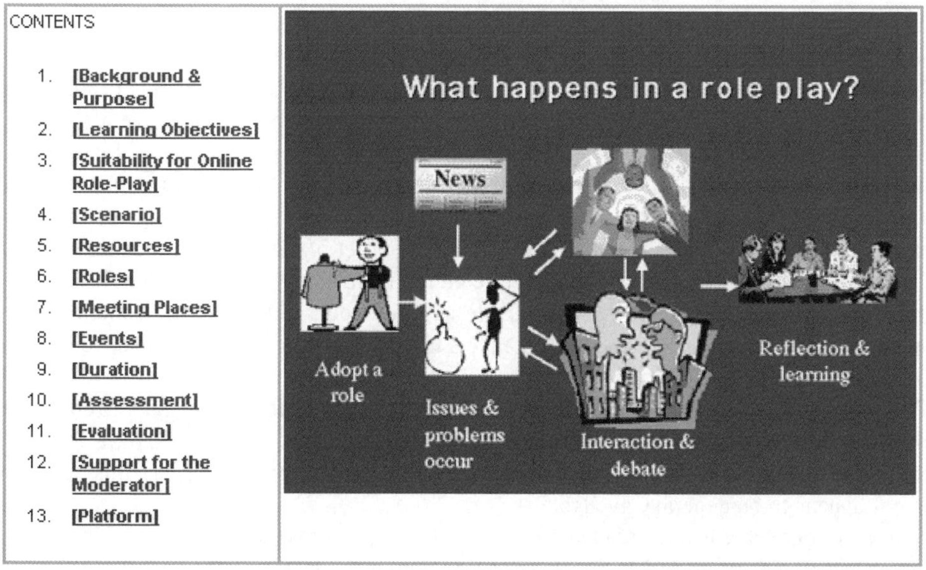

CONTENTS

1. [Background & Purpose]
2. [Learning Objectives]
3. [Suitability for Online Role-Play]
4. [Scenario]
5. [Resources]
6. [Roles]
7. [Meeting Places]
8. [Events]
9. [Duration]
10. [Assessment]
11. [Evaluation]
12. [Support for the Moderator]
13. [Platform]

What happens in a role play?

News

Adopt a role

Issues & problems occur

Interaction & debate

Reflection & learning

Figure 15.1 Summary of role-play activities: Screen shot from Mekong e-Sim (http://learningdesigns.uow.edu.au)

This has a number of implications when students are assessed within a simulation or an online role-play.

Role-plays allow for the creation of an authentic learning and assessment environment. Students are part of a community with a common purpose and are able to use their inherent skills and capabilities, as well as those developed during the course. By taking on a role or persona, students are able to reflect on the impact that their decisions, and those of others, have on the 'community'.

Fablusi™ is an example of an application built specifically to facilitate online role-playing activities (http://www.fablusi.com). The Fablusi™ role-play software allows students to take on a role but remain anonymous to other participants in the role-play; it allows the creation of multiple worlds within which scenarios can be played out; and allows multiple roles such as administrator, moderator and subject matter expert. One of the features of Fablusi™ is its ability to record and archive the entries in the role-play, a feature that assists in assessment. The Fablusi™ website allows access to public role-plays in order to demonstrate the features of the system. Although students can interact with Fablusi™ with any Internet browser, authoring requires a non-Internet Explorer browser such as Firefox, Mozilla or Opera.

The Fablusi™ authoring tool supports 'Dynamic Goal Based Learning', a pedagogy that has been described as being similar to problem-based or case-based learning, scenario-based learning or game-based learning (Naidu et al., 2000). Each of these pedagogical approaches relies on an authentic problem that requires students to find and process information, consider a number of options, and come to, as well as justify, a conclusion or decision. The Fablusi™ methodology provides an initial starting point for the role-play, after which the environment is dynamic. Each time a particular scenario is undertaken, quite different end points or output may result. In a role-play the students learn and produce assessable actions by interacting with each other, by using content and by reflecting on their actions. Role-plays allow the emotional, cultural and social dimensions of decision-making to be investigated, as well as their impact on other participants.

The assessment of role-play activity can involve the process and product of the interactions, as discussed in Chapter 13.2. Teachers need to be very specific about the learning outcomes expected from participation in a role-play, and to ensure that the assessment criteria are aligned appropriately with these objects. Students will not wish to spend significant amounts of time on activities that are not worth an appropriate percentage of the final mark for a course.

Creating a scenario and assigning roles in Fablusi™ is relatively straightforward; the authoring pages use simple text entries and multimedia and web links may be incorporated as required. A screen shot of the authoring page is shown in Figure 15.2.

Teachers will need to give some thought to defining the roles and the level of information that is available to all roles, versus information that is role specific. This can have a significant impact on the initial stages of the student engagement with the scenario. Teachers can facilitate or hinder collaboration between students through the initial information available to various roles. Fablusi™ allows subspaces to be created where specific groups or roles may share information or engage in private discussions. Wills et al. (2002) have provided detailed documentation on constructing and moderating an online role-play, as part of the AUTC project on ICT-based learning designs (http://learningdesigns.uow.edu.au). The website contains design templates, exemplars and interviews with teachers who have moderated and developed different role-plays.

The University of Western Australia has also developed a custom-built application called 'Simulation Builder' for teachers and students to construct and engage in online role-plays (http://www.mmc.arts.uwa.edu.au/studentprojects/staff/simulations). However, this software does not appear to be generally available.

Role-plays generally involve students working in groups so that a community of inquiry can be developed (Linser et al., 2004). Teachers should define the expectations with respect to the quantity and quality of entries that are required and specific criteria about how they will be assessed. It is beneficial if students are offered an initial face-to-face meeting (or synchronous

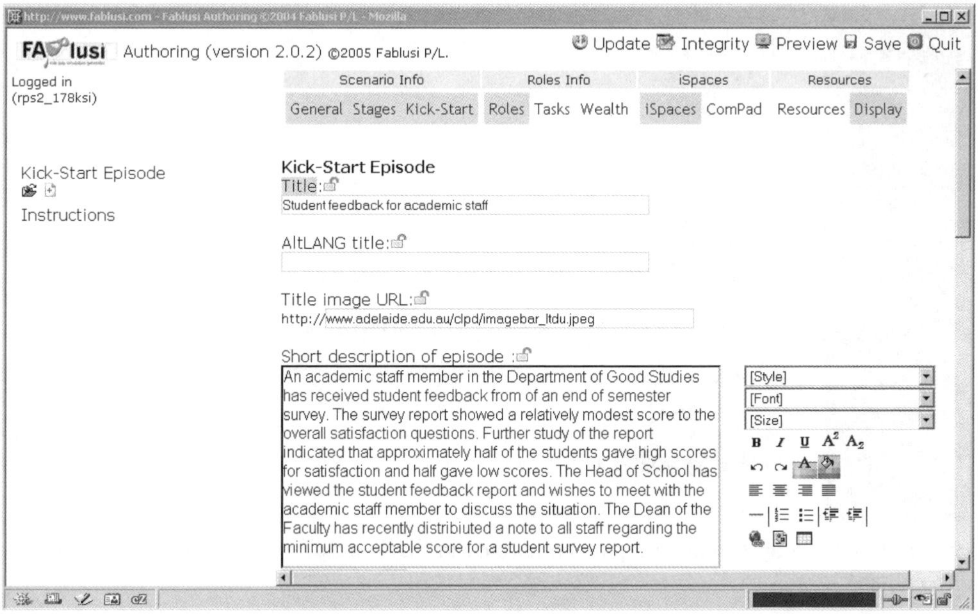

Figure 15.2 Authoring page for role-play software Fablusi™ (http://www.fablusi.com)

online chat session), and also a final meeting to bring closure to the activity and resolve any issues that are remaining from the online activity. Role-plays are particularly appropriate for problems where there are a number of solutions, where the issues are complex and involve decision-making and where social or cultural consequences arise with those decisions. They can be used to assess leadership capabilities and the ability to work in groups in order to achieve a common aim.

Ip (2001) has proposed that four components are required to construct an appropriate learning environment for role-plays. They are:

- scaffolding (tasks designed to achieve stated learning outcomes)
- resources (discipline specific information required to enact the role play)
- interaction facilities (communication tools)
- social structure (a framework for supporting the game).

Role-plays sometimes incorporate a goal or mission which students are required to reach or complete. Naidu *et al.* (2000) have described 'Goal-Based Scenarios' (GBS) in which students assume a main role, usually associated with a defined mission, and are required to use resources (or learn content) in order to carry out their role and complete the mission (which could be the prescribed assessment task). This learning design draws from the literature on authentic environments and problem-based learning, with the emphasis on students learning content to enact a role, rather than accumulating knowledge to pass an exam. The GBS framework can be designed to foster the development of particular skills and capabilities, and the assessment design would be closely linked with the evidence required to show this development.

Role-plays do not necessarily require specific software systems, as all of the major learning management systems discussed in Chapter 5 have discussion boards, group and email facilities that enable online role-plays to be conducted. Examples of role-plays performed within WebCT™ and Blackboard™ are available from the AUTC project site on ICT-based learning designs (http://learningdesigns.uow.edu.au). An example from a role-play conducted using the discussion board, group and email features in Blackboard™ is shown in Figure 15.3.

Role-play activities move participants beyond the prescriptive nature of instructivist and strictly behaviourist learning by allowing a cycle of action, reflection and reaction. Participant

Figure 15.3 Mekong e-Sim role-play conducted in Blackboard™ (http://learningdesigns. uow.edu.au)

behaviour is influenced by the reaction of other participants, rather than by the algorithm in the software, as with simulations and games. An interesting discussion of a role-play activity involving a needle exchange programme in close proximity to a school highlights many of the issues involved in designing and evaluating this type of activity, including setting the learning objectives, assessment in the form of reflective journals and online postings, as well as roles of moderators and administrators (Fannon, 2002). The types of problems encountered within this particular example exemplify for students the complexity of dealing with social, cultural and emotional issues in an authentic situation.

15.2 Assessment of online role-play activity

The assessment of an online role-play will depend on the objectives that have been set for the activity and the features that have been incorporated for student responses and engagement. If the role-play involves group activities, then teachers will need to review the issues discussed in Chapter 13.2 on the assessment of group work. The assessment of role-play activity requires very clear information for students about what is being assessed, whether the process and product of the activity will be assessed and the relative proportions assigned to each component within the activity. Online role-plays often use discussion board features and so the assessment criteria would have similar features (see Chapter 13.3). An example of the assessment and expectation information on the role-play for students in the Mekong e-Sim is shown in Figure 15.4 (Baron et al., 2004).

An example of an assessment rubric from the AUTC project site on ICT-based learning designs (http://learningdesigns.uow.edu.au) is illustrated in Figure 15.5.

Role-plays are designed to model socialized contextual interactions (Ip, 2001) and so the assessment criteria should reflect the important characteristics that are being developed during this type of activity. The assessment marking scheme should be developed during the initial design stages of the role-play to ensure a close alignment between the relative proportions allocated to assessment components and the activity priorities as articulated to students. For example, the Fablusi™ environment allows the use of general discussion forums, discussion with voting, as well as news and bulletins. If students are to spend time developing skills and capabilities in these environments the marks allocated for participation in specific activities should be in proportion to their importance.

Assessment Overview
Both the way that you do things (eg teamwork, participation) during the eSim as well as what you produce (eg reports) will be assessed. The various assessment items and deadlines are given here.

 Quizzes
Two quizzes have been developed covering separate aspects of the Mekong e-Sim that will need to be completed. They are designed to introduce participants to the Mekong region and the various roles involved in the Mekong e-Sim. The quizzes will become available for a limited period of time in accordance with the assessment timetable.

 Role Profile:Strategy
Role Profile:Strategy will help your group to develop a shared understanding of the policies and responsibilities of your role and of the strategies you will implement throughout the e-Sim, as well as critically identifying differences in your interpretation of the persona and the context you are working in.

 Public Inquiry Submission Paper
The public inquiry submission papers allow the development of a deeper understanding of a specific issue and also provide the basis for each group's initial submission to the public inquiries.

 Participation
Your participation in the e-Sim is fundamental to achieving successful learning outcomes from the e-Sim. Due to differences in the various persona and how they would normally participate in these interactions there are a number of different ways you will be assessed.

 Debriefing Report
The aim of the debriefing report is document your learning about the complexity of environmental decision making from the e-Sim. It draws together your experiences and reflections.

Figure 15.4 Assessment rubric for a role-play within Blackboard™ (Baron *et al.*, 2004)

How will it be marked?
Students who wish to score 25% will follow the follow grading and feedback criteria. (A whole page is provided to students) The 25% role play report will be marked using the following feedback and grading checklist. The ticks below indicate where you stand with regard to each set of statements. A tick in the extreme left hand box means that the statement on the left is true and therefore is of distinction quality. The boxes from left to right are abbreviated by H (for High Distinction ie. 85%-100%), D (for Distinction ie. 75%-84%), C (for Credit ie. 65%-74%), P (for Pass ie. 50%-64%) and F (for Fail ie. 0%-49%) respectively. Ticks to the left within a box are better than ticks to the right.

Role play report	H	D	C	P	F	
Clear & focussed introduction, and continues to be interesting						Uninspiring introduction, and continues to be uninteresting and boring
Grammar and spelling accurate						Many spelling and grammatical errors
Logically developed argument and well set out						Rambles, lacks continuity and difficult to follow the logical sequence
Appropriate length (2,500 words) & referencing (10)						Too long/short and minimum 5 relevant references
Effective use of figures & tables						Figures/tables add little to argument
Content						
Objectives achieved						Objectives ignored
Topic covered in depth						Superficial treatment of topic
Accurate presentation of factors						Much questionable or inaccurate evidence
Rigorous critique of key concepts						Lack of demonstration of key concepts
Original and creative thought						Little evidence of originality

Presentation	%	x5%	
Content	%	x20%	
Total			25

Mark Freeman & Michael Adams, UTS

Figure 15.5 Assessment rubric for a role-play (http://learningdesigns.uow.edu.au/guides/info/G1/more/DesignersGuide.html)

An example of a marking sheet from the Mekong e-Sim is shown in Table 15.1, highlighting the distribution of marks between individual and group activities, and includes essential tasks such as planning, reporting and debriefing (Baron *et al.*, 2004).

Online role-playing and games

Table 15.1 Assessment rubric for role-play (adapted from Baron *et al.*, 2004)

Assessment item	Individual or group	%	How to submit	Due date
Quiz: Roles	Individual	5	online submission	
Quiz: Mekong	Individual	5	online submission	
Role Profile Strategy	Group	10	online + hardcopy	
Public Inquiry Submissions	Group	20 (also part of participation)	Media Groups: Relevant news discussion board Non-Media Groups: 1,000 word: Online + hardcopy 400 word: Relevant public inquiry discussion board Decision-Maker Groups: 400 word: Online + hardcopy 1,000 word: Relevant public inquiry discussion board	
Participation	Group	20	Based on emails, discussion group submissions, login statistics, participation in face-to-face discussion, session and peer evaluation.	
Peer Participation Evaluation Survey	Individual	0[#]	Online submission	
Debriefing Report	Individual	40	Online + hardcopy	

[#] however 10% of e-Sim mark will be deducted if not completed

15.3 Scenario-based activity

15.3.1 Scenario-based learning

All disciplines require students to develop problem-solving capabilities and skills in the meta-analysis of the limitations of knowledge and the consequences of making decisions. Students will realize that potential solutions to a problem may be varied and that they may be required to justify a particular solution as a fundamental part of their education. Scenario-based learning allows students to explore complex situations and problems, to follow a path in decision-based activity and analyse the consequences of their actions (Kindley, 2002). The acquisition and integration of knowledge into the scenario is concurrent with process development and meta-analysis of cause and effect; it is an authentic learning environment.

What is the difference between a role-play and scenario-based learning? In role-plays the participant takes on a persona or character, and their behaviours are based on students' perception of how that character might act in a particular context. In scenario-based learning the participant will behave as herself or himself, and act as they believe they should in the context presented.

Scenario-based learning usually occurs in a particular context; it is dependent on situated cognition, where the meaning of the problem and potential solutions are dependent on the

Scene No.: : Beginning the Dialogue

BAT Nurse responds: "I hear there's something going on up at Alice Springs"? RC: "Yes there is. We have just been notified of an explosion up at Lyme Gap, which is a US military facility. Alice Springs hospital have contacted us and said they need some help. They have requested a medical retrieval team to go up there and assist in the management of ...there looks like there is about 10 burns patients. But we really don't know."

The BAT Nurse should respond with ...

Please select from the options below:

▶ Sounds like a job for the Burns Assessment team?

▶ Sounds like we need to get someone to determine whether we need to send a Burns assessment team.

▶ I know just the team. I'll prep them at once.

Documents

Tutorials

Figure 15.6 Screen shot from a Scenariation example for a clinical burns assessment exercise (University of Adelaide)

context, as are the behaviours of the participants. Kindley (2002) has summarized the characteristics of scenario-based learning and the following list is adapted from this work. Scenario-based learning may be characterized as:

- being situated in a real context and based on situated cognition
- aiming for performance improvement and behavioural change
- requiring some boundaries to be in place to allow participants to concentrate on key skill and capability development
- requiring the use of interactive tools and discovery techniques in order to construct and participate in scenarios
- requiring the use of interactive media to generate an engaging participant interface
- requiring an assessment approach that rewards more productive paths and behaviours
- requiring a learning design that highlights more productive and less productive paths in terms of the anticipated learning objectives
- requiring appropriate formative feedback to influence participant behaviour and decisions without necessarily being highly prescriptive.

Scenariation is a web application for designing scenario-based learning objects (http://scenariation.com). Scenariation allows an instructional designer or teacher to build a collection of scenes; each scene has some form of decision-making branching to which the student will respond. The next screen that is presented to the student will depend on their choice at the branching point. The feedback after each choice may include further resources for learning, a revision activity or simply allow the student to follow a particular path and examine the consequences of their decision-making. Figure 15.6 shows an example, from the student perspective, of a decision-making screen from a burns assessment exercise. Students may listen to the multimedia presentation, refer to notes they have previously made online and then respond to the questions presented. Scenario-based learning activities may be implemented as role-plays if students are asked to respond as a particular persona and not as themselves.

15.3.2 Assessment of scenario-based learning

Scenario-based learning activities provide an authentic context in which students will respond to complex issues and problems. The design principles are based on a non-linear paradigm that often attempts to model expert performance and decision-making. The exercises draw out tacit knowledge and acceptable responses from a discipline perspective (Herrington *et al.*, 2000). The assessment of scenario-based learning activities has much in common with that of role-plays, and should be closely aligned with rewarding the development of those skills and capabilities that are valued, not just those amenable to quantitative measurement. Assessment is likely to be continuous and cumulative, and peer and self-assessment activities may be appropriate. The face validity for the assessment of role-play and scenario activities will benefit from the use of online communication tools that are available to all participants, since both informal and formal benchmarking can proceed and standards can be explicitly articulated to students.

Scenario-based learning that emphasizes performance improvements can use aspects of the DECIDE (Define, Exploit, Collect, Investigate, Develop and Expand) methodology as described by Wu *et al.* (2003) and has been adapted to the following summary:

Define the problem and the corresponding learning objectives
Exploit existing individual and group knowledge and skills
Collect various options and potential solutions
Investigate various options and potential solutions
Develop appropriate solutions and define the consequences of this approach
Expand solutions so that they may apply to other problems.

Wu *et al.* (2003) have also described the relationship between scenario-based activities and the corresponding learning objectives and these have been modified to include potential assessment criteria and activities in Table 15.2.

Table 15.2 Relationship between learning objectives, scenario-based activities and assessment items (adapted from Wu *et al.*, 2003)

Learning objective	Activity	Assessment
Improve performance	Students provided with problems that develop performance skills; criteria are explicitly articulated. Feedback used to direct students to appropriate resources	Performance skills assessed before, during and after activity. Diagnostic, formative and summative tools used. Evidence-based approach to measuring performance improvements
Working collaboratively in groups to propose potential solutions to problems	Students working in groups, with defined roles and expectations. Groups required to document their activities and individual contributions	Assessment criteria states individual and group marking scheme. Process and product of group work assessed
Use appropriate resources to propose solutions to problems	Students use authentic tools such as those encountered in the discipline to investigate the problem and propose a solution	Assess the use of the resources and tools, or their incorporation into the solution or justification
Integrate feedback, new knowledge or processes into potential solutions	Students presented with appropriate feedback that included new information sources, processes or tools in response to their activities	Assessment of use of feedback and additional resources, tools or processes to propose final solution
Evaluate proposed solutions to problems	Students required to analyse their proposed solution and justify it through an evidence-based approach	Assess the self and peer-analysis of proposed solutions

15.4 Game-based learning and its assessment

Game-based learning is quite common at primary-school-level education, in business training programmes and for military training exercises; it has been shown to be engaging and effective (Dondi et al., 2002). It has not been as widely adopted at the tertiary education level, perhaps because it is associated with particular types of entertainment activities, such as adventure and fantasy games, or perhaps because the objectives for these types of games might be considered trivial. Entertainment games have a high emphasis on interactivity, appealing graphics and sound, as well as clearly-articulated goals. The player develops skills as she or he proceeds through the game, is provided with feedback in response to particular actions and is rewarded at various milestones. Communities of practice evolve around how to master the skills and capabilities that are required to reach the goal. Each player will approach the journey to the goal in a different way, and mistakes will be made and corrected on the way. All of these characteristics could have been used to describe an effective learning environment in tertiary education.

Many of the principles proposed for good computer game designs match well with those for good learning designs (Prensky, 2001). The relationship between game design (Ahamer et al., 2002) and learning design principles (Oliver, 2000; Chickering et al., 1987; Boud et al., 2002) has been summarized in Table 15.3. Games allow participants to enter a microenvironment that can either closely resemble the real world, or move beyond what is possible in the physical realm. As learning environments move from an instructivist to a more constructivist base, the principles involved in designing games become more relevant to learning designs; the role of the teacher also shifts from that of knowledge deliverer to that of process facilitator, encouraging students to explore different possibilities and suggesting productive strategies rather than prescriptive answers. Games are highly relevant for the development of social and process skills since they allow complexity to be investigated and alternative pathways to a common goal.

Why are computer-based games so engaging to participants? The principles outlined in Table 15.3 highlight the encouragement of a personal commitment in continuing to pursue the game, they draw on the human traits and emotions associated with satisfaction, frustration, excitement, enjoyment and the pride of individual achievement with the associated recognition by peers. Games encompass many of the features already discussed for simulations, role-plays and scenario-based activity. Given the apparent reluctance of tertiary educational institutions to adopt the term gaming in their curricula, it may be appropriate to draw on game design principles and simply relabel them as situational learning.

Prensky (2001) has categorized games into those related to action, adventure, fights, puzzles, role-playing, simulations, sports and strategy. This taxonomy is constructed from the participant's point of view; it describes what type of activity they undertake. Since the entertainment industry is primarily concerned with consumers purchasing their product, much of the initial research into gaming was based on user demographics, their associated attention spans and the level of skill required to complete the tasks presented by the software. Tertiary education programmes are based on developing skills in problem-solving, meta-cognition and decision-making, often in a collaborative environment, and the purpose of learning is not to win but to apply what one has learnt to new situations (Bonk et al., 2005).

Assessing game-based learning will follow the same principles outlined for role-plays and scenario-based learning. For games that are designed to develop a particular skill that is being simulated in the virtual environment, pre and post-testing for this skill in the real physical environment will allow teachers to make judgements about the level of improvement. Games that are developing problem-solving skills can use applications such as IMMEX (http://www.immex.ucla.edu) to monitor and quantify improvements in strategic thinking and the effective use of resources. Games can incorporate selected response items where students must achieve a minimum score before proceeding to the next topic or level, or they can be used in conjunction with online discussions. The assessment can be built into the game itself, which usually increases the complexity of construction of the game, or may use applications independent of the game,

Table 15.3 Design principles for games and learning (adapted from Ahamer *et al.*, 2002; Oliver, 2000; Chickering *et al.* 1987; Boud *et al.*, 2002)

Game design principles	Learning design principles
A clear overall vision	Clear learning objectives articulated
A constant focus on the player experience	Student-centred learning approach, encourages contact between students and faculty, encourages active learning
A strong structure	Chooses the learning activities ahead of the content, emphasizes time on task, uses a structured sequence of different learning activities, allows for flexibility
Highly adaptive	Chooses open-ended and ill-structured tasks, respects diverse talents and ways of learning
Easy to learn, hard to master	Communicates high expectations, challenges students to higher-level learning
Stays within the flow state	Chooses meaningful contexts for the learning
Provides frequent rewards, not penalties	Uses authentic assessment activities, gives frequent and immediate feedback to students on the quality of their learning, has a fair system for assessing and grading students
Includes exploration and discovery	Makes the resources plentiful, uses active forms of learning, rich simulating environments
Provide mutual assistance – one thing helps to solve another	Scaffolds student learning, develops reciprocity and cooperation among students
Has a very useful interface	Provides ready access to learning resources and facilitates group learning
Includes the ability to save progress	Allows construction of student portfolios to demonstrate skill development

which simplifies the construction of the game but introduces issues of alignment between data from the different applications.

A game has a goal, so completion of all the tasks and arriving at the goal could constitute a criterion for assessment. Since a student would be actively engaged in using a variety of skills to complete the tasks, teachers could be confident that learning has taken place if the goal is reached. Games algorithms can minimize the opportunities for guessing, or reduce the probability that the goal can be reached by simply pressing computer keys at random. The game can also be designed so that alternative options are presented to different students so as to minimize the ability of students to engage in non-productive collaboration, such as posting solutions or 'cheats'. This would be similar to using a random selection of items from a question bank or the protocols adopted for adaptive tests to minimize over-exposure of particular items. For criterion-based assessment this would be appropriate, but may not be as directly relevant for norm-referenced assessments, where quantitative data is required so that a score can be calculated.

When using game-based learning, teachers will need to decide whether the product of the activity (reaching the goal) and/or the process of the activity (how the student reached the goal) will be assessed. The previous discussion on the assessment of group work in Chapter 13.2 is therefore relevant. If the process of the activity is to be assessed then the game should facilitate tracking of the path that students have taken towards the goal; data such as the screen time

Figure 15.7 Screen shot from 'The Business Game' (http://www.pixelearning.com)

used to complete the task, non-productive paths followed and information sources requested are important indicators of the strategic thinking of the student.

PIXELearning has developed a proprietary product called LearningBeans that integrates assessment methodologies into its game-based learning programs for business programs (http://www.pixelearning.com/services-learningbeans.htm). LearningBeans allows instructional designers to develop business games that develop leadership and management skills, and RAPID NVQ allows assessment tools to be incorporated into the construction of the game scenario. A screenshot from 'The Business Game' is shown in Figure 15.7, showing how the software recreates a realistic virtual office environment and allows students to access tools that would be commonly available in the real world office.

Section 6 **What about the future?**

16 Future trends in e-assessment

16.1 Current perceptions of where e-assessment is heading

Warburton *et al.* (2003) reported that 'training and support was the highest critical success factor for the implementation of CAA, followed by the importance of reliability and ease-of-use of institutional CAA services and perceived time savings and effectiveness'. The critical success factors necessary for the widespread adoption of e-assessment are often discussed in the literature and at conferences, as is the apparent reluctance of educational institutions to adequately resource assessment processes in general. Many teachers lack the time and confidence to develop e-assessment items appropriate for an interactive online environment and students are often apprehensive about using these items for high stakes, summative assessments (Warburton *et al.*, 2003). As with many issues involving change, stakeholders do not immediately perceive the benefits of moving from the familiar, especially if it involves a significant level of additional work. Why should teachers and students, who have been accustomed to a (perceived) stable and successful framework for learning and assessment, shift to a new paradigm? Will the institution provide teachers with adequate resources, time release and rewards in the form of tenure and promotion, for developing interactive e-assessments? Will students be rewarded with higher grades for developing new skills in being able to use information and communication technologies?

Teachers are particularly reluctant to follow colleagues who are techno-evangelists down an unfamiliar path, especially when the risks appear to be high, the time commitment excessive and the benefits uncertain. Technology, especially in the form of e-learning, appears to promise much but can often fail to deliver when put into an authentic environment. This brief synopsis of comments highlights some of the current concerns repeated in educational institutions. The techno-evangelists, who have seen the light, are bewildered by the lack of enthusiasm of their colleagues; the evangelists present seminars and workshops illustrating the benefits of sophisticated, immersive, authentic, online environments that are currently available and often receive minimum recognition for the scholarship that is present in their activities.

Previous chapters in this book have examined how e-assessment is being used by educational institutions and the models that provide exemplars of the actual and the possible. For teachers and educational administrators interested in the dominant use of e-assessment at the present time, in terms of volume of activity and number of participants, the large-scale standardized tests for literacy and numeracy skills in schools and the GMAT®, AP®, SAT®, MAPP™, PRAXIS™ and TOEFL® tests based in the USA, provide the main examples. Significant research around the efficiencies and efficacies of these e-assessments is available and good practice models have developed from their use (ETS, 2007). These types of assessments are grounded in a standards-based epistemology, and their primary objective is to function as a gatekeeper in a selection process. This role is important and will likely continue into the future for political, social and economic reasons. However, these types of e-assessments do not necessarily have as their primary function the enhancement of student learning. They can be used to develop programmes that enhance student learning, but they are not designed to perform this function in their own right. The economics of assessment development and use favours resources being allocated to these types of standardized tests, and it will be some time before equivalent resources are directed towards large-scale assessments that are coupled directly to enhancements of the student experience.

There is a current assumption that e-assessment will require specialist skills for the writing of appropriate items, particularly those that will be subject to psychometric analysis. The costs associated with the construction of good, reusable, e-assessment items is significant, especially if subject matter experts, multimedia and learning designers and psychometricians are all required. For many teachers this scenario reduces their influence and autonomy over the learning and assessment environment. It impacts on their self-perception of their role and purpose, especially if they are assigned the role of subject matter expert and others dominate the final phases of the assessment construction process. Educational administrators will mount more pressure on assessors to validate their assessment items and for them to meet internationally accepted standards and specifications, such as SCORM, IMS-QTI and ADL. e-Assessment items will need to be written in XML formats, and discipline sub-versions of XML, that are foreign to many teachers, such as MathML and ChemML (http://www.w3.org), as well as proprietary versions of XML such as QML (Question Mark-up Language, http://www.questionmark.com/us/qml/). e-Assessment items will be required to meet accessibility standards and be available in multiple formats. Will we expect individual teachers to be familiar with these details and capable of preparing sophisticated e-assessment environments? If teachers work in multidisciplinary teams to construct items of the appropriate standard, how long will it take to prepare an assessment? Will the cost of the assessment match its purpose? Will more sophisticated assessments become the domain of institutions or companies with more resources?

Currently, e-assessment tends to mimic the objectives and format of paper-based tests, with institutions using them to maximize administrative efficiency, lower costs and provide immediate feedback to students (Raikes *et al.*, 2003). Many of the discussions about why e-assessment should be adopted revolve around reducing teacher marking time, or the efficiencies available in large-scale standardized testing. Such testing appears to be popular for political reasons, or because higher education institutions are not confident in the assessment standards of schools. If e-assessment use is limited to replicating paper-based assessments, then the discussions will continue to revolve around non-educational objectives. The primary purpose for any assessment is to enhance and document skill and capability development, irrespective of its format. e-Assessment allows teachers to rethink the current paper-derived framework of assessment; it can be used as a vehicle for educational change. This change should not be driven by the technology; the technology has simply allowed new possibilities to be explored.

16.2 Drivers for change in assessment

One of the most significant drivers for change in assessment is the formation of a global international marketplace for educational services. Students do not have to be physically close to educational providers; they can access people and content anywhere in the world. This universal access is changing many of the perceptions about what constitutes an educational experience. Graduates are seeking employment opportunities across national and international borders and are expecting a more global experience as part of their education. Participation rates in post-secondary education have risen significantly in the past 30 years, coupled with a rising social expectation that higher education should be accessible to all. Post-secondary education is seen as a social right and culturally coupled to mobility, as well as economic and social stability. Distance education, once the domain of specialist institutions in a limited range of discipline areas is becoming mainstream, with blended learning, as well as fully online activity, becoming more acceptable to institutions, teachers and students alike. Despite some highly publicized failures of fully online institutions, e-learning and e-assessment activity will expand as our ability to implement and facilitate communities of engagement improves.

In the UK the national government is responding to this global pressure by supporting a number of initiatives aimed at changing assessment practices in both secondary and post-secondary education (DfES, Department for Education and Skills). DfES has proposed an e-assessment strategy in response to aspects of recent reviews into secondary and post-secondary education (Tomlinson, 2004). An increase in the use of e-assessment is a central part of the vision for secondary education in the UK (QCA, Qualifications and Curriculum Authority). By 2009, QCA is expecting that:

- all new qualifications should include an option for on-screen assessment
- all awarding bodies should be set up to accept and assess e-portfolios
- all existing standard examinations should be available on-screen
- the first on-demand assessments are starting to be introduced
- at least ten new qualifications, specifically designed for electronic delivery and assessment, should be developed, accredited and live.

One of the conclusions from the report on UK A-level standards (Tomlinson, 2002) was the inability of the GCSE (General Certificate of Secondary Education) assessment model to cater for any further expansion in participation. The current model of invigilated examinations at set times using pen and paper, the requirement for large numbers of assessors to be available for short intensive periods and the time-consuming manner in which examination scripts are marked is not sustainable into the future. The report challenged teachers and educational administrators to reflect on new models for assessment, including the wide-scale adoption of e-assessments with automatic marking and feedback.

The issues around future assessment strategies in the UK provide a useful framework for examining the drivers and directions for e-assessment around the globe. Teachers and educational administrators have reflected on the learning designs and assessment frameworks required in educational institutions. Enhanced problem-solving ability, the meta-analysis of cognitive capacity and more effective group activities and communication skills have all been recognized as critical components in future educational offerings. The requirement for the effective and efficient assessment of these activities on a large scale has provided a catalyst for the exploration of new assessment models. This has led to an in-depth analysis of e-assessment's strengths and weaknesses, and the requirements for the large-scale participation of teachers and students in the culture of adaptation and adoption.

One of the drivers for adaptive change in learning and assessment formats is the ubiquitous spread of mobile and wireless technologies (Evans, 2005). Wireless networks allow learning spaces to be redesigned, and present new opportunities for students to use a wider range of portable and remote devices. For diagnostic and formative assessments that are low to medium stakes, security is not a major impediment to the use of open spaces or disparate physical locations for students. By coupling e-assessments accessed by mobile or wireless technologies with appropriate feedback to students, a powerful learning and assessment environment can be created. Feedback to students is a critical component for developing their ability to undertake a meta-analysis of their own cognitive capacity. Learning is more than just the acquisition of declarative knowledge; it also involves conditional and procedural tasks that build meta-analytic skills. The assessment tasks that are set to demonstrate competence and capability development in meta-analytic skills require more than pen and paper responses. Students require an immersive, authentic and communal environment with which to test their skills and their ability to adopt and adapt behaviours and resources to more productive uses. Access to content and people, and instant feedback to their responses, is an important part of this process.

An important driver for changes to the learning and assessment environment is from students who are digital natives, or net generation (Net Gen) learners, who use technology as an integral part of their everyday lives (Oblinger et al., 2005). For these students the use of computers, mobile phones and the Internet for assessments is an obvious and natural activity. They would likely be puzzled by teachers who are reluctant to exploit the fact that they have instant access to people and resources from across the globe at the push of a button. Social contact and activity is an important part of the everyday life of the Net Gen, so group work and peer feedback and recognition should align well with the preferred learning styles of this group. What does this mean for assessment? Student engagement will depend on the appropriate alignment of learning styles, the learning environment and teacher-prepared assessment tasks. Net Gen students are experiential, immediate and social, but prefer to spend their time on things that matter to them, that align with their values and belief systems (Oblinger et al., 2005). Static assessment tasks that are designed to elicit a single common response from all students acting as separated individuals and that use examples that are unrelated to the real world in which the student operates, are less likely to facilitate engagement, and certainly will not encourage creativity. Teachers can adopt and adapt mobile and wireless technologies to facilitate communication between students and between teachers and students; they can obtain instant feedback on where students are with their learning and assist students accordingly. e-Assessments can incorporate the ability of mobile and wireless technologies to capture and transmit images and audio in real time. Many institutions are now adapting learning and assessment formats so that they are accessible from PDAs (personal digital assistants) and mobile telephony devices (Trinder *et al.*, 2005). It is ironic that as new technologies become available and students use them in their everyday life, examination boards in the UK are banning their presence in traditional pen and paper examinations, and even failing students who bring a mobile phone to an examination centre, whether it is used or not.

Many teachers and institutions would prefer to measure integrative problem-solving skills and procedural knowledge constructs rather than simple MCQs or single-selected response items (Luecht, 2002). One of the problems is how to achieve this in a cost-effective manner using existing hardware, software and current skill levels of teachers? Software that allows ready use of pre-designed templates that can be easily modified, and generates the necessary standards compliant XML code without the teacher having to learn XML, is required. A number of prototypes for such software is available, such as ITD[3] (Luecht, 2002) and CANVAS Learning.

16.3 What will e-assessment be like in the future?

Will all future assessments be immersive and authentic? Will students be presented with a combination of real and virtual environments that test not only declarative knowledge but also conditional and procedural capabilities? Will assessments measure approaches to problem-solving and student responses in terms of efficiency, ethical considerations and the involvement of others?

e-Assessments will become more sophisticated and ubiquitous as the required technology improves and becomes simpler to use (Parshall *et al.*, 2000). Rather than attempt to mimic paper-based assessments, e-assessments in the future will offer authentic problems that will require the student to access resources or use interactive tools in order to propose a solution. The student response will include an analysis of the social and ethical consequences of the proposed solution and include a meta-analysis of the route taken to solve the problem. Clearly this scenario is referring to complex tasks, and not single units of declarative knowledge. These smaller units of declarative knowledge will likely be incorporated into more sophisticated tasks, so that their purpose in the assessment is clearly articulated.

What is the future for the simpler forms of e-assessments such as MCQs? These will still be used in the future but selected response items will incorporate student commentary, and this commentary will form part of the assessment and be automatically marked. The software used to construct e-assessments will assist in the design of questions and lead teachers through the construction of a universal design framework that also automatically generates variations to the question and response formats suitable for universal accessibility. The software will also analyse student responses once an assessment is completed, provide appropriate feedback to the student and also suggest modifications to the question for the teacher to consider.

Networking and hardware improvements will mean that file size and download times will not be an issue in the future, disruptions to the network or power supply will not interfere with a high-stake summative assessment, and access will truly be anywhere, anytime. Universal accessibility will be possible because all assessment items will be rendered in the format suited to the students' needs. Such a scenario is possible now, but it is not available on a large scale. The technical issues associated with the widespread delivery of assessments will all be soluble over time, the real issue is likely to be the level of access to this environment. As assessments become

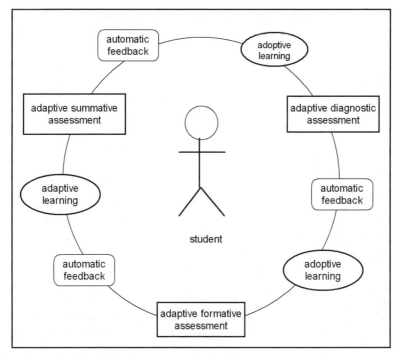

Figure 16.1 Integrated learning and assessment cycle

more sophisticated, and the costs associated with their production and delivery rise, equity issues will be raised. Institutions may be distinguished in the future by the quality of their assessment, rather than the quality of their teaching, particularly as content becomes widely available at minimal costs. This will cause significant changes in the education marketplace, with some teachers choosing to be specialist assessors, rather than teaching generalists who design, deliver and assess a discipline-based course or programme.

Learning and assessment will form an inseparable continuum over the next few years, rather than be viewed as two sequential stages in the educational process (Atkins *et al.*, 2005). Automated feedback will become a normal part of the assessment process, and students will use this feedback to assist in future learning patterns (Figure 16.1). The assessment software will determine if the student should be offered multiple attempts, based on their pattern of responses, and the number of times they have been around the cycle outlined in Figure 16.1. Adaptive assessments will become more the norm, as the software to deliver such tests becomes embedded into virtual learning environments and caters for diversity in abilities and capabilities (Roach *et al.*, 2001; Lilley *et al.*, 2004; Georgiadou *et al.*, 2006). The software for generating adaptive assessments will become more sophisticated, incorporating disability access functions, feedback and analysis of learning styles and problem-solving ability. Adaptive tests will also assist teachers by recommending changes to the questions based on student responses, a process that currently requires a psychometrician and subject matter expert.

Students will use a more portfolio approach to presenting evidence of their skill and capability development. The software used to construct and deliver e-assessments will be capable of automatically assembling the student portfolio. Assessments are likely to be subject to a more rigorous peer review process, and some institutions or teachers may choose to specialize in assessment, offering services to other institutions. For high-stake summative assessments that are available in multiple locations, security will be an important issue. If the student is located in a dedicated assessment centre, then proctoring will occur much as it does today. For those students in remote locations, security measures such as retinal scans or digital fingerprinting over the Internet will likely be used.

Assessments will likely be designed around consensus frameworks, and these will be incorporated into the software to allow teachers to choose a particular framework with which to work. At the present time there is no one iconic framework for e-assessment. Due to the diversity inherent in educational theories and frames of reference, it is unlikely that one assessment framework will be adopted. Early models, such as Parshall's (2000) five-dimensional framework, provided a useful starting point to reflect on what an assessment framework should contain. Parshall's framework included the item format, the response action, the use of multimedia, a description of the level of interactivity and the scoring algorithm to be used in the assessment. The FREMA (Framework Reference Model for Assessment) project, originating through JISC (Joint Information Systems Committee) in the UK, has proposed a very detailed assessment framework and this was discussed in some detail in Chapter 2.2. FREMA attempts to define how the components of an assessment interact in a web service environment with the objective being the seamless integration of commercial, institutional and open source components (http://www.frema.ecs.soton.ac.uk). FREMA uses an entity and process model for the framework and is an example of the significant amount of work that must be undertaken to lay the foundations for e-assessment systems that will be robust, valid and easy to use (Figure 16.2).

e-Assessment allows new possibilities for a dynamic, immersive and responsive environment, not just a static environment based on pen and paper (Ridgway *et al.*, 2003). It allows learning, social interactions and assessment to be blended in a way that enriches the student experience, and ultimately resembles more the real world in which students will be required to operate. Alternative modes of presentation are now possible, adaptive to the different cognitive, social and physical abilities of the student (Boyle, 2005). Assessments will begin to resemble games with role-playing and scenarios; they will involve the creation of assessment environments replicating the real world, including consequences that will evolve from the student responses. More authentic problems will be set; in fact real world problems may be set for assessments, and the combined responses of large numbers of students may be used to propose real solutions to real problems. If one considers the present paper-based examination system, an enormous amount

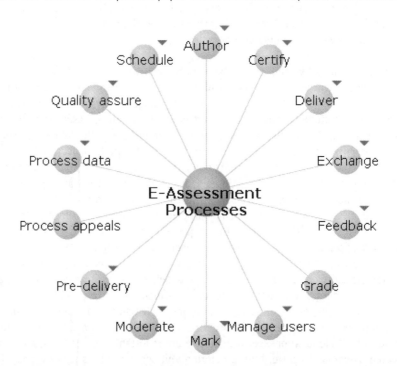

Figure 16.2 Screen shot of FREMA (Framework Reference Model for Assessment, http://www.frema.ecs.soton.ac.uk)

of time and resources are channelled into them, the outcome for the student is usually a grade and the paper-based responses are kept for a short time and then destroyed. By setting authentic problems where the responses may be used as part of a real solution, we would be harnessing a significant cognitive resource. In practice, it would not be possible to design every assessment along this design framework, but units of declarative knowledge could be incorporated into these role-plays and scenarios to ensure compliance with particular outcomes or minimum standards that are required.

By making assessments more interactive and authentic, students will view them as part of the learning process, not as a separate and subsequent process to learning. By incorporating social and process interactions in the assessment design we will be able to better align the educational process with the characteristics of the Net Gen learners. Teachers should not be limited in their thinking about assessment by what the hardware and software can currently deliver. The technology usually provides possibilities well in advance of where the collective consensus of teachers' approaches to assessment resides.

Assessment item banks will likely be more common in the future, and the reuse of assessment resources will be facilitated by software that will automatically provide alternative versions of questions. The technical sophistication of e-assessments will be improved so that current problems associated with the ability to easily write algebraic expressions, the automatic recognition of alternative but equivalent responses, the drawing of graphs or chemical structures, the drawing of three-dimensional objects, schematics or circuit boards, the ability to manipulate objects in a virtual laboratory or the ability to present a virtual performance for music and dance will all be solved.

There is a cultural expectation that all students should be able to achieve a minimum standard in learning and assessment; this is apparent through the introduction of large-scale standardized assessments, particularly in the USA (Pellegrino, 2005). USA state governments are mandating improvements in the general level of skill development and capability resulting from participation in public education. This has resulted in a demand for the external assessment of tests and exams, particularly at school. Almost every USA state has compulsory achievement tests at multiple grade levels in multiple subjects, and all are required to have such tests under current legislation (No Child Left Behind Act, 2001). This has, in turn, generated considerable discussion about assessment practices at all levels of education and the purpose of assessment and its reporting. Pellegrino (2005) has claimed that overall:

> efforts to use assessment to drive academic outcomes provide relatively little evidence that assessment external to an ongoing process of learning and teaching can in fact produce the desired educational outcomes. Rather, the educational assessment community is becoming increasingly aware of the need to embed more valid and complex assessments into the fabric of instruction.

The use of a conceptual framework for assessment design will become more common and integrated with learning designs. Evidence-centred assessment design (as discussed in Chapter 2.2) will become more important as teachers begin to use more formal design principles to determine what capabilities are being developed, how they can be measured and then to design their assessments using the model (Almond et al., 2002). Assessments are likely to be constructed from modular components that have particular characteristics, or for which the characteristics can be inferred readily. Further research on simplifying the use of psychometric parameters and the use of latent trait theory and Rasch models for classroom teachers will allow a more systematic analysis of assessment outcomes and improve the validity of assessments in general.

The construction of e-assessments is likely to be a group activity, with individual teachers less likely to be able to create the interactive and immersive environments required for future assessments (Boyle, 2005). The major role for teachers will be to provide context and relevance to the assessment activities; they will provide a link between the learning and assessment

Table 16.1 Mabry's model of assessment paradigms (from Smith, 2001; McGuire, 2005).

Psychometric	Contextual	Personal or ipsative
Standardized in content and administration	Curriculum-sensitive and group sensitive	Student-sensitive: content setting and time may vary
Objective items and formats	Objective and subjective items and formats	Subjective items and formats. Students involved in selection
External marking (machine)	Teacher marking	Teacher marking
No self-assessment	Self-assessment important	Self-assessment essential
Summative, no feedback beyond score	Formative use of results. Can be used summatively	Formative use of results. Can be used summatively

environments. A more seamless continuum will exist between learning activities and diagnostic, formative and summative assessments, with rich automatic feedback an integral part of the process.

eVIVA (electronic Virtual Ipsative Valid Assessment), from UltraLab in the UK, is an example of a project that made use of communication technologies, such as mobile phones, voice recognition technology and the Internet, to support formative and summative assessment (McGuire, 2005). The eVIVA assessment process made use of student portfolios so that students reflected on their work over time, and shared their thinking and early drafts of their work, as well as receiving meaningful feedback from their teachers and peers. The assessment is not designed to be a high stakes test or examination, its purpose and that of the e-portfolio was to better inform teacher judgement about the student performance. If projects such as eVIVA are to have wider impact on assessment practices, they must provide exemplars of valid and reliable high stakes assessments. This is the key area for changing teacher and student approaches to e-assessments.

Future e-assessment tools will be designed to facilitate a more individualized feedback for both students and teachers (Abell *et al.*, 2004). As e-assessments are developed within a universally designed framework using adaptive approaches to item presentation, students will be provided with individualized feedback based on their particular learning styles, while teachers will be provided feedback on the appropriate teaching style that facilitates maximum student outcomes. Assessments will move from the current psychometric paradigms towards a more personal or ipsative framework (Table 16.1).

16.4 How far are we away from this future?

The Scottish Qualifications Authority (SQA) has published an ambitious set of goals for the period up to 2010 (SQA, 2005). The SQA is anticipating that assessment practices will continue to evolve to include the following characteristics:

- greater flexibility in when and where assessment takes place
- less use of 'one time', 'one place' assessments
- assessment more closely and seamlessly linked to learning
- increased blurring of the distinction between formative and summative assessment
- greater use of diagnostic assessment to establish learning needs and priorities
- greater use of personalized learning programmes requiring personalized assessment
- greater use of personal e-portfolios to capture appropriate evidence of achievement from a wide range of settings
- use of adaptive assessment in which the level of demand adjusts automatically based on the students' responses
- use of technology to capture more information about students' actions during

assessment, for example, capturing time taken for specific tasks, keyboard strokes and steps taken to reach final outcome
- immediate results following an assessment
- information-rich feedback to both the student and the teacher.

There is little doubt that e-assessment is a major contributing factor in the current discussions about the purpose and design of assessments. Many of the goals stated in the SQA document can be achieved with current technology, although not at the level of sophistication, nor with the ease that classroom teachers would find convenient. However, some of the goals, notably less use of 'one time', 'one place' assessments and assessment more closely and seamlessly linked to learning, are aligned with changes in culture, not technology. It is in these areas that development is required, as the technology will eventually be able to provide possibilities beyond the capabilities of most classroom teachers. There is still a considerable lag in the cultural changes required to adapt and adopt new approaches to learning, teaching and assessment.

The technical developments that are still required for e-assessment to be genuinely universally adopted include:

- universal access to high speed networks for all students and teachers
- universal access to high-performing mobile computing and telephony devices
- greater access to multimedia resources in an appropriate format with clearer copyright and usage rights
- the ability to readily capture synchronous activity in multiple formats
- less reliance on hardware such as keyboards and a mouse for on-screen navigation and interactivity
- more appropriate hardware and software tools for delivering, facilitating and capturing enquiry-based activities, group activities, and authentic activities.

Highlighting the benefits of adopting sophisticated e-assessment formats will not convince the majority of current teachers to change their existing assessment practices. e-Assessment should not be seen as a solution seeking a problem, nor a product in search of a context; it is not an end in itself but rather one component of a continuous cycle of adaptation and adoption. For those teachers and academic developers whose epistemologies are grounded within the culture of adaptation and adoption, the use of e-assessment is a natural progression along the enhancement continuum. It is part of their scholarly approach to learning, teaching and assessment. e-Learning and e-assessment are not disruptive technologies to these teachers. The adoption of the online environment does not require bridges to be built across quantum gaps in understanding or approaches. For these teachers and academic developers, often referred to as early adopters, the use of e-assessment is just one variation in a series of experiments designed to improve assessment. These teachers are continuously seeking new methods to engage students in a richer, more sustaining, learning environment. They have already allocated time to participate in the culture of adaptation and adoption, it is part of their teaching day, so the time required to become proficient in the use of a piece of software, or to design a new assessment framework is not burdensome or a threat to their other professional activities.

Instead of recommending that the short amount of time the majority of teachers will allocate to attending development programmes about online education to highlight the benefits of sophisticated e-assessment formats, it would be more productive to develop a community of practice where teachers become active participants in a culture of adaptation and adoption. These are core values that can be applied to all aspects of professional practice. Teachers can ensure their own future by not being rooted in static paradigms, but by embracing continual adaptation. Technology itself should not be seen as the driver for the changes that are necessary in learning, teaching and assessment, although this is a premise often held about technology and its impact on education; rather technology should take its place as an enabler in the culture of adaptation and adoption.

Section 7 Appendices, Glossary, References, Index

Appendix A

Table A.1 Example of an assessment rubric without marks for an online discussion

Category	Indicators
Triggering	Recognizing the problem. Sense of puzzlement
Exploration	Divergence within online community. Divergence within single message. Information exchange. Suggestions for consideration. Brainstorming. Leaps to conclusions
Integration	Convergence among group members. Convergence within a single message. Connecting ideas, synthesis. Creating solutions
Solution	Vicarious application to real world. Testing solutions. Defending solutions

Table A.2 Example of an assessment rubric with marks for an online discussion

Mark	Evidence
0	No entries in discussion board
1	Minimum participation that did not address the task, or provided only minimum information for other group members. No use of other entries
2	Minimum participation on the task topic, added to knowledge of group, no reflection on issues directly related to task. No use of other entries
3	Adequate participation, added to knowledge of group, minimum reflection on issues directly related to task. Minimum use of the entries from others by critiquing them or extending them

Table A.3 Rubric for the assessment of contributions to an online discussion (adapted from Baron *et al.*, 2003)

Criterion	Exemplary	Acceptable	Below standard
Writing style and presentation			
Title	Title is concise and informative so others can anticipate the content	Title gives a general indication of the material covered in the contribution, but others have to read the document to fully appreciate what is covered	Linkage between the title and the text is not clear
Introduction	Clearly indicates main purpose of the contribution and suggests the plan of organization	Indicates the main purpose of the contribution in general terms	Introduction does not give an overview of the contribution

Criterion	Exemplary	Acceptable	Below standard
Main Body	Makes connected points that clearly build the argument so the text flows from introduction to conclusion in a logical manner	Presents a number of points that assist in understanding the argument, but some lapses in the writing	Not well structured so the reader must try to make sense of the text
Conclusion	Clearly indicated and reinforced so the reader can remember it	Main point is indicated, but may be stated in an unconvincing manner	Does not reinforce or revisit the main points
Written expression	Sentences and paragraphs are well structured and clear. Each paragraph has a topic sentence that indicates the subject matter	Minor lapses in sentence structure, such as run-on sentences and unnecessarily complex sentence structures. Paragraphs present a complete argument, but may not flow well	Many sentences are poorly structured. Many paragraphs lack topic sentences or have poor flow so the main points and linkages among explanatory text are not clear
Grammar, punctuation and spelling	Grammar, spelling and punctuation are excellent, which allows the reader to focus on the message	Some minor errors in grammar, spelling and/or punctuation detract from the quality of the text, but do not impair the communication	Many errors in grammar, spelling and/or punctuation make reading the text difficult and communication is impaired
Concepts and arguments are well developed			
Accuracy	All information is accurately reported using appropriate terminology so the information is reliable	Information is largely accurate but imprecise language could lead a reader to misinterpret aspects of the text	Some information is incorrect; there are problems with the interpretation of it
Relevance	Connections between the contribution and the main topic of the discussion are clearly indicated	Connections between the contribution and the main topic of the discussion are indicated or implied	Text is relevant, but not clearly indicated, so the reader must guess how the text relates to the main topic
Significance	Clearly described and discussed so the reader takes the contribution seriously	Touched on but not elucidated, reader must make some interpretations about the contribution's significance	The contribution may include significant material but this is not indicated, so the reader must guess it
Clarity	Main points and new technical terms are clearly described and/or explained; no ambiguity about what was written	Text is clear to informed audiences, but unexplained points may be misinterpreted	Key points and new technical terms are not explained so the reader is confused

Criterion	Exemplary	Acceptable	Below standard
Independence	The contribution is completely self-contained	Reader can understand the main point without further reading, but some parts of the text are not clear without consulting other sources of information	Text is written in a manner that presumes considerable prior knowledge
Contribution is responsive to another contribution	Links ideas submitted by others to own contribution in a manner that strengthens the group's efforts to resolve the main problem	Makes references to earlier works that are a starting point for new ideas but not much information is incorporated	The text mentions other contributions but neither explains the reference nor substantially adds to it
Text is supported by references			
Sources indicated	All information and ideas that are not commonly known are supported with references to sources	Most sources are indicated	Few or no references are supplied for information and ideas that are not the author's
Relevant references	Information, concepts and opinions are supported with references to published literature, especially primary (original) sources of information, rather than review articles or textbooks	One or a few references are used to support the text. Some general references to textbooks are made	Information comes from websites or other sources that have no recognized authority
Citation style	References cited appropriately in the text, and the correct format is used	Minor lapses in citation format do not prevent the reader from finding the sources	Citation format incorrect or poorly placed in the text
Bibliographic information	The reference list contains complete bibliographic information (author's name(s), publication date, title, source, date web page accessed)	Bibliographic information largely complete, but some information missing	Not all references are listed, information in the reference list is incorrect or important information is missing from the reference list

Table A.4 Assessment rubric for online discussion (adapted from http://scope.citl.ohiou. edu/FLC/ActiveLearning/Docs/Assessment.doc)

Criteria	4 marks	3 marks	2 marks	1 mark
Articulation of ideas, clarity of expression	Clear thesis, supported with convincing evidence; appropriate language; well-organized, mechanically correct; acknowledges opposing views, strong voice	Adequate thesis but lacks convincing support; clear language, organized with reasonably correct sentences; fails to address opposing views well; needs to show more conviction	Ambiguous thesis; insufficient supporting details; no clear focus with stereotypical arguments; word choices are appropriate; mostly correct sentences but weak voice	Some ideas, but no clear focus and support is unconvincing; lacks organization; word choices are limited; sentence errors and weak voice
Appropriate logic and examples	Clear and logical statements; clear explanations; appropriate examples to support ideas; displays good insight	Mostly clear and logical statements; some explanations; appropriate examples to support ideas; displays some insight	Some clear statements; some explanations; some examples to support ideas; some ambiguous or confusing points. No insight	Few clear statements or explanations; few examples to support ideas; mostly ambiguous or confusing points. No insight
Breadth and depth of analysis	Considers multiple perspectives on an issue; uses relevant research knowledge to analyse an issue; employs a higher-order discussion strategy using analogy, stipulation or resolution	Demonstrates knowledge of important ideas related to an issue; states an issue for the group to consider and presents more than one viewpoint; supports a position with reasons or evidence	Makes statements about the issue that express only personal attitudes; mentions a potentially important idea but does not pursue it in a way that advances the group's understanding	Remains silent or contributes no original thoughts, makes only surface-level comments

Appendix B

Examples of interactivity using simulations, Java applets and role-plays.

ACD structure drawing Java applet

(http://www.acdlabs.com/download/sda.html)
This is an example of an interactive Java applet that allows students to draw a chemical structure within a web browser. Students can be expected to draw individual chemical structures, or reaction sequences, in response to assessment items.

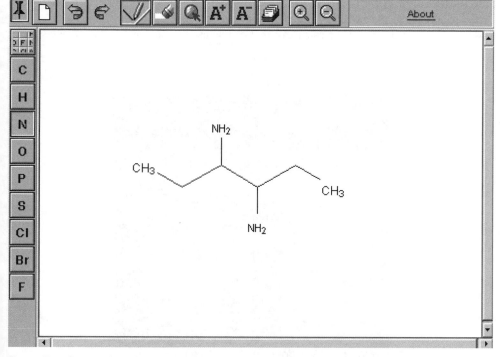

Figure B.1 Screen shot from the ACD chemical structure drawing applet

ANADIGICS Receiver Model

(http://www.anadigics.com/engineers/Receiver.html)

This is an example of a Java applet that allows students to explore the effects of changing input values such as gain, noise and dynamic range on output values.

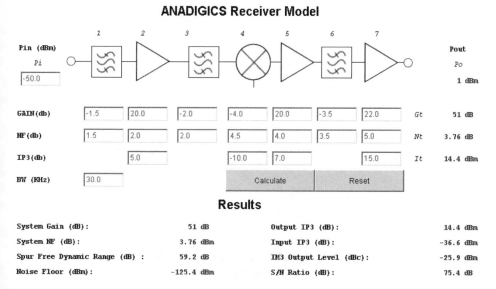

Figure B.2 Screen shot from a Java applet describing circuits

Calculator Java applet

(http://mc2.cchem.berkeley.edu/java/Calc/Calc6/calculator.html)

This is an example of a scientific calculator that can be used by students during an assessment.

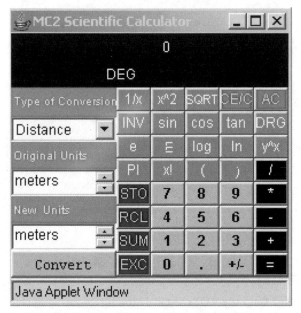

Figure B.3 Screen shot from a Java applet scientific calculator

Chemis 3D

(http://chemis.free.fr/mol3d/)

This is an example of a Java applet that allows three-dimensional representations of complex molecules to be presented through a web browser. Students may rotate a molecule, and measure physical properties such as bond angles and bond distances.

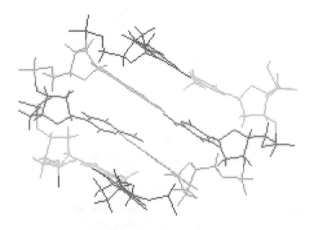

Figure B.4 Screen shot from a Java applet that allows three-dimensional chemical structures to be displayed and rotated in a web browser

Chemistry boiling point Java applet

(Goodman *et al.*, 2000 http://www.ch.cam.ac.uk/magnus)
This is an example of an interactive Java applet that allows students to explore the variation in boiling point of a liquid at various pressures. Questions requiring both quantitative and qualitative responses can be set by the teacher.

The variation of boiling point with pressure

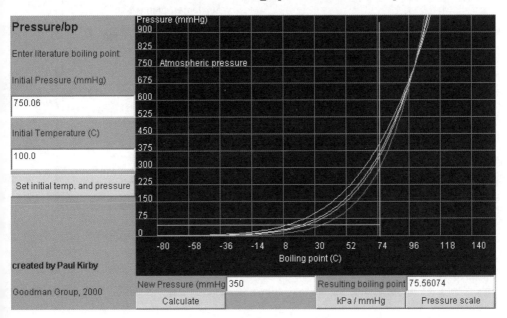

Figure B.5 Screen shot from a Java applet that shows variation of boiling point with pressure

Chemistry titration Java applet

(http://chemmac1.usc.edu/Bruno/java/titration)
This is an example of an interactive Java applet where students can explore the concepts of chemical titration. This applet can be used within an assessment to present alternative scenarios for students to explore. Questions requiring both quantitative and qualitative responses can be set by the teacher.

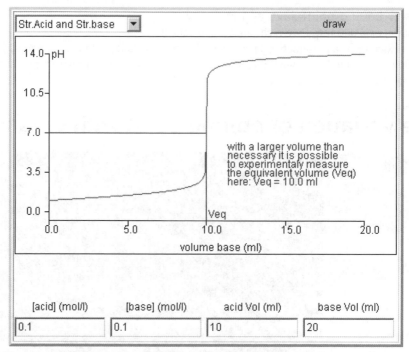

Figure B.6 Screen shot from a chemistry titration Java applet

Circuits

(http://www.falstad.com/mathphysics.html)

This is an example of a Java applet that allows students to explore the properties of a simple circuit.

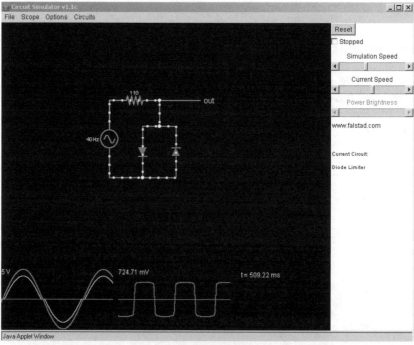

Figure B.7 Screen shot from a simple circuit simulation

CGView Applet
(http://wishart.biology.ualberta.ca/cgview/index.html)
This is an example of a Java applet that allows Circular Genome Viewer.

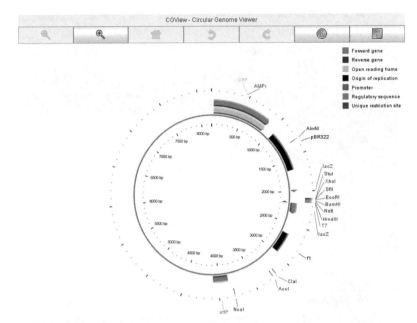

Figure B.8 Screen shot from the CGView Applet showing maps of circular genomes

Electric Sounding Applet
(http://www.ifg.tu-clausthal.de/java-d.html)
This Java applet calculates the apparent resistivity of a layered subsurface model, interactively adjustable to fit field observations.

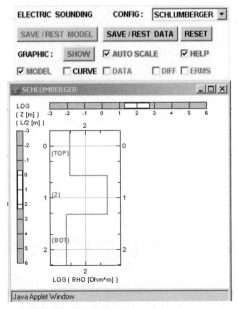

Figure B.9 Screen shot from the Electric Sounding Applet

Geology Explorer

(http://oit.ndsu.edu/menu/home.ie.htm)

This is an example of a simulation game where participants assume the role of a geologist on a new planet. Students can be provided with authentic problems where they are expected to use geological concepts to locate particular minerals.

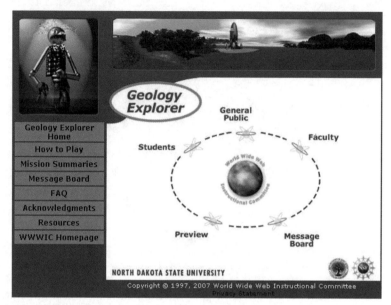

Figure B.10 Screen shot from the simulation game 'Geology Explorer'

General motion physics Java applet

(http://www.surendranath.org/Apps.html)

This applet traces the motion of the centre of mass of a dumbbell shaped object.

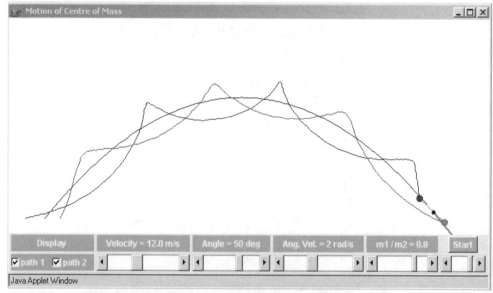

Figure B.11 Screen shot from a centre of mass motion simulation

GIDEON

(http://www.gideononline.com)

An online application for health science and medical students that facilitates the development of skills in the diagnosis of infectious diseases.

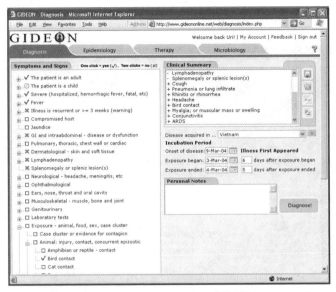

Figure B.12 Screen shot from the simulation package GIDEON

Java Molecular Editor

(http://www.molinspiration.com/jme/)

This is an example of an interactive Java applet that allows students to draw a chemical structure within a web browser. Students can be expected to draw individual chemical structures, or reaction sequences, in response to assessment items. The editor can generate SMILES text strings or MDL mol files for created structures and these outputs can be used as responses in assessments.

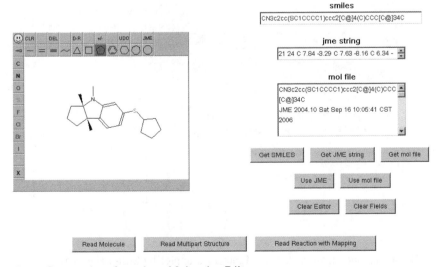

Figure B.13 Screen shot from Java Molecular Editor

NeuroLab
(McGrath *et al.* 2003)

An introductory computer laboratory simulation package designed for first-year university health science students. The simulation allows students to undertake a series of simulated experiments on neurons including measuring resting membrane potentials, threshold potentials, refractory periods and the effects of different concentrations of sodium and potassium ions.

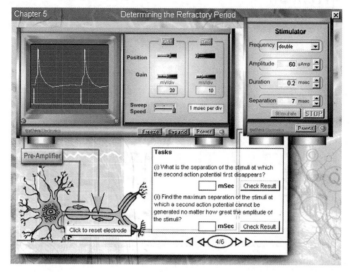

Figure B.14 Screen shot from NeuroLab (http://advan.physiology.org/cgi/content/full/27/3/120)

Periodic Table of the elements Java applet
(http://chemmac1.usc.edu/java/ptable/ptable.html). Example by Bruno Herreros, Department of Chemistry, University of Southern California.

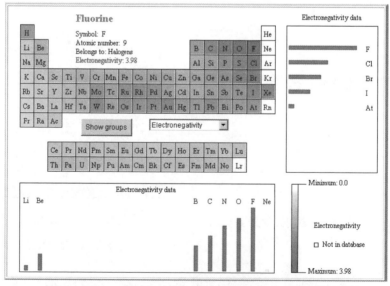

Figure B.15 Screen shot from a Periodic Table Java applet by Bruno Herreros

Physlets

(http://webphysics.davidson.edu/Applets/Applets.html)

This Java applet allows students to explore the consequences of changing numerous variables on an object in motion.

Linear Air Resistance on a Projectile

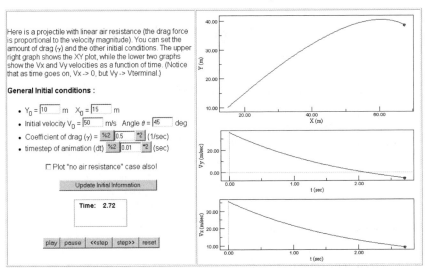

Here is a projectile with linear air resistance (the drag force is proportional to the velocity magnitude). You can set the amount of drag (γ) and the other initial conditions. The upper right graph shows the XY plot, while the lower two graphs show the Vx and Vy velocities as a function of time. (Notice that as time goes on, Vx -> 0, but Vy -> Vterminal.)

General Initial conditions :

- $Y_0 = $ `10` m $X_0 = $ `15` m
- Initial velocity $V_0 = $ `50` m/s Angle $\theta = $ `45` deg
- Coefficient of drag (γ) = `%2` `0.5` `*2` (1/sec)
- timestep of animation (dt) `%2` `0.01` `*2` (sec)

☐ Plot "no air resistance" case also!

[Update Initial Information]

Time: 2.72

[play] [pause] [<<step] [step>>] [reset]

Figure B.16 Screen shot from a Physlet Java applet example showing projectile motion

Acceleration physics Java applet

(http://www.phy.ntnu.edu.tw/ntnujava)

This Java applet allows students to explore the consequences of changing velocity, time and displacement variables on two different objects accelerating in the same direction.

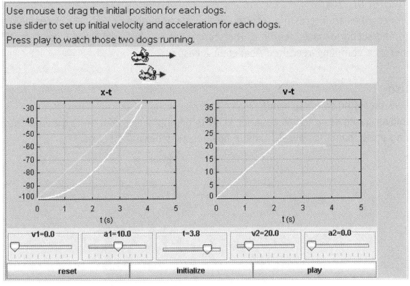

Figure B.17 Screen shot from a kinematic simulation acceleration

Refraction physics Java applet
(http://www.netzmedien.de)
Daniel Roth – Law of Refraction.

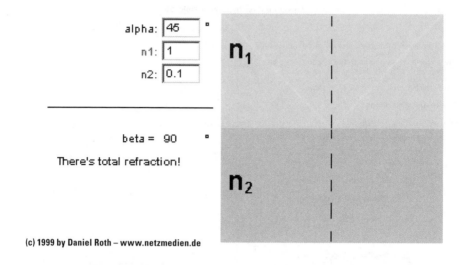

alpha: 45 °

n1: 1

n2: 0.1

n_1

beta = 90 °

There's total refraction!

n_2

(c) 1999 by Daniel Roth – www.netzmedien.de

Figure B.18 Screen shot from Daniel Roth – Law of Refraction simulation

Road Map: Israeli / Palestinian Negotiations
(http://www.simplay.net/clients.html)
A publicly available example of a role-play using the Fablusi™ software.

Role-play
(Agostinho *et al.*, 2005)
This paper describes an interesting learning design for an online activity that uses elements from role-plays and scenario-based learning. The scenario uses a 'remote' Chief Executive Officer and the teacher as a company-recruited Academic Advisor.

Zapitalism
(http://www.lavamind.com/zap.html)
A multi-player game designed to enhance skills in being a successful and strategic entrepreneur by allowing participants to invest funds in businesses, stocks and bonds.

GLOSSARY

ADL: Advanced Distributed Learning. US Department of Defense sponsored project for standards and interoperability (http://www.adlnet.org).

AERA: American Educational Research Association (http://www.aera.net).

AICC: Aviation Industry Computer-Based Training Committee. Develops guidelines for computer-based training materials for the aviation.

Angoff method: used to determine a minimum acceptable score where a panel of judges assigns a probability to each item on a test. The sum of the probabilities determines the acceptable score.

API: application program interface, how the computer application communicates with the operating system.

Assessment: an evidenced-based approach used to draw inferences about the level of knowledge, skills or capabilities of a person, or group of people, for a specific purpose.

Authentic assessment: assessment that is related to tasks that are relevant to professional practice or real life.

BSI: British Standards Institute. UK-based organization concerned with the development of standards and codes of best practice.

CAA: computer-assisted assessment.

CAT: computer adaptive testing. Tests where the next question offered to a test-taken is dependent on how the test-taker has responded to previous questions.

CBT: computer-based training.

CETIS: Centre For Educational Technology Interoperability Standards. A UK-based organization representing the tertiary education sector on international committees concerned with learning technology standards.

Chem ML: a version of XML for writing chemical structures and molecular properties for display and distribution through a web browser (http://www.w3.org/Chem).

CMC: computer-mediated communications.

CMS: content (course) management system. Software that assists in organizing content for courses.

Coefficient Alpha: an internal consistency or reliability coefficient; also referred to as Cronbach's alpha (α), or for dichotomous items, KR 20.

Construct validity: a measure of the ability of an assessment to indicate the relationship between the theoretical and real ability of a student.

Content package: IMS Content Packaging. A specification for exporting learning resources from one software application to another.

Content validity: an indicator of the degree to which the assessment items cover the intended content.

Convergent response: where the answer depends on recalling or restating a generally accepted fact.

Correlation: the degree to which two variables are related; often reported as a fraction in the range -1 to $+1$.

CRESST: Center for Research on Evaluation, Standards, and Student Testing. A process model for collaborative problem-solving (http://www.cse.ucla.edu).

Criterion-referenced: a method that measures student progress toward specific outcomes or standards. Scores are determined relative to predefined performance standards and are independent of other student scores.

Cronbach's alpha (α): an internal consistency or reliability coefficient.

DCMI: Dublin Core Metadata Initiative. Metadata standards that assist interoperability.

DECIDE: acronym for Define, Exploit, Collect, Investigate, Develop and Expand, approach described by Wu *et al.* (2003).

DfES: Department for Education and Skills. UK government education department.

Diagnostic assessment: used to identify students' prior knowledge for the purpose of defining future learning.

Discrimination: a measure of the ability of an assessment item to distinguish between students of different abilities.

Distracter: an incorrect option in an objective item such as a multiple-choice question.

Divergent response: where the answer depends on opinion or analysis.

EMI: extended matching item. A variation on the traditional multiple-choice-question format; a common stem is used for a group of multiple-choice questions and all the options are grouped together.

ETS: Educational Testing Services, a US-based organization offering standardized assessments (http://www.ets.org).

Examination: A summative assessment used to measure a student's knowledge or skills for the purpose of documenting their current level of knowledge or skill.

Extensible: a word usually used in the context of metadata, to describe an element that may contain sub-elements.

Facility: a measure of the difficulty of an assessment item.

Formative assessment: an assessment where a qualitative or quantitative judgement about a participant's achievement is used to provide feedback in order to direct future learning.

GBS: goal-based scenarios. A type of educational pedagogy.

GCSE: General Certificate of Secondary Education. The UK qualification resulting from successfully completing specific requirements at secondary school level.

GMAT®: Graduate Management Admission Test®. Standardized assessment used for entry into business courses.

GNU: a project to develop an open-source operating system. Lead to the development of Linux operating system. Developed the GNU General Public Licence for open-source software.

GRE®: Graduate Record Examinations®. Standardized assessment measuring verbal and quantitative reasoning, critical thinking, as well as analytical writing skills.

High stakes assessment: where the results from an assessment will be used to determine specific objectives such as completing a programme of study, receiving certification or moving to the next level of a programme of study.

HTML: hypertext markup language. A standardized way of preparing web pages for display on the Internet.

ICT: Information and Communication Technology.

IEEE: Institute of Electrical and Electronics Engineers. Responsible for the LOM standard.

IMMEX: Interactive Multi-Media Exercises. Software that allows teachers to assess the processes involved in solving a problem, in addition to the solution itself.

IMS: IMS Global Consortium Inc. The body responsible for the QTI specification.

Interoperability: the ability import and export content and data from one software application to another with minimum changes.

IP address: Internet Protocol address. A set of numbers describing the unique address given to electronic devices that are connected to the Internet.

Ipsative referencing: where a student compares their own performance over a period of time, or in different assessment tasks.

IRT: item response theory. A test model assumes that latent variables are responsible for test-taker responses.

ISO: International Standards Organization.

ISP: Internet Service Provider. A service that allows users to connect their computer or portable electronic device to the Internet.

Item: an individual question, and associated content, in an assessment or item bank.

Item bank or pool: a database of questions and their associated content, from which individual items may be selected in order to prepare or deliver an assessment.

JeLSIM: Java eLearning SIMulations (http://www.jelsim.org).

JISC: Joint Information Systems Committee, a UK-based organization which advises the further and higher education sectors on issues relating to the use of information and communication technologies (http://www.jisc.ac.uk).

Key: the correct option in an item such as a multiple-choice question.

LAN: local area network. A local computer network allowing a group of computers to communicate with each other.

Learning design: the conceptual framework underpinning a learning activity and associated assessment tasks. The formal IMS Learning Design is a specification used to describe learning scenarios so that they may be shared between software applications.

LOM standard: Learning Object Metadata. Standard for describing metadata, approved by IEEE.

MathML: a version of XML for writing maths for display and distribution through a web browser (http://www.w3.org/Math).

MCQ: multiple-choice question. The most commonly used form of objective assessment, consisting of a stem (the question), numerous options (the choices) and a key (the expected response).

Mean: the arithmetic mean of a set of scores.

Median: the middle score of a set of scores that have been rank-ordered.

Meta-analysis: a method for analysing data to determine the degree of relationship between the variables that influence the overall result.

Metadata: data that describes other data.

MIDI: Musical Instrument Digital Interface. Standard specification for electronic music on computers.

Mode: the most frequently occurring score in a set of scores.

MOO: *m*ud *o*bject *o*riented, where mud is a *m*ultiple *u*ser *d*omain, and is based on role-playing games.

NCLEX-RN® and NCLEX-PN®: National Nurse Licensure Examinations for Registered and Practical Nurses.

Normal distribution (curve): a theoretical description of the expected distribution of scores for an assessment where the performance of a group of students is influenced by a variety of independent factors.

Norm-referenced: scores that are assigned relative to those of others undertaking the same assessment. Usually used to describe scores that may vary depending on the general level of achievement of the specific group taking the assessment.

Ontology: a formal description of objects or beliefs and their relationships.

Option: describes the choices that are presented to a student in an objective test (such as a multiple-choice question).

PDA: personal digital assistant. A portable electronic device capable of communication and interactivity.

Percentiles: a number representing the percentage relative position of a student's score in relation to a norm-referenced cohort.

Portfolio: a repository containing examples of a student's work. A portfolio may be used for assessment purposes and also as evidence of the student's ability for employment purposes.

PRAXIS™: standardized assessments for academic skills.

Proctor: a person, or group of people, who invigilate, or administer, an assessment and usually certify that the assessment was completed under specific conditions.

PRS: personal response system. Hand-held alpha-numeric keypad device that allows students to select a response to objective questions.

QCA: Qualifications and Curriculum Authority. An organization which develops the national curriculum and associated assessment tasks for the UK education sector.

QML: Question Mark-up Language. A propriety version of XML for writing e-assessment items (http://www.questionmark.com/us/qml/).

QTI: Question and Test Interoperability. A specification which allows different software systems to exchange assessment data such as questions, assessments, responses and results.

Quiz: usually a diagnostic or formative assessment used to estimate a student's level of understanding in order to provide feedback to inform learning.

RAM: random-access memory. Computer memory used by software to perform their tasks.

Reliability: a measure of the consistency of an assessment. There are different methods used to estimate reliability, including the statistical analysis of scores, the use of multiple markers and administering the assessment multiple times.

RELOAD: Reusable eLearning Object Authoring and Delivery. An application that contains a content packager and metadata editor, and allows SCORM-compliant content to be viewed over the Internet.

Rubric: a set of scoring guidelines that can be used by students and teachers to assist in defining the relative importance of the components in an assessment task.

SAT®: Student Aptitude Test. A form of standardized assessment often used for enrolment selection processes.

Scaled scores: scores from an assessment that have been subject to some form of statistical or mathematical adjustment.

SCORM: Sharable Content Object Reference Model. A technical model for describing learning objects so that they can be readily shared across multiple virtual learning environments. A method for sharing content in different software applications.

SEM: Standard error of measurement. A measure of the difference between the theoretical true score and the actual score obtained. SEM uses the standard deviation and the estimated reliability for the assessment.

Shareware: software that users may trial free, but if they continue to use the software after the trial period they are usually required to pay a nominal fee.

Smart Phone: a portable electronic device that combines personal information, management and mobile phone capabilities.

SME: subject matter expert. Usually refers to the discipline expert in a team.

SOAP: Simple Object Access Protocol. An XML-based protocol for exchanging information in a distributed, online environment.

SPARK: Self and Peer Assessment Resource Kit, an open source self and peer-assessment application (http://www.educ.dab.uts.edu.au/darrall/sparksite).

SQA: Scottish Qualifications Authority. An organization in Scotland responsible for the development, accreditation, assessment and certification of qualifications other than degrees.

SSL: Secure Sockets Layer. A security method used whereby encrypted information may be transferred over the Internet.

Standard deviation: a measure of the spread of a set of scores.

Standardized assessment: an assessment where all students take the same test under the same conditions.

Stem: the term typically used in an objective-test question (most often a multiple-choice question) to describe the question or statement to which participants will respond.

Summative assessment: an assessment where a quantitative judgement about a participant's achievement is required. This type of assessment is normally undertaken at the completion of a learning sequence.

Survey: a tool to measure the attitude or perceptions of a person or group of people.

Test: an assessment to measure the extent of a student's knowledge or skills.

TOEFL®: Test of English as a Foreign Language™. An assessment used to measure English language proficiency.

TOEIC®: Test of English for International Communication™. An assessment used to measure English language proficiency.

True score: the hypothetical true ability of an individual taking an assessment.

URL: uniform resource locator. In common usage it is a description of where to find a resource on the Internet.

Validity: how well an assessment measures what you are attempting to assess.

Variance: a measure of the distribution of scores from an assessment. The square root of the variance is the standard deviation.

VLE: virtual learning environment. Software that allows learning activities and assessment tasks to be delivered through the Internet.

VorteX: software for estimating the contribution of individual group members to group work in the design of Java computer code (http://www.studentcentredlearning.com).

Web-based assessment: tests or exams that are accessed through the Internet using a web browser.

Weighted scoring: a method for scoring an assessment where the value of each question may be different.

W3C: World Wide Web Consortium. An organization which develops specifications and guidelines to assist with interoperability over the Internet.

XML: eXtensible Markup Language. A standard for displaying structured information over the Internet.

REFERENCES

AAHE, http://www.fctel.uncc.edu/pedagogy/assessment/9Principles.html.

Abell, M., Bauder, D. and Simmons, T. (2004), 'Universally designed online assessment: Implications for the future', *Information Technology and Disabilities*, Vol. X (1), http://www.rit.edu/~easi/itd/itdv10n1/abell.htm.

AERA (2000), http://www.aera.net/policyandprograms/?id=378

Agostinho, S., Meek, J. and Herrington, J. (2005), 'Design methodology for the implementation and evaluation of a scenario-based online learning environment', *Journal of Interactive Learning Research*, 16, 229–42.

Ahamer, G., Dziabenko, O., Haywood, J., Macleod, H., Pivec, M. and Schinnerl, I. (2002), *UniGame: Game based learning in universities and lifelong learning. Deliverable 1.2 'Conceptual Design'*, http://www.unigame.net/html/case_studies/D2.pdf.

Almond, R. G., Steinberg, L. S. and Mislevy, R. J. (2002), 'Enhancing the design and delivery of assessment systems: A four process architecture', *The Journal of Technology, Learning, and Assessment*, 1, http://www.bc.edu/research/intasc/jtla/journal/v1n5.shtml.

Anderson, L. W. and Krathwohl, D. R. (eds) (2001), *A Taxonomy for Learning, Teaching and Assessing: A Revision of Bloom's Taxonomy of Educational Objectives*. New York: Longman.

Angoff, W. H. (1971), 'Scales, norms, and equivalent scores', in R. L. Thorndike (ed.), *Educational Measurement*. Washington, DC: American Council on Education.

ANTA (2002), 'Assessment and Online Teaching: Australian Flexible Learning Quick Guide Series', Australian Flexible Learning Framework, Australian National Training Authority, http://www.flexiblelearning.net.au/guides/assessment.pdf.

ANTA (2003), 'E-assessment strategies and models research analysis – issues and implications', Australian Flexible Learning Framework, Australian National Training Authority, http://www.flexiblelearning.net.au/projects/resources/OASM_Res_analysis.pdf.

Atkins, S. and O'Connor, G. (2005), 'Re-purposing learning objects as assessment instruments', The 10th Annual Roundtable Conference *AR+t: Assessment Reporting & Technology*, http://www.vcaa.vic.edu.au/roundtable/papers/sagcoatkins.pdf.

ATP (2002), *Guidelines for Computer-Based Testing*. Washington, DC: Association of Test Publishers.

Baker, F. B. (2001), *The Basics of Item Response Theory*. ERIC Clearinghouse on Assessment and Evaluation, University of Maryland, College Park, MD. http://edres.org/irt/baker/.

Baldwin, L. and Sabry, K. (2003), 'Learning styles for interactive learning systems'. *Innovations in Education and Teaching International*, 40, 325–40.

Ball, S. A. (2005), 'Checklist for inclusive assessment: getting started with accessibility', 9th CAA Conference, http://www.caaconference.com/pastConferences/2005/proceedings/BallS.pdf.

Barak, A. (2003), 'Ethical and professional issues in career assessment on the Internet'. *Journal of Career Assessment*, 11, 3–21.

Baron, J. and Keller, M. (2003), 'Use of rubrics in online assessment', Assessment and Evaluation Conference, Adelaide, Australia, http://www.unisa.edu.au/evaluations/Full-papers/BaronFull.doc.

Baron, J. and Maier, H. (2004), 'A Community of Inquiry evaluation of Mekong e-Sim: An online collaborative simulation', ICET2004 Conference Proceedings (CD-ROM), Singapore, September 9–11, http://icet2004.hku.hk.

Barstow, C., Mckell, M., Rothberg, M. and Schmidt, C. (2002), 'IMS Guidelines for Developing Accessible Learning Applications, Version 1.0', http://www.imsglobal.org/accessibility.

Bartram, B and Coyne, I. (2005), 'International Guidelines on Computer-Based and Internet Delivered Testing, Version 2005', International Testing Commission Council, http://www.intestcom.org/itc_projects.htm.

Bates, A. W. (1995), *Technology, Open Learning and Distance Education*. London, Routledge.

Bejar, I. I., Lawless, R. R., Morley, M. E., Wagner, M. E., Bennett, R. E. and Revuelta, J. (2003),

'A feasibility study of on-the-fly item generation in adaptive testing'. *Journal of Technology, Learning, and Assessment,* 2(3), http://www.jtla.org.

Belton, M. and Knopf, S. (2002), 'Creating assessments that conform to W3C accessibility guidelines', 6th CAA Conference, http://www.caaconference.com/pastConferences/2002/proceedings/belton_m1.pdf.

Benfield, G. (2002), 'Designing and managing effective online discussions', Learning and Teaching Briefing Papers Series, Oxford Centre for Staff and Learning Development, http://www.brookes.ac.uk/services/ocsd/2_learntch/briefing_papers/online_discussions.pdf.

Bennett, R. E. (2002), 'Inexorable and inevitable: the continuing story of technology and assessment', *Journal of Technology, Learning, and Assessment,* 1(1), http://www.jtla.org.

Bennett, R. E., Jenkins, F., Persky, H. and Weiss, A. (2003), 'Assessing complex problem solving performances', *Assessment in Education,* 10, 347–59.

Beretvas, S. N. (2004), 'Comparison of Bookmark difficulty locations under different item response models', *Applied Psychological Measurement,* 28, 25–47.

Biggs, J. B. (1979), 'Individual differences in study processes and the quality of learning outcomes', *Higher Education,* 8, 381–94.

Biggs, J. B. (1999), *Teaching for Quality Learning at University.* London: Society for Research into Higher Education and Open University Press.

Biggs, J. B. (2002), 'Aligning teaching and assessment to curriculum objectives', LTSN Imaginative Curriculum Guide IC022, http://www.ltsn.ac.uk/application.asp?app=resources. asp&process=full_record&section=generic&tid=154.

Biggs J. and Collis K. (1982), *Evaluating the Quality of Learning: the SOLO taxonomy.* New York: Academic Press.

BIOSCIENCE (2005), 'Assessment Audit Tool', Higher Education Academy, LTSN Bioscience Network, http://www.bioscience.heacademy.ac.uk/resources/Audit.htm.

Bonk, C. J. and Dennen, V. P. (2005), 'Massive Multiplayer Online Gaming: A Research Framework for Military Training and Education', Technical Report 2005-1 Advanced Distributed Learning (ADL) Initiative, http://www.adlnet.org/downloads/189.cfm.

Booth, R., Clayton, B., Hartcher, R., Hungar, S., Hyde, P. and Wilson, P. (2003), 'The development of quality e-assessment in vocational education and training: Volume 1', NCVER National Centre for Vocational Education Research Australia, http://www.ncver.edu.au/publications/962.html.

Boud. D. and Prosser, M. (2002), 'Key principles for high quality student learning in higher education: A framework for evaluation'. *Educational Media International,* 39(3), 237–45.

Boyle, A. (2005), 'Sophisticated tasks in e-assessment: What are they? And what are their benefits?', 9th CAA Conference, http://www.caaconference.com/pastConferences/2005/proceedings/BoyleA2.pdf.

Boyle, A. and O'Hare, D. (2003), 'Finding appropriate methods to assure quality computer-based assessment development in UK higher education', 7th CAA Conference, http://www.caaconference.com/pastConferences/2003/procedings/boyle.pdf.

BPS (2002), *Guidelines for the Development and Use of Computer-based Assessments,* Leicester: British Psychological Society, Psychological Testing Centre, http://www.psychtesting.org.uk.

Brandon, P. R. (2004), 'Conclusions about frequently studied modified Angoff standard-setting topics'. *Applied Measurement In Education,* 17, 59–88.

Brem, S. (2002), 'Analyzing online discussions: ethics, data, and interpretation', *Practical Assessment, Research & Evaluation,* 8(3), http://PAREonline.net/getvn.asp?v=8&n=3.

Brinkerhoff, R. O. (1987), *Achieving Results from Training.* San Francisco, Jossey-Bass.

Broadfoot, P. and Black, P. (2004), 'Redefining assessment? The first ten years of assessment in education', *Assessment in Education,* 11, 7–20.

Brown, S., Race, P. and Bull, J. (1999), *Computer Assisted Assessment in Higher Education.* London: Kogan Page.

BSI (2002), British Standard Institute, BS 7988, 'A code of practice for the use of information technology for the delivery of assessments', Guildford Educational Services Ltd, http://www.bsi-global.com.

Bull, J. and Danson, M. (2004), 'Computer-assisted assessment (CAA)', Assessment LTSN Generic Centre Series, No. 14, http://www.heacademy.ac.uk/embedded_object.asp?id=20388&filename=ASS093.

Bull, J. and McKenna, C. (2003), *Blueprint for Computer-assisted Assessment*. London, RoutledgeFalmer.

Bull, J., Zhao, P., Foulkes, A. and Thomas, P., *Web-Based Learning. A Guide for Postgraduate Tutors and Lecturers*, http://www.glow.ac.uk/resources/part4/soar4.pdf.

Burghof, K. L. (2001), 'Assembling an item-bank for computerised linear and adaptive testing in geography'. *International Education Journal*, 2, 74–83.

Burton, R. F. (2001), 'Quantifying the effects of chance in multiple-choice and true/false tests: question selection and guessing of answers'. *Assessment & Evaluation in Higher Education*, 26, 41–50.

Burton, R. (2005), 'Multiple-choice and true/false tests: myths and misapprehensions'. *Assessment & Evaluation in Higher Education*, 30, 65–72.

Burton, R. F. and Miller, D. J. (1999), 'Statistical modelling in multiple-choice and true/false tests: ways of considering, and of reducing, the uncertainties of guessing'. *Assessment & Evaluation in Higher Education*, 24, 399–411.

Bush, M. (2001), 'A multiple choice test that rewards partial knowledge'. *Journal of Further and Higher Education*, 25,157–63.

CAA Centre, http://www.caacentre.ac.uk/resources/objective_tests/assertion.shtml.

Canvas, http://www.the-can.com

Carneson, J., Delpierre, G. and Masters, K. (2002), 'Designing and managing multiple choice questions', http://www.le.ac.uk/castle/resources.

Case, S. M. and Swanson, D. B. (2002), *Constructing Written Test Questions for the Basic and Clinical Sciences*, Third Edition. Philadelphia, PA: National Board of Medical Examiners, http://www.nbme.org/PDF/ItemWriting_2003/2003IWGwhole.pdf.

Cassidy, S. (2004), 'Learning styles: An overview of theories, models and measures'. *Educational Psychology*, 24, 419–44.

CASTLE Toolkit, http://www.le.ac.uk/castle/resources/mcqman/mcqchp4.html.

Challis, N., Houston, K. and Stirling, D. (2004), 'Supporting Good Practice in Assessment in Mathematics, Statistics and Operational Research. Briefings Guide for Heads of Departments Guide for Lecturers', Maths, Stats & OR Network, Higher Education Academy, UK, http://mathstore.ac.uk/publications/staff.pdf.

Chalmers, D. and McAusland, W. D. M. (2002), 'Computer-Assisted Assessment', http://www.economicsnetwork.ac.uk/handbook/printable/caa_v5.pdf.

Chang, W. C., Hsu, H. H., Smith, T. K. and Wang, C. C. (2004), 'Enhancing SCORM metadata for assessment authoring in e-learning'. *Journal of Computer Assisted Learning*, 20, 305–16.

Cheang, B. C., Kurnia, A., Limb, A. and Oon, W-C. (2003), 'On automated grading of programming assignments in an academic institution'. *Computers & Education*, 41, 121–31.

Chen, C-M, Lee, H-M. and Chen, Y-H, (2005), 'Personalized e-learning system using Item Response Theory'. *Computers & Education*, 44, 237–55.

Chickering, A. W. and Gamson, Z. F. (1987), 'Seven principles for good practice in undergraduate education'. *AAHE Bulletin*, 39(7), 3–7.

Chung, G. K. W. K., O'Neil, H. F., Jr and Herl, H. E. (1999), 'The use of computer-based collaborative knowledge mapping to measure team processes and team outcomes'. *Computers in Human Behavior*, 15, 463–94.

Clariana, R. and Wallace, P. (2002), 'Paper-based versus computer-based assessment: key factors associated with the test mode effect'. *British Journal of Educational Technology*, 33, 593–602.

CODE (2004), 'Code of practice for the assurance of academic quality and standards in higher education. Section 2: Collaborative provision and flexible and distributed learning (including e-learning), Quality Assurance Agency for Higher Education, http://www.qaa.ac.uk.

Cohen, Y., Ben-Simon, A. and Hovav, M. (2003), 'The effect of specific language features on the complexity of systems for automated essay scoring', IAEA 29th Annual Conference, Manchester, UK, http://www.aqa.org.uk/support/iaea/papers/ben-cohen-hovav.pdf.

COLEG On-Line Assessment Project.

COLA (2003), http://www.cetis.ac.uk/profiles/uklomcore/toia_cola_metadata_v1p2.doc.

Coyne, I. and Bartram, D. (eds) (2005), 'International guidelines on computer-based and Internet delivered testing', http://www.intestcom.org/guidelines/index.html.

Crisp, G. (2002), 'Using Java applets to help make online assessment interactive', ASCILTE 2002 Conference, Auckland, NZ, http://www.ascilite.org.au/conferences/auckland02/proceedings/papers/096.pdf.

Cronbach, L. J. (2004), 'My current thoughts on coefficient alpha and successor procedures'. Educational and Psychological Measurement, 64, 391–418.

Davies, W. M., Howard, Y., Millard, D. E., Davis, H. C. and Sclater, N. (2005), 'Aggregating assessment tools in a service oriented architecture', 9th CAA Conference, http://www.caaconference.com/pastConferences/2005/proceedings.

DfES, http://www.dfes.gov.uk.

Dondi, C. and Moretti, M. (2002), 'UNIGAME: Game-based learning in universities and lifelong Learning. Deliverable 1.1: Survey on online game-based learning', http://www.unigame.net/html/publications.html.

Downing, S. M. (2003), 'Item response theory: applications of modern test theory in medical education'. Medical Education, 37, 739–45.

Draper, S. W., 'Electronic voting systems and interactive lectures: entrance lobby', http://www.psy.gla.ac.uk/~steve/ilig/.

Draper, S. W., Cargill, J. and Cutts, Q. (2002), 'Electronically enhanced classroom interaction'. Australian Journal of Educational Technology, 18, 13–23.

Dunn, L., Morgan, C., O'Reilly, M. and Parry, S. (2004), The Student Assessment Handbook. New Directions in Traditional and E-assessment. London, RoutledgeFalmer.

Dutch, S. (2003), http://www.uwgb.edu/dutchs/Exams/ExamMaster.htm.

Eggen, T. J. H. M. (2001), 'Overexposure and underexposure of items in computerized adaptive testing', Measurement and Research Department Reports, http://download.citogroep.nl/pub/pok/reports/Report01-01.pdf.

Eggen, T. J. H. M. and Straetmans, G. J. J. M. (2000), 'Computerized adaptive testing for classifying examinees into three categories'. Educational and Psychological Measurement, 60, 713–34.

Ehrmann, S. C. (2002), 'Evaluating (and improving) benefits of educational uses of technology', http://www.tltgroup.org/resources/Flashlight/Benefits.html.

Ellis, W., Ratcliffe, M. and Thomasso, B. (2003), 'Promoting fairer grading of group based assessment using collaborative IT tools', 7th CAA Conference, http://www.caaconference.com/pastConferences/2003/procedings/ellis.pdf.

Elwood, J. and Klenowski, V. (2002), 'Creating communities of shared practice: The challenges of assessment use in learning and teaching'. Assessment & Evaluation in Higher Education, 27, 243–56.

Entwistle, N. and Ramsden, P. (1983), Understanding Student Learning. London: Croom Helm.

ETS (2007), http://www.ets.org.

Evans, C. and Sabry, K. (2003), 'Evaluation of the interactivity of web-based learning systems: principles and process', Innovations in Education and Teaching International, 40, 89–99.

Evans, D. (2005), 'Potential uses of wireless and mobile learning', http://www.jisc.ac.uk/uploaded_documents/Potential%20Uses%20FINAL%202005.doc.

Fahy, P. J. (2005), 'Two methods for assessing critical thinking in computer-mediated communications (CMC) transcripts'. *International Journal of Instructional Technology and Distance Learning, 2,* http://www.itdl.org/Journal/Mar_05/article02.htm.

Fannon, K. (2002), 'A role-play simulation. Transformative learning in complex dynamic social systems', http://www.flexiblelearning.net.au/leaders/fl_leaders/fll02/papers/roleplay_fannon. pdf.

Freeman, M. and McKenzie, J. (2002), 'SPARK, a confidential web-based template for self and peer assessment of student team work: Benefits of evaluating across different subjects'. *British Journal of Educational Technology,* 33, 551–69.

Gao, H., Baylor, A. L. and Shen, E. (2005), 'Designer support for online collaboration and knowledge construction'. *Educational Technology & Society,* 8, 69–79.

Garrison, D. R., Anderson, T. and Archer, W. (2001), 'Critical thinking, cognitive presence, and computer conferencing in distance education'. *The American Journal of Distance Education,* 15, 7–23.

Georgiadou, E., Triantafillou, E. and Economides, A. A. (2006), 'Evaluation parameters for computer-adaptive testing', *British Journal of Educational Technology,* 37, 261–78.

Gibbs, G. and Simpson, C. (2004), 'Measuring the response of students to assessment: the Assessment Experience Questionnaire', in C. Rust (ed.) *Improving Student Learning: Theory, Research and Scholarship.* Oxford: Oxford Centre for Staff and Learning Development.

Gilbert, P. K. and Dabbagh, N. (2005), 'How to structure online discussions for meaningful discourse: a case study'. *British Journal of Educational Technology,* 36, 5–18.

Glaser, B. G. (2005), *The Grounded Theory Perspective III: Theoretical Coding.* Mill Valley, CA: Sociology Press.

GMAT (2007), http://www.gmac.com.

Goodman, J. M., Kirby, P. D. and Haustedt, L. O. (2000), 'Some calculations for organic chemists: boiling point variation, Boltzmann factors and the Eyring equation', *Tetrahedron Letters,* 2000, 41, 9879–82.

Gunn, C., French, S., McLeod, H., McSporran, M. and Conole, G. (2002), 'Gender issues in computer-supported learning'. *Association for Learning Technology Journal,* 10, 32–44.

Hara, N., Bonk, C. J. and Angeli, C. (2002), 'Content analysis of online discussion in an applied educational psychology course'. *Instructional Science,* 28, 115–52.

Harper, R. (2003), 'Correcting computer-based assessments for guessing'. *Journal of Computer Assisted Learning,* 19, 2–8.

Hartford, T. (2005), 'Facilitation and assessment of group work using web-based tools', BEEj-5, http://www.bioscience.heacademy.ac.uk/journal/vol5/beej-5-5.htm.

Harwood, I. A. (2005), 'When summative computer-aided assessments go wrong: disaster recovery after a major failure'. *British Journal of Educational Technology,* 36, 587–97.

Hattie, J. A. C. and Brown, G. T. L. (2004), 'Cognitive processes in asTTle: The SOLO taxonomy. asTTle', Technical Report #43, University of Auckland/Ministry of Education, http://www.tki. org.nz/r/asttle/pdf/technical-reports/techreport43.pdf.

Herd, G. and Clark, G. (2003), 'Computer-aided Assessment – Final Report and Guidelines for Implementation: Implementing CAA in the FE Sector in Scotland', http://eprints.soton. ac.uk/14113/.

Herrington, J., Oliver, R. and Herrington, T. (2000), 'Towards a new tradition of online instruction: using situated learning theory to design web-based units', 17th Annual Conference of ASCILITE, http://www.ascilite.org.au/conferences/coffs00/papers/jan_ herrington.pdf.

Herrington, J. and Standen, P. (1999), 'Moving from an instructivist to a constructivist multimedia learning environment', EdMedia Conference, Seattle, Washington, USA, http:// dl.aace.org/4230.

Higgins, E. and Tatham, L. (2003), 'Assessing by multiple choice question (MCQ) tests', http:// www.ukcle.ac.uk/resources/trns/mcqs/index.html.

Higgins, J., Russell, M. and Hoffmann, T. (2005), 'Examining the effect of computer-based passage presentation on reading test performance'. *Journal of Technology, Learning, and Assessment,* 3(4).

Honey, P. and Mumford, A. (1992), *The Manual of Learning Styles* (3rd edition). Maidenhead: Peter Honey.

Hughes, P. and Boyle, A. (2005), 'Assessment in the earth sciences, environmental sciences and environmental studies', GEES Learning and Teaching Guide, http://www.gees.ac.uk/pubs/guides/assess/gees%20assesment.pdf.

Imrie, B. W. (1995), 'RECAP – Assessment for learning: quality and taxonomies'. *Assessment & Evaluation in Higher Education,* 20, 175–89.

IMS QTI (2005), 'IMS Question and Test Interoperability Information Model Version 2.0 Final Specification', 2005 IMS Global Learning Consortium, Inc., http://www.imsproject.org/question/.

Ip, A. (2001), 'Ideal features of web-based role-play generator'. *Educational Technology & Society,* 4(2). http://ifets.ieee.org/periodical/vol_2_2001/discuss_summary_feb2001.html.

Jacobsen, M. (2003), 'Multiple choice item construction', http://www.ucalgary.ca/~dmjacobs/portage/.

James, R., McInnis, C. and Devlin, M. (2002), 'Assessing learning in Australian universities: ideas, strategies and resources for quality in student assessment', Centre for the Study of Higher Education, The University of Melbourne and The Australian Universities Teaching Committee, Canberra, Australia, http://www.cshe.unimelb.edu.au/assessinglearning.

JISC, http://www.jiscinfonet.ac.uk/InfoKits/system-selection.

Jodoin, M., Zenisky, A. and Hambleton, R. (2002), 'Comparison of the psychometric properties of several computer-based test designs for credentialing exams', National Council on Measurement in Education, New Orleans, http://www.psych.umn.edu/psylabs/CATCentral/PDF%20Files/JO02-01.pdf.

Johnstone, A. (2004), 'LTSN Physical Sciences Practice Guide: Effective Practice in Objective Assessment. The Skills of Fixed Response Testing', http://www.physsci.ltsn.ac.uk/Publications/PracticeGuide/EffectivePracticeInObjectiveAssessment.pdf.

Joinera, R. and Issroff, K. (2003), 'Tracing success: graphical methods for analyzing successful collaborative problem solving'. *Computers & Education,* 41, 369–78.

Juwah, C., MacFarlane-Dick, D., Matthew, B., Nicol, D., Ross, D. and Smith, B. (2004), 'Enhancing student learning through effective formative feedback', The Higher Education Academy Generic Centre, York, http://www.heacademy.ac.uk/resources.asp?process=full_record&section=generic&tid=353.

Kendle, A. and Nothcote, M. (2000), 'The struggle for balance in the use of quantitative and qualitative e-assessment tasks', 17th Annual Conference of ASCILITE, http://ascilite.org.au/conferences/coffs00/papers/amanda_kendle.pdf.

Ketterlin-Geller, L. R. (2005), 'Knowing what all students know: procedures for developing universal design for assessment'. *Journal of Technology, Learning, and Assessment,* 4(2), http://www.jtla.org.

Kindley, R. W. (2002), 'Scenario-based e-learning: A step beyond traditional e-learning', http://www.learningcircuits.org/2002/may2002/kindley.html.

Kirkpatrick, D. L. (1998), *Evaluating Training Programs* (2nd edition). San Francisco: Berrrett-Koehler.

Kleeman, J. and Osborne, C. (2002), 'A practical look at delivering assessments to BS 7988 recommendations', 6th CAA Conference 2002, http://www.caaconference.com/pastConferences/2002/proceedings/kleeman_j1.pdf.

Kolb, D. A. (1984), *Experiential Learning: Experience as the Source of Learning and Development.* New Jersey: Prentice Hall.

Koper, R. and Olivier, B. (2004), 'Representing the learning design of units of learning'. *Educational Technology & Society,* 7, 97–111.

Lampe, T. and Eggen, T. (2003), 'Innovative item types in computer based testing: Scoring of multiple response items', IAEA Conference, http://www.aqa.org.uk/support/iaea/papers/EGGEN-LAMPE.PDF.

Landauer, T. K., Foltz, P. W. and Laham, D. (1998), 'Introduction to latent semantic analysis'. *Discourse Processes*, 25, 259–84.

Landauer, T. K., Laham, D. and Foltz, P. (2003), 'Automatic essay assessment'. *Assessment in Education*, 10, 295–308.

Laurillard, D. (2002), *Rethinking University Teaching: A Conversational Framework for the Effective Use of Learning Technologies* (2nd edition). London and New York: Routledge.

Leacock, C. and Chodorow, M. (2003), 'C-rater: Automated scoring of short-answer questions'. *Computers and the Humanities*, 37, 389–405.

LearningMate (2004), 'Scenario-based learning: An effective and efficient approach to improving text-centric learning by interactive adjuncts', A LearningMate™ White Paper, http://www.learningmate.com/whitepaper.htm.

Leung, C-K., Chang, H-H. and Hau, K-T. (2003), 'Computerized adaptive testing: A comparison of three content balancing methods'. *Journal of Technology, Learning, and Assessment,* 2(5), http://www.jtla.org.

Li, Y. H. and Schafer, W. D. (2005), 'Increasing the homogeneity of CAT's item-exposure rates by minimizing or maximizing varied target functions while assembling shadow tests'. *Journal of Educational Measurement*, 42 (3), 245–69.

Lilley, M., Barker, T. and Britton, C. (2004), 'The development and evaluation of a software prototype for computer-adaptive testing'. *Computers & Education*, 43,109–23.

Linser, R. and Ip, A. (2004), 'Creating learning opportunities using an RPS authoring tool', AUSWEB 2004, http://ausweb.scu.edu.au/aw04/papers/refereed/ip/paper.html.

Linser, R., Waniganayake, M. and Wilkes, S. (2004), 'A different lunch: Role-play simulations in preparing early childhood leaders', IASTED Conference, Web-based Education, 2004, http://www.simplay.net/papers/dlunch.html.

Lipponen, L. and Lallimo, J. (2004), 'Assessing applications for collaboration: From collaboratively usable applications to collaborative technology'. *British Journal of Educational Technology*, 35, 433–42.

Livingston, S. A. (2004), 'Equating test scores (without IRT)', Educational Testing Service, http://tigger.uic.edu/~georgek/HomePage/EdMeasurement/livingston.pdf.

LOM (2002), IEEE Learning Technology Standards Committee Draft Standard for Learning Object Metadata, IEEE 1484.12.1-2002, New Jersey: IEEE Standards Department, http://ltsc.ieee.org/wg12/files/LOM_1484_12_1_v1_Final_Draft.pdf.

LTSN (2001), 'Assessment: A guide for lecturers', LTSN Series on Assessment, http://www.heacademy.ac.uk.

Luecht, R. M. (2002), 'From design to delivery: engineering the mass production of complex performance assessments', Annual Meeting of the National Council on Measurement in Education, New Orleans, LA, http://www.ncme.org/repository/incoming/102.pdf.

Mabry, L. (1999), *Portfolio Plus: A Critical Guide to Alternative Assessment*. Thousand Oaks: Corwin Press.

McAlpine, M. (2002a), 'Principles of assessment', CAA Centre, University of Luton, http://caacentre.lboro.ac.uk/dldocs/Bluepaper1.pdf.

McAlpine, M. (2002b), 'A summary of methods of item analysis', CAA Centre, University of Luton, http://caacentre.lboro.ac.uk/dldocs/Bp2final.pdf.

McAlpine, M. (2002c), 'Design requirements of a databank', CAA Centre, University of Luton, http://caacentre.lboro.ac.uk/dldocs/Bp3final.pdf.

McAlpine, M. and Ware, W. (2003), 'Introducing computer-assisted assessment in Scotland: Laying the foundations for an integrated approach', 29th International Association for Educational Assessment Conference, Manchester, http://www.aqa.org.uk/support/iaea/papers/mcalpine-ware.pdf.

McCabe, M. and Barrett, D. (2003), 'It's a MUGS game! Does the mathematics of CAA matter in the computer age?', Maths CAA Series, http://ltsn.mathstore.ac.uk/articles/maths-caa-series/apr2003/index.shtml.

McCabe, E. M. and Lucas, I. (2003), 'Teaching with CAA in an interactive classroom: Death by Powerpoint, life by discourse', 7th CAA Conference, http://www.caaconference.com/pastConferences/2003/procedings/mccabe2.pdf.

Macdonald, R. and Savin-Baden, M. (2004), 'A briefing on assessment in problem-based learning', The Higher Education Academy Generic Centre, York, http://www.heacademy.ac.uk/resources.asp?process=full_record&section=generic&id=349.

MacDonald, J. (2003), 'Assessing online collaborative learning: Process and product'. *Computers & Education*, 40, 377–91.

McGrath, P., Kucera, R. and Smith, W. (2003), 'Computer simulation of introductory neurophysiology'. *Advances in Physiology Education*, 27, 120–9.

McGuire, L. (2005), 'Assessment using new technology'. *Innovations in Education and Teaching International*, 42, 265–76.

McKenna, C. and Bull, J. (1999), 'Designing effective objective test questions: an introductory workshop', http://caacentre.lboro.ac.uk/dldocs/otghdout.pdf.

McMillan, J. H. (2000), 'Fundamental assessment principles for teachers and school administrators'. *Practical Assessment, Research and Evaluation*, 7, http://PAREonline.net/getvn.asp?v=7&n=8.

Maron, F. and Saljo, R. (1976), 'On qualitative differences in learning: Outcomes and process'. *British Journal of Educational Psychology*, 46, 4–11.

Mason, R., Pegler, C. and Weller, M. (2004), 'E-portfolios: an assessment tool for online courses'. *British Journal of Educational Technology*, 35, 717–27.

Mavrikis, M. and Maciocia, A. (2003), 'Incorporating assessment into an interactive learning environment for mathematics', Maths CAA Series: June 2003, Higher Education Academy, http://ltsn.mathstore.ac.uk/articles/maths-caa-series/june2003/index.shtml.

MESA (2005), 'Managing assessment: Student and staff perspectives', Managing Effective Student Assessment (MESA), Higher Education Academy, http://www.heacademy.ac.uk/799.htm.

Millard, D. E., Howard, Y., Bailey, C. P., Davis, H. C., Gilbert, L., Jeyes, S., Price, J., Sclater, N., Sherratt, R., Tulloch, I., Wills, G. B. and Young, R. (2005), 'Mapping the e-learning assessment domain: Concept maps for orientation and navigation', e-Learn 2005, Vancouver, Canada, http://www.aace.org/conf/elearn/.

Mislevy, R. J., Almond, R. G. and Lukas, J. F. (2004), 'A brief introduction to evidence-centered design', CSE Technical Report 632, Educational Testing Service, Princeton, NJ, http://www.cse.ucla.edu/reports/r632.pdf.

Mislevy, R. J., Steinberg, L. S., Almond, R. G., Breyer, F. J. and Johnson, L. (2001), 'Making sense of data from complex assessments', CSE Technical Report 538, http://www.cse.ucla.edu/CRESST/Reports/RML%20TR%20538.pdf.

Moreale, E. and Vargas-Vera, M. (2003), 'Genre analysis and the automated extraction of arguments from student essays', 7th CAA Conference, http://www.caaconference.com/pastConferences/2003/procedings/moreale.pdf.

Murphy, E. and Rodriguez Manzanares, M. A. (2005), 'Reading between the lines: understanding the role of latent content in the analysis of online asynchronous discussions'. *International Journal of Instructional Technology and Distance Learning*, 2, 23–32.

Naidu, S., Ip, A. and Linser, R. (2000), 'Dynamic goal-based role-play simulation on the web: A case study'. *Educational Technology & Society*, 3, 190–202.

Naidu, S., Menon, M., Gunawardena, C., Lekamge, D. and Karunanayaka, S. (2005), 'Quality teaching and learning in the Master of Arts in Teacher Education (MATE – International) programme at the Open University of Sri Lanka', 17th Biennial Conference of the Open and Distance Learning Association of Australia, Adelaide, http://www.unisa.edu.au/odlaaconference/referred-papers.htm.

Naidu, S, and Järvelä, S. (2006), 'Analyzing CMC content for what?' *Computers & Education*, 46, 96–103.

Nichols, P. D. (1994), 'A framework for developing cognitively diagnostic assessments'. *Review of Educational Research*, 64, 575–603.

Northcote, M. (2003), 'The influence of pedagogy on the construction of students' epistemologies'. *Issues in Educational Research*, 13, 66-84.

Oblinger, D. G. and Oblinger, J. L. (2005), *Educating the Net Generation*, Washington, DC: Educause, http://www.educause.edu/books/educatingthenetgen/5989.

Oliver, R. (2000), 'When teaching meets learning: design principles and strategies for web-based learning environments that support knowledge construction', 17th Annual Conference of ASCILITE, http://www.ascilite.org.au/conferences/coffs00/papers/ron_oliver_keynote.pdf.

O'Neil Jr, H. F., Chung, G. K. W. K. and Brown, R. (1997), 'Use of networked simulations as a context to measure team competencies', in H. F. O'Neil, Jr (ed.) *Workforce Readiness: Competencies and Assessment*. Mahwah, NJ: Erlbaum, pp. 411–52.

O'Neil, Jr., H. F, Chuang, S-H. and Chung, G. K. W. K. (2003), 'Issues in the computer-based assessment of collaborative problem solving'. *Assessment in Education*, 10, 361–73.

Palmer, K. and May, C. (2004), 'Using learning styles theory to improve on-line learning through computer assisted diagnosis', 8th CAA Conference, http://www.caaconference.com/pastConferences/2004/proceedings/Palmer_May.pdf.

Parshall, C. G., Davey, T. and Pashley, P. J. (2000), 'Innovative item types for computerized testing', in W. J. Van der Linden and C. A. W. Glas (eds) *Computerized Adaptive Testing: Theory and Practice*. Dordrecht, Netherlands: Kluwer Academic Publishers, pp. 129–48.

Parshall, C. G., Spray, J. A. and Davey, T. (2002), *Practical Considerations in Computer-Based Testing: Issues and Applications*. New York, NY: Springer-Verlag New York, Inc.

PASS-IT, 'Good practice guide in question and test design. Project on assessment in Scotland – using information technology', http://www.pass-it.org.uk/resources/031112-goodpracticeguide-hw.pdf.

Patelis, T. (2000), 'An overview of computer-based testing', http://www.collegeboard.com/research/pdf/overview_of_computer__10507.pdf.

Paul, J. (1998), 'Improving educational assessment by incorporating confidence measurement, analysis of self-awareness, and performance evaluation: The Computer-Based Alternative Assessment™ (CBAA™) Project', http://www.jodypaul.com/ASSESS/CBAA.pdf.

Pellegrino, J. W. (2005), 'The evolution of educational assessment: Considering the past and imagining the future', The Policy Evaluation and Research Center at ETS, http://www.ets.org/Media/Research/pdf/PICANG6.pdf.

Pellegrino, J. W., Chudowsky, N. and Glaser, R. (2001), 'Knowing what students know: The science and design of educational assessment', Committee on the Foundations of Assessment, Board on Testing and Assessment, Center for Education, Division of Behavioral and Social Sciences and Education, National Research Council, http://www.nap.edu/books/0309072727/html.

Pena-Shaffa, J. B. and Nicholls, C. (2004), 'Analyzing student interactions and meaning construction in computer bulletin board discussions'. *Computers & Education*, 42, 243–65.

Penuel, W. R. and Yarnall, L. (2005), 'Designing handheld software to support classroom assessment: analysis of conditions for teacher adoption'. *The Journal of Technology, Learning, and Assessment*, 3, http://www.jtla.org.

Poggio, J., Glasnapp, D. R., Yang, X. and Poggio, A. J. (2005), 'A comparative evaluation of score results from computerized and paper-and-pencil mathematics testing in a large scale state assessment program'. *Journal of Technology, Learning, and Assessment*, 3(6), http://www.jtla.org.

Pommerich, M. (2004), 'Developing computerized versions of paper-and-pencil tests: Mode effects for passage-based tests'. *Journal of Technology, Learning, and Assessment*, 2(6), http://www.jtla.org.

Pomplu, M. and Ritchie, T. (2004), 'An investigation of context effects for item randomization within testlets'. *Journal Educational Computing Research*, 30, 243–54.

Prensky, M. (2001), *Digital Game-Based Learning*. San Francisco: McGraw-Hill.

QAA Assessment (2000), 'Code of practice for the assurance of academic quality and standards in higher education, Section 6: Assessment of students', http://www.qaa.ac.uk/academicinfrastructure/codeOfPractice/section6/COP_AOS.pdf.

QCA (2004), 'The Basic and Key Skills (BKS) E-assessment Experience Report', http://www.qca.org.uk/6992.html.

QTI (2006), 'IMS Question & Test Interoperability: Specification, Version 2.1', http://www.imsproject.org/question/qtiv2p1pd2/imsqti_oviewv2p1pd2.html.

QTILITE (2002), 'IMS Question & Test Interoperability. QTILite Specification, Final Specification, Version 1.2', http://www.imsglobal.org/question/qtiv1p2/imsqti_litev1p2.html.

Quellmalz, E. and Kozma, R. (2003), 'Designing assessments of learning with technology'. *Assessment in Education*, 10(3), 389–407.

Race, P. (2003), 'Designing assessment to improve physical sciences learning', LTSN Physical Sciences Practice Guide, http://www.physsci.heacademy.ac.uk/Publications/PracticeGuide/guide4.pdf.

Race, P. and Bull, J. (1999), *Computer-assisted Assessment in Higher Education*. London: Kogan Page.

Rafaeli, S., Barak, M., Dan-Gur, Y. and Toch, E. (2004), 'QSIA – a web-based environment for learning, assessing and knowledge sharing in communities'. *Computers & Education*, 43, 273–89.

Raikes, N. and Harding, R. (2003), 'The horseless carriage stage: replacing conventional measures'. *Assessment in Education*, 10, 267–77.

Ricketts, C. and Wilks, S. J. (2002), 'Improving student performance through computer-based assessment: insights from recent research'. *Assessment & Evaluation in Higher Education*, 27, 475–9.

Ridgway, J. and McCusker, S. (2003), 'Using computers to assess new educational goals'. *Assessment in Education*, 10, 309–28.

Roach, M., Blackmore, P. and Dempster, J. (2001), 'Supporting high level learning through research-based methods: A framework for course development'. *Innovations in Education and Training International*, 38, 369–81.

Rose, D. and Meyer, A. (2002), 'Teaching every student in the digital age: Universal design for learning', Alexandria, VA: Association for Supervision and Curriculum Development, http://www.cast.org/teachingeverystudent/.

Rust, C., O'Donovan, B. and Price, M. (2005), 'A social constructivist assessment process model: how the research literature shows us this could be best practice'. *Assessment & Evaluation in Higher Education*, 30, 231–40.

Salmon, G. (2000), *E-moderating: The Key to Teaching and Learning Online*. London: Kogan Page.

Salter, G. and Hansen, S. (1999), 'Modelling new skills for online teaching', 16th Annual Conference of ASCILITE, http://www.ascilite.org.au/conferences/brisbane99/papers/salterhansen.pdf.

Samuelowicz, K. and Bain, J. D. (2002), 'Identifying academics' orientations to assessment practice'. *Higher Education*, 43, 173–201.

Sawyers, J. and Alexander, S. (1998), 'A centralised approach to the adoption of a university-wide web-based learning tool', 15th Annual Conference of ASCILITE, http://www.ascilite.org.au/conferences/wollongong98/ascpapers98.html/sawers0132.pdf.

Schaeffer, G. A., Henderson-Montero, D., Julian, M. and Bené, N. H. (2002), 'A comparison of three scoring methods for tests with selected-response and constructed-response items'. *Educational Assessment*, 8, 317–40.

Sclater, N. (2003), 'TOIA-COLA Assessment Metadata Application Profile, Version 1.2', University of Strathclyde, http://www.cetis.ac.uk/profiles/uklomcore/toia_cola_metadata_v1p2.doc.

Sclater, N. (2004), 'Item Banks Infrastructure Study', JISC, http://www.toia.ac.uk/ibis/IBIS-Item-Banks-Infrastructure-Study.pdf.

Sclater, N., Boyle, E., Bull, J., Church, C., Patrick Craven, P., Cross, R., Danson, M., Halliday, L., Howie, I., Kelly, J. X., Lay, S., Massey, M., McAlpine, M., McDonald, D., MacDonald, M., Rogers, S. and White, S. (2005), 'Defining the infrastructure for a national item bank service', 9th CAA Conference, http://www.caaconference.com/pastConferences/2005/proceedings/SclaterN_etal.pdf.

Sclater, N. and Howie, K. (2003), 'User requirements of the "ultimate" online assessment engine'. *Computers & Education*, 40, 285–306.

Sclater, N. and Low, B. (2002), 'IMS Question and Test Interoperability: An idiot's guide'. CETIS Assessment Special Interest Group, http://www.scrolla.ac.uk/resources/s2/idiots_guide.pdf.

SCROLLA, http://www.scrolla.ac.uk/.

SENDA (2001), 'Special Educational Needs and Disability Act', http://www.opsi.gov.uk/acts/acts2001/20010010.htm.

Sevenair, J. P. (2001), 'Materials to accompany a presentation on multiple choice questions, examinations, and test banks', http://webusers.xula.edu/jsevenai/objective/objective.html#anchor358593.

Shea, V. (1994), *Netiquette*. California: Albion Books, http://www.albion.com/netiquette/book/index.html.

Shepherd, E., Kleeman, J., Phaup, J., Fair, K. and Belton, B. (2003), 'Delivering computerized assessments safely and securely', White Paper, QuestionMark Corporation, http://www.questionmark.com/us/news/pressreleases/assessment_security_white_paper_september_2003.htm.

Sherratt, R. and Jeyes, S. (2005), 'Assis: Final Report', http://www.hull.ac.uk/esig/downloads/Final-Report-Assis.pdf.

Smith, K. (2001), 'Children's rights, assessment and the digital portfolio: is there a common denominator?', in A. Pulverness (ed.), *IATEFL Brighton Conference Selections (Whitstable, IATEFL)*, 55–68.

Smythe, C. and Roberts, P. (2000), 'An overview of the IMS Question & Test Interoperability Specification', 4th CAA Conference, http://www.caaconference.com/pastConferences/2000/proceedings/smythec.pdf.

SQA (2003), 'SQA guidelines on e-assessment for further education', Scottish Qualifications Authority, Glasgow, http://www.sqa.org.uk/files_ccc/GuidelinesForOnlineAssessment(Web).pdf.

SQA (2005), 'SQA's vision and strategy for e-assessment', http://www.sqa.org.uk/files_ccc/SQAsPlansForE-assessment-March2005.pdf.

Squires, P. (2003), 'Concept paper on an item bank approach to testing', http://www.appliedskills.com/whitepapers/files/AnItemBankApproachtoTesting.pdf.

Stemler, S. (2001), 'An overview of content analysis'. *Practical Assessment, Research & Evaluation*, 7(17), http://PAREonline.net/getvn.asp?v=7&n=17.

Stephens, D., Bull, J. and Wade, W. (1998), 'Computer-assisted assessment: Suggested guidelines for an institutional strategy'. *Assessment & Evaluation in Higher Education*, 23, 283–94.

Stevens, R. and Palacio-Cayetano, J. (2003), 'Design and performance frameworks for constructing problem-solving simulations'. *Cell Biology Education*, 2, 162–79.

Stevens, R., Johnson, D. F. and Soller, A. (2005), 'Probabilities and predictions: Modeling the development of scientific problem-solving skills', *Cell Biology Education*, 4, 42–57.

Stevens, R., Soller, A., Cooper, M. and Sprang, M. (2004), 'Modeling the development of problem solving skills in chemistry with a web-based tutor', in J. C. Lester, R. M. Vicari and F. Paraguaca (eds), *Intelligent Tutoring Systems*. Berlin, Heidelberg: Springer-Verlag, pp. 580–91, http://www.immex.ucla.edu/docs/publications/pdf/its_paper.pdf.

Strijbos, J. W., Martens, R. L. and Jochems, W. M. G. (2004), 'Designing for interaction: Six steps to designing computer-supported group-based learning'. *Computers & Education*, 42, 403–24.

Sukkarieh, J. Z., Pulman, S. G. and Raikes, N. (2003), 'Auto-marking: using computational linguistics to score short, free text responses', 29th Annual Conference of the International Association for Educational Assessment, http://www.aqa.org.uk/support/iaea/papers/sukkarieh-pulman-raikes.pdf.

Sung, Y. T., Chang K. E., Chiou S. K. and Hou, H. T. (2005), 'The design and application of a web-based self- and peer-assessment system'. *Computers & Education*, 45, 187–202.

Tam, M. (2000), 'Constructivism, instructional design and technology: Implications for transforming distance learning'. *Educational Technology & Society*, 3, 50–60.

Thomas, P. G., Price, B., Paine, C. and Richards, M. (2002), 'Remote electronic examinations: an architecture for their production, presentation and grading'. *British Journal of Educational Technology*, 33(5), 539–52.

Thomas, R., Ashton, H., Austin, B., Beevers, C., Edwards, D. and Milligan, C. (2004), 'Assessing higher order skills using simulations', 8th CAA Conference, http://www.caaconference.com/pastConferences/2004/proceedings/Thomas_R.pdf.

Thomas, R. and Milligan, C. (2004), 'Putting teachers in the loop: Tools for creating and customising simulations'. *Journal of Interactive Media in Education*, 2004 (15), http://www-jime.open.ac.uk/2004/15.

Tomlinson, M. (2002), *Inquiry Into A Level Standards*. London: DfES, http://www.dfes.gov.uk/alevelsinquiry/.

Tomlinson, M. (2004), '14–19 Curriculum and Qualifications Reform: Interim Report of The Working Group On 14–19 Reform'. London: DfES, http://www.dfes.gov.uk/14-19/.

Torrance, H. (ed.) (1994), *Evaluating Authentic Assessment: Problems and Possibilities in New Approaches to Assessment*. Buckingham: The Open University.

Torrance, H. and Pryor, J. (2001), 'Developing formative assessment in the classroom: using action research to explore and modify theory'. *British Educational Research Journal*, 27, 615–31.

Trinder, J. J., Roy, S. and Magill, J. (2005), 'Using PDAs for CAA: Practicalities, problems, apathy', 9th CAA Conference, http://www.caaconference.com/pastConferences/2005/proceedings/TrinderJ_RoyS_MagillJ.pdf.

Trochim, W. M. (2005), *The Research Methods Knowledge Base* (2nd edition), http://trochim.human.cornell.edu/kb/index.htm.

Tuckman, B., http://www.businessballs.com/tuckmanformingstormingnormingperforming.htm.

Tuckman, B. and Jensen, M. (1977), 'Stages of small group development'. *Group and organizational studies*, 2, 419–27.

Valenti, S., Cucchiarelli, A. and Panti, M. (2002), 'Computer based assessment systems evaluation via the ISO9126 Quality Model'. *Journal of Information Technology Education*, 1, 157–75.

Valenti, S., Neri, F. and Cucchiarelli, A. (2003), 'An overview of current research on automated essay grading'. *Journal of Information Technology Education*, 2, 319–30.

Vendlinski, T. and Stevens, R. (2002), 'Assessing student problem-solving skills with complex computer-based tasks'. *Journal of Technology, Learning, and Assessment*, 1(3), http://escholarship.bc.edu/jtla/vol1/3/.

Vygotsky, L. S. (1978), *Mind in Society*. Cambridge, MA: Harvard University Press.

Vygotsky, L. S. (1986), *Thought and Language*, Cambridge, MA: The MIT Press.

Wainer, H. and Kiely, G. L. (1987), 'Item clusters and computerized adaptive testing: A case for testlets'. *Journal of Educational Measurement*, 24, 185–201.

Walter, L., Turner, A., Antonis, C. and Stylianou, B. (2004), 'The IT advantage assessment model: Applying an expanded value chain model to academia'. *Computers & Education*, 43, 249–72.

Walvoord, B. E. and Johnson-Anderson, V. (1998), *Effective Grading: A Tool for Learning and Assessment*. San Francisco: Jossey-Bass.

Wang, L. (2004), 'New methods for CBT item pool evaluation', Annual Meeting of the American Educational Research Association (AERA), April 2004, San Diego, CA, http://www.psych.umn.edu/psylabs/CATCentral/pdf%20files/wa04-02.pdf.

Wang, X., Bradlow, E. T. and Wainer, H. (2002), 'A general Bayesian model for testlets: theory and applications'. *Applied Psychological Measurement*, 26, 109–28.

Warburton, B. and Conole, G. (2003), 'CAA in UK HEI's – the state of the art?', 7th CAA Conference, http://www.caaconference.com/pastConferences/2003/procedings/warburton.pdf.

Warburton, B. and Conole, G. (2005), 'Whither e-assessment?', 9th CAA Conference, http://www.caaconference.com/pastConferences/2005/proceedings/WarburtonB_ConoleG.pdf.

Weinberger, A. and Fischer, F. (2006), 'A framework to analyze argumentative knowledge construction in computer-supported collaborative learning'. *Computers & Education*, 46, 71–95.

Whetton, C. (2005), 'E-assessment of English', National Foundation for Educational Research, http://www.nfer.ac.uk/publications/pdfs/journal/eassessmentwhetton.pdf.

White, C. (2004), 'Assessing key skills by video or audio presentation', The Higher Education Academy Generic Centre, York, http://www.heacademy.ac.uk.

Wiles, K. and Ball, S. (2003), ' Constructing accessible CBA: minor works or major renovations?', 7th CAA Conference, http://www.caaconference.com/pastConferences/2003/procedings/wiles.pdf.

Wiliam, D. (1994), 'Towards a philosophy for educational assessment', British Educational Research Association, 20th Annual Conference, Oxford, www.kcl.ac.uk/education/papers/philosophy.pdf.

Williams, R. (2001), 'Automated essay grading: an evaluation of four conceptual models', 10th Annual Teaching Learning Forum, Perth, http://lsn.curtin.edu.au/tlf/tlf2001/williams.html.

Wills, S. and Ip, A. (2002), 'enRole, research, react, resolve, reflect: developing and using online role play learning designs', http://learningdesigns.uow.edu.au/guides/info/G1/index.htm.

Winn, W. D. (2002), 'Current trends in educational technology research: the study of learning environments'. *Educational Psychology Review*, 14, 331–51.

Wirth, J. and Klieme, E. (2003), 'Computer-based assessment of problem solving competence'. *Assessment in Education*, 10, 329–45.

Wise, S. L. and Kingsbury, G. G. (2000), 'Practical issues in developing and maintaining a computerized adaptive testing program'. *Psicológica* 21,135–55.

Wood, E. J. (2003), 'What are extended matching sets questions?' *Bioscience Education eJournal*, 1-2, http://www.bioscience.heacademy.ac.uk/journal/.

Wright, B. D. (1977), 'Solving measurement problems with the Rasch model'. *Journal of Educational Measurement*, 14, 97–116.

Wu, H-J., Huang, K-T., Chen, H. and Wu, H-P. (2003), 'Scenario-based learning – an application for the National Digital Library', http://www.taskco.com.tw/en/kt/k06.htm.

Yang, H-L. and Liu, C-L. (2006), 'Process-oriented e-learning architecture in supporting mastery learning'. *International Journal of Innovation and Learning*, 3, 635–57.

Zakrzewski, S. and Steven, C. (2000), 'A model for computer-based assessment: The Catherine wheel principle'. *Assessment & Evaluation in Higher Education*, 25, 201–15.

Handbook of Online Education

Shirley Bennett, Debra Marsh, and Clare Killen

Available now!
The perfect companion volume to The Handbook of e-Assessment

This resource book provides a range of practical, innovative ideas to promote active learning online. For teachers, trainers, and course writers there are a selection of ready-made, adaptable activities which can be used as a basis for eLearning activities. All of the activities in this book have been developed by experienced online tutors with over sixty clearly presented and easy-to-use e-Activities for motivating online learners. The activities are suitable for using on a course or as a departure point for development, independent work and/or discussion. Each section is structured with a theoretical overview along with suggestions for further reading and personal action research.

PB 9780826472960
HB 9780826472953

DATE DUE
